I Wish You Love

I Wish You Love

A Memoir

GLORIA LYNNE

WITH KAREN CHILTON

A TOM DOHERTY ASSOCIATES BOOK

New York

I WISH YOU LOVE

A Forge Book
Published by Tom Doherty Associates, LLC
175 Fifth Avenue
New York, NY 10010

www.tor.com

Forge® is a registered trademark of Tom Doherty Associates, LLC.

Design by Lisa Pifher

ISBN 0-312-87031-0

First Edition: February 2000

Printed in the United States of America

0 9 8 7 6 5 4 3 2 1

This book is dedicated to those who have suffered abuse in their lives. I only hope that the chapters in this book will help you realize that when you are abused by the hands of another, it is not your fault. Abuse started in childhood far too often repeats itself into adulthood. I believe this happens because we blame ourselves. Hopefully, my story will encourage you to relieve yourself of any guilt or blame. I feel lucky and blessed to be able to tell this story.
—GL

For my parents.
—KC

Contents

Acknowledgments

To my family and friends, who've been there for me through thick and thin. I thank you, appreciate you, and share this with you: my son, Richard Alleyne, Duke Wade, Neil Cole, Bernice Lundy, Cardella Di Milo, Dr. Vicky Ghoulson, Helen Singleton Carey, Kenneth Carey Sr., Ernestine Singleton, Geralyn Carey, Bernard Carey, Kenneth Carey Jr., Lenny Triola (Tavern on the Green), Susan Jenkins (Rhythm & Blues Foundation/The Smithsonian Institute), David Hinckley (*New York Daily News*), Greg Wright (*Crosswalk*), Mark Green (*Public Advocate*), Gwen Nelson, Phyllis White, Rosemary Sterrett, Elaine Patterson, Robert Layne and family, especially Stephanie, Khali, and Lee Lukemann, Rodney Jones (producer), Chuck Niles, James Genese, Lloyd Williams (Harlem Chamber of Commerce), Dr. Marie Saunders, Paul Williams, Dorthann Kirk, Cooley Anderson, Jim Cato, Thurston Briscoe, Daryl Banks, Rudy Crew, Maxine Waters, Governor Pataki, H. R. McCall, Susan Taylor, Tina McCray, Representative Charles Rangel and his wife, Alma, Andrew Young, Paul Williams, H. B. Barnum, Congressman John Conyers, Don Cornelius (*Soul Train*), and Charles McMillan, Henry Nash, Eddie October and family, Monty Bram, Lita Taracido, and Linda Braun.

Many thanks to ASCAP, SAG, AFTRA, AGVA.

For Percy Sutton: Thank you for being my friend all these years. You've always been there when I needed you.

For Robert Layne and family, especially Stephanie, my "granddaughter": Thank you for your undying love and support. You've always been in my corner and I love you for it.

Many thanks to Barbara Jackson and family.

Thank you to all of the gifted musicians I've had the pleasure of working with down through the years: Earl May, Herman Foster, Grassella Oliphant, Mickey Bass, Roy Meriwether, Leon Dorsey, Vince Ector, Michael Fleming, Jimmie Jones, Ron Kalina, Larry Farrow, Bill Upchurch, Lucky Millinder, David Benoit, Karen Hernandez, Allen Jackson, Frank Wilson, Richard "Pistol" Allen, Bross Townsend, Kenny Burrell, Ram Ramirez, "Wild" Bill Davis, Gene Ammons, Billy Kaye, James Wideman, Nat Adderly Jr., Melba Liston, Marty Paich, Leroy Holmes, Raymond Scott, Luchi DeJesus, Lionel Hampton, Duke Ellington Orchestra, Mercer Ellington, Larry Fallon, Jimmie Sabini, Don Costa, Harry "Sweets" Edison, "Philly" Jo Jones, Hugh Lawson, Ike Isaac, Marvin Jenkins, Hal Mooney, George Duvivier, Jerry Butler, Jerry Peters, Ed Townsend, Jimmie Smith, Ernie Wilkins, Kenny Dixon, Vic Cenicola, Buddy Scott, Bobby Scott, Jimmy Radcliffe, Chris Radcliffe, Grady Tate, Art Blakey, Barbra Streisand, Tony Bennett, Dionne Warwick, Louis Armstrong, Count Basie, Pearl Bailey, Billie Holiday, Johnny Carey (Jazz Mobile), Dave Bailey (Jazz Mobile), Billy Taylor, Nancy Wilson, Marian McPartland, Gloria Cooper, Randy Cauldwell, Greg Skaff, Ray Gallon, Walter Perkins, Danny Mixon, Tony Shur, Damita Jo and Buddy Wood, Rodney Jones, Hank Crawford, Kinichi Shamazu, Donald Smith, Greg Bandy, Lou Donaldson, Stan Gilbert, Shirley Scott, Preacher Robbins, and Garrick King.

Special thanks to all of the radio station and jockeys who've supported me down through the years: WBLS, WDAS, WBGO, KALN, WRTI, WNEW, WQEW, WYNJ, WSIE, WWRL, Leo Cheers, Symphony Sid, Del Shears, Sid Mark, Von Harper, Chuck Niles, James Genese, Gary Byrd, Hal Jackson, Bob Perkins, Kenny Washington, Stan Martin, Ed Smith, Pat Prescott, Michael Bourne, Annette Williams, Annette Smith, Al Monroe, Eddie O'Jay, Sonny Schwartz, Tommy B, Hervis Span, McKee Fitzhue, Tommy Small, Jack Walker, and Eddie Bee.

And thank you to the folks at Target Transportation.

—GL

For our editor, Bob Gleason: Thank you for trusting, supporting, and believing in this project from start to finish. Thank you for indulging us all of our ideas, thoughts, and opinions and giving us the freedom to put pen to paper with honesty and truth. What enthusiasm! We couldn't have done it without you.

For our literary agent, Susan Gleason: Thank you for your diligence, patience, and support.

An extra special thanks to Dell Long for bringing us together and *knowing* we'd all make a perfect match.

—GL and KC

To my entire family, whose love and support is never ending, especially, my mother and father, Richard and Telia Chilton; my brothers, Richard Chilton and Steven Chilton; my sister, Kim Griffith, who held my hand every step of the way; my brother-in-law, Howard Griffith, who supplied all the fun along the way; and my nephew and niece, Howard Griffith II and Stephanie Chilton (and for the little one who's on the way).

For Lewis—I couldn't have done it without you!

To my friends who shared with me, more love and more laughs: Ingrid Grimes-Myles, Dominic A. Taylor, Ken Roberson, H. Chip Johnson Jr., Aston Penn, Michelle M. Robinson, Sharon Wilkins, Judi Edwards, Simone Cooper, and D'Juana Jones.

Special thanks and appreciation to Melvin Van Peebles and Isabel Helton.

And for Mama Lil—Always and Forever.

—KC

Foreword

Gloria Lynne . . . what a voice . . . what a lady. Gloria and I go back a ways to an era filled with excitement. An era filled with thrills and heartache . . . success and failure and an atmosphere that can never be replaced.

Tin Pan Alley. What a world. What characters. Writers, publishers, singers, musicians, agents, producers, all hustling every day to make it in the world of music. Names like Otis Blackwell, who wrote "Fever" under the name of Eddie Cooley at BMI while writing a string of Elvis Presley tunes under his own name at ASCAP; Charlie Singleton, cowriter of "Strangers in the Night"; Titus Turner, who penned "If I don't love you, baby, grits ain't groceries . . . eggs ain't poultry and Mona Lisa was a man." And the singers of the day all out there on that small stroll from Forty-ninth Street and Broadway to Fifty-seventh Street. Jackie Wilson, Bobby Darin, the Drifters, the Coasters, Tony Williams of the Platters. The watering holes, the Turf Bar, where everybody stopped to have a taste and connect with the power. Jim & Andy's, the world-famous musicians bar; Al & Dick's, the publishers' steak house/bar hangout and more. Everybody had their own clientele and personality and history.

Of course, the music business attracted other elements, too. The gangsters, scammers, loan sharks, drug dealers, and just plain old "take advantage of the talent" scumbags, but the good outweighed the bad. New York City was truly the music capital of the world then. Tin Pan Alley was humming. Harlem was hot. Jersey and Long Island were the homes of all grades of nightclubs, where young talent could work and develop. Manhattan had the Copa, the Village Vanguard, the Village Gate, the Blue Angel, and so many other music magnets. The track was fast, the ladies were fine, and the action was constant. Those were the days that caused Ray Charles to say, "When you leave New York . . . you ain't goin' nowhere." We used to say, "When you leave New York, you're just out of town." That was our world, our Mecca, our roots.

Gloria was there, and that's when I met her. Fresh off her Everest hit "I'm Glad There's You," the world knew this was a sound to make room for, at least I did, and I was right. That voice soared through the airwaves and into your heart. I became a fan from the very start (and I still am). As a young songwriter when I got the opportunity to present some music to Gloria, it happened in a way that only the spirits could have fashioned. . . .

Arthur Prysock and Gloria were sharing the bill at the Apollo Theater. My partner, Jimmy Radcliffe, and I were backstage in Arthur's dressing room, rehearsing him on some tunes of ours for an upcoming recording. Arthur sent us upstairs to see Gloria (bless his soul), we met, and it was like we had done this before, and the rest is history. I'm sure it is somewhere in this book. That also happened to be the night of the infamous New York City blackout. No lights anywhere. There we were backstage at the Apollo with no lights. What do you do? You get some candles and sing those tunes for Gloria Lynne. . . . That's what you do. Next thing I knew we were in New Jersey at Gloria's house and her ever charming mother was filling us with food. I mean the real deal. The greens, cornbread, ribs, etc. The lady could burn! Come to think of it, Gloria sets a mean table herself. I know, I have set my feet beneath it a few times.

Well, I don't think the foreword should be longer than the book, so I'll wrap this up with this. Gloria comes from the good days and when she's around the days are still good. Lady Lynne, I wish you love because the odds of making it in the music business are a million to one but you have become one in a million. We love you.

—Buddy Scott

Harlem

Harlem is my home. I'll never stop loving it.

It is what it is because of the people. To understand the rhythm of it, the style and flavor of it, you just watch the people. You can read their lives by paying attention to the action on the streets. And one Saturday afternoon will give you all the information you need. Pretty women fluttering up and down 125th Street, picking up this, that, and the other, little necessities for their Saturday night dates. Walking fast, dropping in dime stores for stockings and lipstick, sharing the details of the night before or the night to come with their girlfriends, who they spot on the avenue and holler out at them, waving. Sometimes you see them in hair curlers and head rags making a beeline for the corner store. That's when you know the lady's on the go, when time is truly wasting and she's got to get something she forgot to get earlier but can't go without.

Jazz musicians may hit the downtown spots to make their money, but by the early morning hour, they all come creeping home: Harlem. They breeze by in their fancy getups and shining cars, riding slow and blowing horns. Or they come pimping out the Lenox Avenue subway, looking good with an unmistakable stride.

It hasn't been long since the Renaissance of the twenties was in full swing. And though we're in the thirties now, traces of its style and sophistication left their impressions on everybody. The men keep up their polished profiles with their slick hair and cigarettes. And don't forget the celebrities—Sugar Hill is lined with them. Big-time black folks who didn't leave the neighborhood after hitting it big—

Duke Ellington, Billy Strayhorn, Dinah Washington, Langston Hughes, Madame C. J. Walker—all Harlem residents.

Uptown. Every other corner there's a church, a liquor store, a bar room, and an undertaker. Plenty of Negroes have businesses, a lot of them are West Indians who came over from the Bahamas and such. Barbershops are jampacked on Saturdays, just like the beauty shops. Policemen walk the beat, strolling the neighborhood in full uniform. They know everybody's name and everybody knows their faces. That's just how it is.

Good food is a stone's throw away, unlike good jobs. You can get what you need in the neighborhood, whether it's good music, fast women, or a hot crap game. It's all to be had up in Harlem. Here, people live hard and party hard to make up for the hard living. Jewish immigrants own everything—the grocery stores, the liquor stores, drugstores, and jewelry stores. They've got the cleaners, the tailor shops, clothing stores, and the meat market. You never have to worry about food for your children or milk for your babies; you can get it on credit, until your relief check comes at the end of the month.

There are a million different ways to make your money in Harlem. Some legit, some not. Numbers running is a regular gig for some. And don't let your number hit! That quick money comes in handy for a rainy day . . . it ain't bad on a sunny day either. Yeah, gambling, bootlegging, scuffling for a dollar all come with the territory. There's marijuana and bathtub gin, King Kong and hot plates of food, even women—for sale. When things get a little tight, you can always throw a rent party to bail you out. Rent parties are a regular thing up here. Just fry some chicken and make a potato salad, get some bottles of beer, turn on the music, and invite your friends. If you're not careful, the whole neighborhood might show up, and everybody pays twenty-five cents to get in. This little money keeps people going and nobody ever thinks twice about helping out because you never know when your turn might come around.

Southern immigrants (and there are plenty!) come with smiles and wide eyes, only to find that time moves faster here and you better learn quick how to watch your own back. Seems like every day somebody's cousin or uncle or half sister is getting off a train at Grand Central and asking for directions to Harlem. I suppose Minton's Playhouse and Small's Paradise made news all the way across the Mason-Dixon line. While those are nice joints, don't be fooled. The talent might be black but the patrons are white, white, white. They're able to enjoy these clubs more than any of us living within walking distance. They got the money and the law on their side. Negro performers are pure entertainment for wealthy, white patrons, which isn't a new thing, but don't nobody bring up the fact that they're forced to use back doors, coming and going, while getting dolled up in cracked mirrors and using old closets for dressing rooms. Ump.

The streets stay crowded, what with people getting their relief checks just days before and needing to pick up the week's groceries. All of the single mothers flood the streets pushing baby buggies with one hand and holding their five-year-olds with the other. You have to be a single, unemployed woman with children to qualify for Home Relief. From time to time, always unexpected and definitely unannounced, officials will come to your house to see if you are, in fact, going it alone. They check your closets and bathrooms for men's clothing and toiletries. If they find anything "suspicious" you'll get cut off from all further assistance.

We stay on the lookout for these out-of-place professionals swarming through our neighborhood. Usually a white woman in a blue or gray skirt suit who walks at an unsteady but swift pace. Perhaps it's her suit, her shoes, or her job that makes her move that way. It's hard to say. She's carrying a briefcase or an attaché of some kind. Sticking out like a sore thumb but holding fast to her assumed badge of authority, she presses on through, block after block, like she owns the place. From Lenox Avenue to Amsterdam, she's always on foot, hitting each household with her clipboard and questions. Over time, we have all gotten hip to these methods and know dozens of ways around the interrogations. Because the truth of the matter is, a lot of women sneak out to do domestic work on the side, in order to earn a little extra cash. No matter where you're from, personal survival is the first instinct and we, up in Harlem, ain't no different.

We see the Relief people stepping up to each brownstone, going up the steep staircases of these grand old buildings that stand neck and neck. On the front stoop, we play our girlish games, listen to grown women gossip, and laugh about things we can hardly comprehend. There's something about the brownstones in Harlem that makes you feel indestructible. As if, no matter what happens to you or around you, these buildings will never crumble and can hold you up. They line the streets, allowing little glints of sunlight to cut through. It's really quite ominous. You can't help but notice their beauty. Harlem is a beautiful place.

No matter what, there's always some fun to be had. There are the movie shows and live performances by big name stars, school dances, and church functions. On Saturdays, we go to the movie house on 125th Street and Seventh Avenue, the Alhambra Theater, or sometimes, we end up at the Renaissance, on 137th Street. The Harlem YMCA has a million things for kids to do. We all flock to the Friday night basketball games. The neighborhood boys compete so *hard, like basketball is going out of style. After the games, there is usually a dance held in the same place. If we get permission, we can stick around and dance awhile to celebrate with the winning team.*

I have lived all over Harlem, in many different buildings. One hundred thirty-fourth Street off of Lenox Avenue sticks out in my mind the most. On my block, everybody knows each other and everybody's mama on the block is your mama, too. Parents are strict and kids respect their parents. End of discussion. If you do something wrong on one end of the block, you can be sure that before you reach the other end, your mother will know about it. Children are taught the basics from home—reading, writing, and arithmetic. I spent about one week in the first grade, then my teacher recommended that I go straight to the second-grade class. I was able to read, write, and count before I ever stepped foot in a school, thanks to my mother.

Harlem is so full and rich and colorful that when I hear people call it a ghetto, I get angry. Ghetto? Not to this little girl, Gloria Mai Wilson, who runs its streets and loves its city lights. To call my neighborhood a ghetto is to call it dark, unsafe, poor, and dirty. Such a dreary, lowdown place has never existed in my mind. People look out for each other where I come from. We all just keep living and enjoying what we do have. Spirits are high in Harlem. The Village of Harlem: It's got that something special. And something good has to come out of being here.

1

Homespun

*M*emory. It's a funny thing. Some folks can't remember five minutes ago and others, like me, can go all the way back to the crib.

I remember my mother screaming, running down the street with me in her arms, calling out for help. I was just a baby, no more than one or so. I wasn't walking or talking then, just taking it all in. My mother, beaten and hysterical, was trying to protect me from something horrible. Who or what that was exactly, I wasn't sure, but I knew enough to be afraid. The violent sounds would often sting my ears. The actual picture of what the hell was going on took a little longer to come clear. I learned the source of my mother's fear as I grew older. I clung to her.

Maybe God was trying to tell me I'd have to learn how to hold on in life.

Early memory. I wished it all would stop. All of the loud noises, shouting, and fighting that surrounded me. Fists and hands slapping faces, arms swinging, things crashing and falling to the floor. We were in constant chaos and commotion. And even though I was just knee-high to the curb, I remember.

Vivid memory. He had been beating her ass again, physically and verbally abusing her, and once she got loose from his grip, she would run.

We'd go flying through the streets, time after time, in search of help from somebody, *anybody* that could free us from my father's madness. What was he so upset about? I didn't know. Was it something she said, something she did, or nothing at all? Was it her fault? My fault? What could possibly make one man so mad? I still don't know. From the time I was a baby and throughout my childhood, every single day in my house was filled with abuse. She suffered the blows. He dished them out.

My mom, Mary Wilson, was a pretty lady of Creole blood. Everybody told her she was pretty. She grew up in the backwoods of Louisiana. Lake Charles, Louisiana. She had very refined ways. Now, most of her background, I've had to piece together over the years. She rarely talked about her family or her past. Every now and then she would give you a tidbit or two and you'd have to piece it together for yourself. I suspect she followed my father, John Wilson, to New York to get out of Lake Charles. She wanted something different, something more for herself. Exactly what that was, she probably didn't know, but leaving was a move toward it. I suppose youth did to her what it does to all of us, gave her ambition and longing. And she was young, maybe twenty or twenty-one years old. My father was twenty years her senior and he treated her more like a child than a wife.

My father, John Wilson, was a longshoreman. He worked for the Clyde Maryland Shipping Company, which was based in Texas. This was considered a real good job in that day, though it amounted to packing and unpacking, loading and unloading cargo when the ships came into the dock. When he found out his company had boats off the coast of New York, he was itching to leave. His request for a transfer came in 1931 and he and my mother took off. She left behind the women she loved most—her mother and five sisters, trusting her man and his big city dreams. My grandmother didn't know what to think about all of this. She had lived and worked on a plantation most of her life, so them coming as far as New York City from Lake Charles was damn near as close to a miracle as you could get. Well, I came with them too, because Mom, before leaving Louisiana, found out she was pregnant.

I don't believe my parents were ever really married. Not in the legal sense. They didn't have any papers between them. But they came on to New York and set up house like newlyweds. They both wanted big city living, so they thought, but neither one of them knew what to expect.

They were country people and all that New York City had to offer astounded them. It took them a minute to get used to the harshness and the edge of the city. After riding for hours by bus, when they reached Manhattan, the two of them did what most black folks do—sought out the black neighborhoods and headed straight to Harlem. It was understood during that time that stumbling into the "wrong" (meaning, white) neighborhood could get you in a hell of a lot of trouble. They found a small flat together uptown, at 124 West 135th Street, and got busy living.

Since Mom was pregnant, she didn't get out much, but my father fell, fast and hard, into the grips of city life. Temptation was everywhere. It didn't take but a minute before he started running around with women, hanging out at bars, and staying out all night. He had a huge presence, so it wasn't like you were going to go up against him and question him about anything. He was very tall, about six four or six five, and dark, with beautiful black skin and a strong build. It's a wonder he didn't kill my mother when he hit her. He was so strong.

My father felt well within his rights, as the man of the house and the breadwinner, to do whatever he damn well pleased. The tension in the house grew worse. Days and weeks of bad arguments and fights turned into years of abuse. As strange as it may seem, I really do remember my infant years, my early childhood. I can recall the sounds, the noise, all of the disruption. Some things are hazy in my mind, but other, more traumatic experiences, I remember like yesterday.

He beat my mother nonstop. If it wasn't a fist in her face, it was some awful words he'd spit out at her to make her feel like shit. I believe my premature birth, at eight months, had something, if not everything, to do with my father beating Mom while she carried me. I was born on November 23, 1931, at Harlem Hospital. I weighed only three pounds at birth and stayed sick during most of my childhood.

Mom became pregnant with my brother John while living through hell with my father. The birth of more children seemed to do nothing to make him act right. Things only got worse. We did what he said, or said nothing at all. My father was a mean, mean man. I remember thinking if he would just get out of the picture, everything would be all right. I was too young to understand the emotional tie my mother had to him. None of it made any sense to me, because what kind of love was that? Somebody whipping your behind, day in and day out, making you cry out and shout, can't be love. But it was something, because my mother didn't leave. Not right away, anyway. We all just kept living under his rule and dealing with his madness. I was so frightened of my father that I could not find it in myself to ever get too close to him. He scared the shit out of me. I stuck up under my mother most of the time.

When my brother John was born, the effects of physical abuse showed on him like a bad rash. There was no mistaking that he had been traumatized in the womb. John was such a nervous baby. Mom tried everything to comfort him, but eventually he had to be placed in an institution for the mentally retarded. My father didn't show any signs of care or remorse. He continued with his wickedness. I used to pray for the day that we could leave that house. It was too much to take. By the time I was three years old, all I had been exposed to were the violent rages of my father, the whimpering and wailing of my mother.

Mom never talked much. She was a shy woman. Quiet and polite. Young and naive. And far away from home. Her dependence on my father's financial support kept her bound to him. Although she didn't talk much about her life in Lake Charles, I'm sure she missed her family. Suffering the way she was suffering, New York couldn't have felt much like home. She didn't go out much or make many friends. Whenever I would ask her about what it was like where she was from, she mostly gave me warnings about Louisiana: "Don't go down there. Don't ever live there. Ain't nothing down there for you." I wasn't sure why, just, "Leave the South where it is."

In the deepest, darkest areas of the South, you could always find such stories, terrific tales—some good, some bad, and some that made you weep in your tracks. Mom gave me just a glimpse of what her life was like down there and it was hard to believe. When I heard her horror story, I could not understand why Mom chose to live through a repeat performance of the same madness in her adult life. However, realizing what my mother lived through in her own young life, everything else made a little more sense. It was still crazy and uncalled for, but her place in it became clearer to me.

In my mother's childhood home there was violence. There were twelve children altogether, seven boys and five girls, all named after people in the Bible. Well, it turns out that my grandmother, Rebecca Jackson, withstood umpteen years of physical attacks by my great-grandfather, Isaac Jackson.

He was a black Indian, a Cherokee, and he grew tobacco down there. He was one of the few Indians who owned his own property and had a few dollars. Mom said he would make my grandmother get down on her knees while he called all of her children in, all twelve of them, to watch him beat her. His violence was sheer sport. Or maybe, he believed it was his duty. He took some kind of twisted pleasure in having an audience of his grandchildren to watch him beat this woman, his daughter and their mother, into submission. I believe there was some strange mixing going on there, because all twelve of the children had very different looks. They were all different colors, with all different daddies, I believe. Some were pitch-black and others looked damn near white. Mom had one sister who looked identical to her, just like a twin, except she was very dark and Mom was light brown. Now, that happens in black families, but something about my aunts and uncles just struck me as strange. It's hard to explain. Mom said very little about all of this, except that her brothers used to terrorize her when she was growing up, calling her a "red, rhiny bitch" and one of them had broken a broom over her back before. There was very little love between them. So, I guess the first person to come through there and tell my mother he loved her and wanted to marry her, she left.

I understood her wanting to make a clean break out of there, but she walked dead into the same situation. I often wondered why she didn't leave our house at the first blow of my father's fist, but she stayed. She found it somewhere in herself to stay with him. I guess she loved him. Maybe it was just that simple. It was very common, back in those days, for women to stand by their men, no matter what. Especially if you had children by him. Women stayed and suffered. It was considered the "right thing to do." When you think about it, where would she have gone? When you're running away from a lowdown past, running back is not in the plan, so what else is there? You just keep going, keep moving toward something else, hoping it will get better. "Everything will be all right." I heard those words a million times from Mom when we lived with my father. "Don't worry. Everything will be all right, Gloria." I trusted her and really believed that, one day, we would be free from all of the pain and aggravation. From a child's point of view, a parent's walking away might seem like a simple enough thing to do. But it would take me years to find out how the burden of your emotions can be so heavy that it, alone, can weigh you down till you can't budge.

After John, there was Harry, my youngest brother. When he was born, we stood by, frozen with hope that this one would make it. "Yes, you'll make it," I used to hear Mom whisper to the baby. Harry was a very sick baby, nervous, too, and mentally handicapped. As it turned out, Harry didn't fare any better than John. This was tearing my mother apart inside. Her face began to look sad and drawn. She even began to carry herself differently, slightly slumped over with a dazed look in her eye. The weight of this was more than she could bear. This same little doll-faced woman with the lovely shape and gorgeous gait was bent by exhaustion.

Harry was institutionalized with John. Neither one of them had the benefit of a mother's loving arms or touch. And I missed them. I could have used a companion. They both stayed in the mental institution for years, and my mother visited them regularly. She would take them boxes of all kinds of good things, but she never took me. I suppose she thought the hospital atmosphere would be too upsetting, because I was still very young. But, God knows, I wanted to see my brothers. I would beg her to take me. Instead, she would take pictures of them during her visits, so I could see what they looked like. I wanted us all to live together. I was their big sister and I wanted to be close to my little brothers. I remember one picture she took of them in these cute little matching short suits. Both of them were wearing bow ties. They looked so cute, really adorable. I needed them desperately and I blamed my father. It was his fault that we weren't able to be a real family.

I was raised as an only child. Very few people knew that my mother had two other children. If they did know, they thought they were in Lake Charles being raised by my grandmother. I was a young thing but I had seen enough and heard enough to know that strength was needed in order to make it in this world. Backbone is what they used to call it. I was always a fast learner. I was a smart little girl who never missed a beat. I packed away all of these memories and prayed for better days ahead. In spite of it all, I always felt my mother's love. Her nurturing and attention gave me the feeling of being protected.

I learned heartbreak at a very young age. My brother Harry had a twin, our sister, Helen. I was so happy about having a sister, I didn't know what to do. Helen was a pretty little baby, but small—born too early, suffering before arriving, with just enough strength to manage birth. My mother had Helen checked out early. The doctors said she was fine mentally, but she was physically weak. Helen hung in there for a while and we thought she would make it. Mom never let her out of her sight, giving every bit of motherly know-how she had. My father wasn't around much to do anything for us. He stormed in and out of the house, ranting about one thing or the other, then slapping Mom around whenever the mood hit him.

Mom was worried to death about Helen. She had a feeling that keeping her alive was going to be hard. Helen contracted pneumonia at nine months old and Mom's hopes were sunk. She had to use every kind of home remedy imaginable, because no doctors were called, and they made no hospital visits. This was my father's order. Mom did her best to nurse Helen back to health. She begged my father every day to let her take Helen to the hospital, but he flat out refused. He kept Helen from getting the medical care she needed and her condition only got worse. Her frail body could no more withstand the pneumonia that was clogging her lungs than my mother could stand watching her suffer. It was a slow but steady torture taking place between the two of them. My father sat back and watched. I was helpless and of no help at all. I was too young to be of any assistance to my mother, but old enough to know that sick babies need doctors. The only thing I could do was mind my mother and stay out of the way. Mom finally broke down and faced up to my father, insisting that Helen be taken to a doctor. Between the time they wasted arguing over taking her to the doctor and the time they actually arrived at Harlem Hospital, over three weeks had passed and Helen was fading. Come to find out, she was beyond care at this point. Three days later, she died at home. The help she needed came too late.

Mom was devastated by Helen's death. All of her children were suffering—my brothers, mentally, Helen, physically, and me, emotionally. After all that had happened, my father never softened. In fact, it seemed like his beatings became more frequent and more intense. God only knows what would make a man carry on like he did. He charged up and down our small apartment, knocking Mom around like a piece of garbage. I'm sure the neighbors could hear all of this, but no one ever came to our aid. People minded their own business and stayed away. Mom never called the police or sought help outside the home. I suppose she saw herself as a prisoner, since she had no money of her own and no life of her own, outside the one they had created together, as shabby as it was. My father was without remorse. He just got meaner and more miserable over time. Mom never forgave him for this. You could see it in her face. The pain and anger were etched in her expression, framed in the tone of her voice.

Finally, after several severe beatings, one after the other, and all in one week, Mom had hit her limit. One day, she grabbed me while my father was at work and told me, "Gloria, gather up all your things. Quick!" Then, before I could even take hold of a single toy, dress, or extra pair of shoes, she grabbed my hand and we left right that second. We left with nothing but the clothes on our backs—with no direction, no place to go, no money, no home. We just got up and left.

We wandered through the streets of Harlem and I could feel my mother's hand shaking in mine. She was nervous, yes, but more than that, she was angry. Mom walked and walked, bruised and in pain, thinking of a plan for us. She dropped me off at someone's house. I can't say if this woman was a friend or not, because I don't remember my mother getting out long enough to make any friends. Mom left me there with the woman and her three children.

She said to me, "Be a good girl, Gloria. I'll be back as soon as I can."

I was terrified.

I began to cry and shout, "Why can't I go with you?"

She went out of that door and I really didn't think I'd ever see her again. I was much too young to be suffering with bad nerves and anxiety, but I was. I was a worried little girl who hardly ever smiled. A nervous wreck. No child in the world should have thoughts heavy enough to weigh them down. I don't wish that kind of burden on any kid.

The woman who I was left with lived on the first floor of a brownstone, just blocks from where we had been living. It was a small apartment with one bedroom, hardwood floors like ours, and a big living room. I didn't want to do anything to cause trouble, so I kept quiet. I left the other kids' things alone and kept to myself. All I wanted was my mother to come back and get me. She didn't come back that day. In fact, it was days before I saw her again. And that woman starting talking about my mother like a dog. She made all kinds of vicious comments about us, making sure that I was in earshot to soak up every last one of her bitter words.

One day, she told me, "Unless your mama brings some money in here soon, you won't get very much to eat."

If I had to starve on top of everything else, then so be it, but that woman wasn't going to get a peep out of me. I was already underweight and very sickly, but food didn't interest me in the least. I only wanted my mother. I didn't dare open my mouth to say a thing. I never responded to her threats. I was too afraid. Her kids were teasing me like crazy, saying my mother was never going to come back. Three days had passed, maybe more. It felt like forever.

When Mom finally showed up, she burst through the door smiling. She was really happy about something.

Her first words to me were, "We're going to take a trip on a boat."

After living with that awful woman and her kids, I didn't care where we went as long as we left there. A boat trip sounded good to me. This, like everything else during this time, was all out of the blue. But I was so happy to see my mother, I'd go anywhere. She had our tickets in her hand and was nearly out of breath. I noticed her talking fast and smiling a nervous smile at that woman, while at the same time, giving me a once-over to make sure I was intact. I remember her handing me a shopping bag full of new clothes for our trip. Then I saw Mom give that woman some money, and I recall feeling so relieved at the sight of that exchange. Then Mom left again. She said she had another stop to make before we could leave for good. She promised to be back in a few hours to pick me up. I cried and cried after her. I begged to go with her. All of this mystery filled me with fear. Those awful kids had started up again, "Your mother's not coming back to get you ever again. If she wanted you, you wouldn't be here at our house." They kept right on with their mess, staring me up and down, eyeing the new clothes my mother bought me.

It was late at night when Mom made it back. She had with her a brand-new suitcase and the same smile from earlier, just a bit more worn. I was half asleep but I helped her pack up my things so we could leave. I was rushing to the door with my little bag of things in my arms, trying to reach for the doorknob, when Mom made me turn around and say good-bye and thank-you to that woman and those kids. There was a taxi waiting for us outside and I couldn't wait to get in it. On our ride out of the neighborhood, I started telling Mom what a terrible time I had and how awful those people were. She stopped me halfway through my pitiful report and said, "No matter how mean they were, they've done me a big favor by keeping you until I got things together. It never hurts to be as nice as you can be."

We spent the night at another lady's house, then left the next morning on the boat. We took a taxi downtown to the pier and I remember seeing all of these people lined up, with bags and parcels, waiting to get on the biggest, most incredible boat in the world. I had never seen anything like it. It was fantastic. Mom and me leaving together, all of the confusion from the past behind us. Talk about wanting time to stand still. Even as a child, I could understand that. If only the two of us could have stayed right there, in that moment. No more New York. No more Daddy. No more problems.

Children pick up on everything and I was an observant child. I distinctly remember my mother's expression changing on that trip. Her worried look had softened and we both were breathing easier. I didn't know if we were ever coming back or not. Like I said, Mom never talked much. I still don't know where her windfall of cash came from, but Mom was spreading money around like crazy. When the boat docked temporarily in Florida, we got off so she could buy some gifts for her mother and sisters. I was going to meet my grandmother and aunts for the first time. Pulling into Baton Rouge, I remembered my mother's warnings about the South: "Don't ever live down South. Ain't nothing down there for you."

One of my aunts picked us up from the dock and we drove awhile into Lake Charles, to my grandmother's house. Lake Charles is just west of Lafayette, not far from the Texas border. My most vivid memories of the town are of heat and mosquitoes. I remember they had a lot of land. We spent a lot of time outdoors and all of the women were constantly cooking. I remember lots and lots of good food. My mother and her sisters would sit up all night, talking and laughing, way past the time that I went to bed. The scenery down South was so different from what I had grown accustomed to. I enjoyed the fresh air and sunshine. I felt like a little girl. For the first time, I was carefree, without a worry in the world. What a childhood should be—butterflies and ice cream, puppies and bicycles. The warm weather made us sleepy and we used to take naps in the middle of the day, then wake up to something sweet to eat that my grandmother had baked. Well, judging from the outer appearance, things looked perfect. I overheard the grown-ups' conversations, all of it having to do with my mother and father, his abusive behavior and the two of us being alone in New York. Mom insisted that we'd be all right by ourselves. She spent a lot of time trying to convince my grandmother that we were safe and everything was going to turn out just fine. She assured her over and over, "Mama, everything will be all right." My grandmother said, "Well, at least leave Gloria here with me." She figured with all I had seen, I could have used a change in environment. And from the looks of it, things down there had calmed down quite a bit, since everybody was grown. My great-grandfather must have been too old to carry on like he used to. Honestly, I don't even remember the man being around, maybe he was dead.

Another one of Mom's tidbits, which she revealed to me much, much later: She admitted that she would have left me in Lake Charles with my grandmother if my father hadn't threatened her. He told her if she took me away, he would kill her. Here we were hundreds of miles away from the man and he still haunted us. I couldn't believe what I was hearing. Mom told me this years later but it hurt like yesterday. This is the same man that refused to support his children. My brothers were being carried by state funds, my sister was in the grave, and if Mom so much as asked him to buy me a new school dress or a pair of shoes, he would flat-out refuse. Instead, he used her asking as ripe ground to start a fight. I didn't feel connected to my father at all. And from childhood on, that never really changed.

We had been in Lake Charles about three months when Mom decided it was time for us to go back to Harlem. She found an apartment for us on 135th Street between Seventh and Eighth Avenues. It was owned by a West Indian couple, Professor Lorin Phillips and his wife. They lived in the building and had set up a small grocery store in one of the apartments. Professor Phillips ran a music studio from their flat on the first floor. We lived on the second floor in a one-room apartment, a kitchenette, they used to call it. All of the tenants shared the one bathroom, which was on the second floor. The Phillipses kept the building spotless. It was very well maintained. The hardwood floors in the hallways were always swept and clean, sparkling from fresh coats of varnish. The stairs out front were always clear of litter. And best of all, there was always music coming from Professor Phillips's place, which gave the building a very homey feeling.

Professor Phillips was a tall, stately man. He looked almost like an ambassador or something. He was the first black professor I had ever met or even heard of. I think the word "professor" was even new to me then. Mrs. Phillips was a teacher, too. She was a petite woman, very fair-skinned with tight, kinky hair and a friendly face. What impressed me most about both of them was the way they talked. They spoke such clear, beautiful English. They had British accents, very clear and distinct. I don't remember which island they were from, but I know it was somewhere in the British West Indies.

Mom made our small kitchenette beautiful. She had a knack for decorating and somehow was able to turn the one room into two. We didn't have much but we made do. Our neighbors, the Singleton family, became our friends. Elsie was a single mother and she had a daughter my same age, named Helen, who clicked with me right away. It didn't take but a minute for us to be joined at the hip. We spent all of our time together. I always thought Helen was a special blessing. It was ironic that she and my little sister who passed away had the same name. I always believed that God had sent my sister back to me.

Aunt Elsie was a pretty lady with reddish hair and freckles. She and my mother became very close. They would take us everywhere. We went all over the place—uptown, downtown, Brooklyn, and the Bronx. On nice afternoons, we'd go to the movies or shopping. I remember a place called Under the Bridge, where my mother used to shop on Saturdays. For about twenty city blocks, there were stores, side by side, with all kinds of food, jewelry, clothes, everything you could imagine. It started from about 135th Street and went down to 110th on Third Avenue, right under the Third Avenue El train. The four of us would hit the streets and stay out for hours. Mom and Aunt Elsie would have us girls fixed up so cute. Helen was a little browner than her mother with what we called "good hair" and a happy little face. We were both about the same height back then, short. Well, Helen would have on her cute little outfit and so would I. We were two happy-go-lucky little girls. On Saturdays, we would go to the movies at the Alhambra Theater or to the Renaissance on 137th and Seventh Avenue. Now, my mother was very strict, but if something was happening in the community, she'd usually let me go. We went to the YMCA to see basketball games on Fridays, and after the games there were dances. This was when Helen and I were a little older. We would go to the Y together, unchaperoned, which was, of course, a very big deal.

Mom picked up work where she could find it, usually somewhere in the Harlem community. We were doing fine on our own. Money was tight, but wasn't it always? Mom knew how to stretch out a dollar and make it last. I mean, that woman could hold on to a dollar. We hadn't seen much of my father, but he was still up in Harlem somewhere. The families in the neighborhood became my extended family. Everybody knew each other on the block. I guess everybody has a special affection for where they grew up. I know I do. It's funny how I can remember exact details about our block, the people who lived there, and some of the everyday life that took place. I remember the Stewarts, the Joneses, the Tates, and the Bullocks. The Savoys, the Woodards, the Mannings, the Askews, the Palmers, the Robinsons, the Newkirks, the Gilliams, the Locketts, and the Webbs.

I remember one couple who lived in a brownstone on our block. Every weekend the husband would get drunk, and every weekend the wife would throw him out. I mean, this was a regular thing with them. She would be hollering at him as she placed his behind right outside the fence. She'd turn around and go on back in the house like she had just taken out the garbage or something. Then the husband, bent over drunk, would get to talking to the fence. He would talk to the fence as if it was the wife. He'd say, "Woman, listen, I'm gonna kill your ass—don't say nothing back to me—don't you open your fucking mouth! I'll beat your ass! Shut up, shut up, woman! I'm talking!" Oh, he'd cut the fool. We would run to the window to see him perform. All the kids on the block got a big kick out of him. Well, after a while the police would come to get him. They'd throw him in the tank until he got sober, then they'd send him on back home. The police, of course, got to know him because this went on every single weekend. At about the same time, every Saturday night, their front door would open, you'd hear the woman screaming, "Get on out here, man!" The gate would swing open, then the man would get started with the fence. He used to wear that fence out! Anybody who was living around 134th Street at the time will know exactly who I'm talking about, because this went on for years.

Mom and I spent many days just hanging around the house listening to music. My mother loved gospel music. Around this time, Billie Holiday was the hot ticket. Duke Ellington, Count Basie, Billy Eckstine—these were the top people when I was growing up. We would listen to them on the radio, coming to you live from somewhere up in Harlem. The Apollo Theater was close by, so we'd all go on Friday nights to hear the live bands and see the concerts. My mother loved the Apollo. Sometimes we'd go for rides on the double-decker tour buses that rode up and down the entire island of Manhattan. Helen and I would always insist on sitting on the top deck. Boy, we would ride! We were in seventh heaven, honey. All the way to Chinatown and everywhere in between. A Saturday afternoon meant lunch at a neighborhood diner, ice-cream cones, and walks in Riverside Park on the West Side. In the summertime, we hit the beaches out on

Coney Island and spent I don't know how many hours at the amusement park. We filled our days and nights with lots of laughter, just enjoying each other's company.

Helen and I were the best of friends. We were inseparable. We went to different schools, but we'd walk each other to a point halfway in between, then split up. Helen went to Catholic school and I went to public school, P.S. 119. Everything else we did together. We were always running through the building, in and out of each other's apartments. But usually Mom and Aunt Elsie were somewhere sitting together, talking and laughing, in one apartment or the other. We had made friends. Real friends. I hadn't realized, until I met Helen, what I was missing. I had a friend of my own that I could talk to and share things with. I think little girls need that. What we had really done was form a family. There were no daddies or men around, but it didn't matter. We leaned on each other. These were the happy, happy times. Fond memories.

One unforgettable event was when the First Lady, Eleanor Roosevelt, came to Harlem along with Mary McLeod Bethune, the black educator. I was just a kid but Mom thought I should witness the occasion. I don't remember the venue. It could have been the Audubon Ballroom or the Renaissance, I'm not sure. After the speeches were over, Mom took me up to meet both women, so I could shake their hands. Although I couldn't fully appreciate it then, I knew that I was taking part in something very special. Later, I realized what a powerful woman Mary McLeod Bethune was and how influential she had been in fighting for civil rights for black people, long before the civil rights movement of the sixties. More than the actual speeches, I remember my mother's expression of pride and joy throughout the whole afternoon. She was quite pleased with herself and had, by this time, become a very proud Harlem lady. She worked the polls at election time and campaigned diligently for the Democratic Party every year. When President Roosevelt organized the Works Progress Administration, my mother, with her third-grade education, applied to the WPA and got a job working with the public school system as a dietician. This was the time in her life when she felt most satisfied with herself.

Harlem was a different place in those days. Powerful people came through the neighborhood all the time. Art, culture, and politics were all part of the neighborhood's makeup. I remember the black-owned newspaper, New York Age. Their offices were on 135th Street, right in our neighborhood. With Franklin Roosevelt as president and Fiorello La Guardia as the mayor of New York, people were really able to get by. Both of these politicians were *for* the people. New York hasn't seen the likes of a La Guardia since. He gave a damn about how people lived, that jobs were available, that opportunity was accessible. He always found a way to distribute food to needy families. There were milk stations all over Harlem where kids could get a small carton of milk for a penny. And if you didn't have it, they'd give it to you anyway. If you ask any Harlemites who were around during his term, they'll tell you, that man did a fantastic job as mayor. People may have been poor, but nobody went hungry. Back then, you just didn't see all the homelessness and degradation you see in the streets today. When I was growing up, if you saw somebody on the street, you could go up to them and ask them where their family was or offer them a place to stay. People came in and out of our house all the time. If you didn't have a place to lay your head, you could make a pallet on the floor and stay the night, or the week, or month, whatever it was. No one allowed another living soul to sit out on the street and go hungry.

And after the Depression and after the war, all Americans, not just black folks, could use a little extra assistance. There were lots of single mothers, raising their children on what is now known as welfare. Then, it was called Home Relief. Mom and I were no exception. Even women who had husbands would sometimes claim "single" status in order to qualify for Home Relief. Back then, this assistance program was designed solely for single mothers. When the investigators would come by your house, they would ask to look into your closets and medicine cabinets to check for men's things. If they found as much as a bottle of Aqua Velvet or Murray's Pomade, you could be cut off from further assistance. You weren't supposed to get any work on the side either. Of course, there were ways around the system, but you had to be careful.

I remember my mother would give me money to pick up groceries, and other odds and ends, from a small store right near our house. The owners got to know us well. So, Mom made arrangements for me to get my lunch on school days from them and she'd pay at the end of the month. This particular store was on Seventh Avenue between 134th and 135th Streets, right next door to Small's Paradise. I grew up in Harlem at a time when you could go into the stores, say hello to the owners, shake hands, wave good-bye—they knew you. They would let you buy things on credit because everybody was struggling. This was in the thirties, after the Depression, so everybody was trying to get back on their feet. Home Relief was foreign to no one, anybody that could get on it, got on it.

Now, of course, things are entirely different. You can hardly use a credit card up there, let alone get credit. Everybody's got bars on their doors. And you go into some of these shops and there's bulletproof glass separating the owners from the customers. So, you've got to holler out your order like you're in a jungle somewhere. I find this extremely hostile and I think it's such an awful image for young kids. It just wasn't this way when I grew up. People spoke to each other, talked, carried on conversations, and knew each other's names.

It's interesting, because back in that day, families, in whatever form they came in, were very close-knit. There were a lot of single women raising their kids alone, then there were those who had two and three generations living in the same apartment. People made it the best way they could. Family meant different things to different people, depending on your circumstances. Women used to take their kids everywhere, even to grown folks' parties. Nobody left their kids with baby-sitters or at home alone. They just brought them along. Whoever was throwing the party would set up all the kids in one room and then go on with the party.

There's one party in particular I can recall. I had to have been around seven years old or so. I don't know who threw the party, but it was in a very large apartment. All of the rooms were off the long hallway and the party was going on in the front room where people were talking, listening to music, and drinking. My mother put me to bed in one of the bedrooms in the back. She would come in to check on me, occasionally, during the night. I remember lying in that big bed. I should have been asleep but I couldn't get comfortable. Suddenly, I looked out into the dark and thought I saw someone standing there. At first, I thought it was my mother. I kept looking and wondering why she didn't turn on the light like she always did. I kept trying to make out the figure in the dark but my eyes deceived me. And maybe my mind was playing tricks on me. Anyway, as I was looking up in the dark, I felt something fall into my eyes. It was a very soft gel-like substance. I wiped my eyes in an attempt to get rid of it, but whatever it was had landed on the inside of my eyes, not the outside. Because I was so young, and perhaps just scared of the dark, I don't know if someone was there and had put something in my eyes, or not. I eventually went on to sleep.

The next morning, I couldn't open my eyes. I told my mother and she was shocked. She tried to open them, but couldn't. Whether or not we went to see the doctor about it, I can't recall, but I do know when my eyelids opened, I still could not see. I was temporarily blind. Every day, my mother would ask me to try to see. She would even tell me that if I would see, she would take me to Coney Island or some of my other favorite places. I tried but I really could not see a thing. I relied on my sense of sound to get through each day, which, naturally, enhanced my hearing, and to this day, I can hear grass grow. Perhaps that's why this happened. We never could come up with a logical explanation.

The condition went away as fast as it had come. One morning, I woke up and could see again. My sight was restored, but with a very distinct difference. Nothing looked as it had before. Not my mother or any of the people that I knew. Everything appeared differently. It was as if things had become extremely clear, like I was seeing for the first time. What this experience actually meant, physically, emotionally, or spiritually, I don't know. Why it happened, what caused it, is anybody's guess. But it had a profound effect on how I viewed the world. It's difficult to explain. It was a strange occurrence, but then again it seemed just as natural as anything.

2

Helen Smith was one of my mother's other good girlfriends. (All these Helens kept showing up in our lives.) Helen had two daughters, Gwendolyn and Marian, who were around my same age. Every summer, Miss Helen would send her girls to her hometown in Farmville, North Carolina. One summer, my mother decided to send me along with them. By this time, I had grown into a chubby little girl. Actually, I was fat. Marian and Gwendolyn used to tease me about my weight all the time. And because I didn't feel like being teased all summer long, I really didn't want to take this trip. I couldn't tell my mother because she was really happy that I was getting the chance to go. She thought it would be fun for me to spend time on a farm and get a change in atmosphere.

So we left right after school was out for the summer.

When we arrived in Farmville, Miss Helen's uncle met us at the train station and took us out to their farm. It was a great big huge place. Once I got there, I was thrilled to death. I was so glad my mother had sent me down there. For as far as my eyes could see, there was land, with livestock, fruit trees, corn, tomatoes, peppers, watermelons, collard greens, string beans. Everything was homemade—butter, milk, cheese, ice cream. It took me a minute to get used to the food. The taste was so different from what I was accustomed to. They told me it was because everything was fresh. I tell you, you'd see a chicken running across the grass and the next time you saw that bird it was on the dinner table, cooked and ready to be eaten with all the trimmings.

We went everywhere in Farmville, on hayrides and to dances on Saturday evenings, and visiting with the other families in the area. Gwendolyn and I picked fruit and vegetables almost every day. The meal for the evening was planned around our pickings. I loved it all, everything except the peaches. When you pick them fresh from the tree, they are covered with fur, which gets all over your hands and itches something terrible. It takes forever to get the fuzz off your skin. Other than this small inconvenience, I was having a great time.

One day we were outside playing when Gwendolyn's boy cousin started teasing me about my weight. Now, he made it his business to do this nonstop, but he was in rare form on this particular day. I paid him no mind, but he persisted. He got my attention when he started talking about my mother:

"Your mama's so fat and smelly."

Well, he didn't know my mother and I asked him to stop talking all that mess. He just kept right on. Then he decided to put a caterpillar down my back, and that's when I couldn't stand it anymore. So, I picked up a brick and threw it at him. Well, it hit him in the head. I really didn't mean to hurt him, but he *was* getting on my nerves. Of course, the blood flew all over, and he ran to his mother, hollering and screaming.

Her first response after she saw what happened was: "I told you to leave that fat-ass gal from New York alone." And with that, she shook him.

This sort of spoiled things for me. I was ready to go back home to New York. About three days before we were set to leave, the little boy's mother called me over to their house. I didn't know what she wanted, but I went over there anyway. She never mentioned the incident. She said, "I just want to fix your hair before you go back home." When my mother sent me down there, my hair was in two long braids. Well, this woman cut my hair off. In two snips, she cut my braids in half, for no other reason than to get back at me for hitting her son with the brick. I couldn't think of any other reason. When my mother picked me up at the train station and saw me with these little short pigtails, she had a fit. She asked me what happened and I told her everything. Mom was livid. She turned to Miss Helen and said:

"I didn't give anyone permission to cut Gloria's hair. If your sister ever steps foot in New York, I'm going to have a little talk with her."

I think this really put a dent in their friendship. Miss Helen came around every once in a while, but it was never the same. My mother never forgot what happened. I didn't see Marian and Gwendolyn much after this.

Something else happened with Gwendolyn and Miss Helen that I never will forget. Some time after our Southern trip together, Miss Helen came by to see my mother. They sat in the kitchen talking for hours and Miss Helen was crying the whole time. Apparently, Gwendolyn had gone to the doctor in the neighborhood, and during her visit, the doctor raped her. She was only thirteen years old when this happened. The doctor was a German man who was well known in the Harlem community.

I remember hearing Mom and Miss Helen talk about how they weren't able to get any justice for Gwen, because he was a white man and we were Negroes. Miss Helen went to as many people as she could to solicit some help, but nobody wanted to get involved. When she went to the authorities, they actually tried to blame Gwen for what happened.

How are you going to blame a thirteen-year-old kid?

They did their level best to degrade and embarrass her. It was really unbelievable. No one wanted to blame this white man for wrongdoing. Miss Helen tried everything. My mother tried to help her as much as she could, but they were two poor black women living in Harlem and who cared?

After this happened, Miss Helen suddenly became very ill and was taken to the hospital. She had a very bad cold that my mother thought might be a touch of pneumonia. We took her to the hospital, but she didn't last two days. After her death, the talk through the community was they must have done something to her, because Miss Helen was a young woman, in her thirties. And the medical community knew about the allegations she had made against that German doctor. We'll never know, but we all smelled a rat.

It was a horrible time for Gwendolyn. And to make matters worse, she was pregnant with the doctor's child. This was a real live mess. It sounds like a soap opera, but it's God's honest truth. Gwen was really in a bad way. The only mother she had now was my mother. We helped her as much as we could, but she was a confused and hurt child. It was a real shame.

As time went by, Gwendolyn grew stronger and she made a way for herself. She had the baby. It was a beautiful little girl. And she went on and raised her the best she could. She may not have had the law on her side, but she had strength. Gwen pushed on past all of this turmoil and came out the other side just fine. She went on to do great things in her life. She worked out in Brooklyn for one of the local congressmen. She stayed there for thirty or forty-odd years, working in city government. Her daughter grew up to be a lovely young woman, smart and successful. Gwendolyn passed away recently, and I must say, she was a real survivor. She didn't let life get her down. Looking back, it is astounding how much courage that woman must have had. And if that doctor was around today, his ass would be peeping out from under the nearest jail.

I don't recall the precise time when my friend Helen and I decided that we wanted to be singers and study with Professor Phillips. All of that music coming from his apartment made us curious. We'd watch his students come to their lessons and we'd compare notes on who sounded the best on which day. One day, we ganged up on our mothers and talked them into paying for half-hour voice lessons. Well, we were beside ourselves when they agreed. We carried our little hips downstairs once a week, taking turns and learning all we could from Professor Phillips. This was serious business, you see. Helen and I just knew we were bad. We practiced our scales religiously and later on, he gave us a few songs to learn. We were so proud of ourselves, just tickled to death. You couldn't tell us nothing!

"Girl, you sound good today. You must have practiced that song a million times!"

"Professor Phillips says I'm coming along, that I've got a fine voice."

"You better practice harder if you want to get as good as me!"

"Girl, we sound as good as any of those chicks on the radio."

My mother had a fine voice. She could have been another Billie Holiday. She loved gospel music and she sang in the choir at church. We both did. I sang in the young people's choir at the A.M.E. Zion Church on 137th Street. Reverend Price was minister then. Mom taught me a lot of songs. Mom spoke French patois and she grew up listening to Cajun music.

When I was a little girl she used to sing these songs to me and I never forgot them. Beautiful ballads she'd sing in her dialect.

I would love to do an album one day, *Songs My Mother Taught Me*.

Down on Fifty-seventh Street there used to be a theater called the Little Carnegie. It was a fine arts theater situated right inside Carnegie Hall. They showed a lot of European films, ballets, musicals, so it attracted lots of artists. My mom worked at the Little Carnegie for a while, as a cleaning lady. She found it fascinating to see all of these interesting, artsy people passing by. Actually, when I think of it, the Little Carnegie was probably my first real exposure to the artistic world. Mom used to take me with her to work sometimes so I could see the movies. The woman who had helped my mother get the job, Miss Hattie Jones, would always compliment me on my voice:

"That Gloria's got a voice!"

She would tell everybody. Miss Hattie lived in our neighborhood. She used to take all the kids out on field trips. She took me to the World's Fair, and to city museums, the Bronx Zoo, Central Park, children's theaters. In some ways, she was like a guardian angel. She exposed me to the arts at a very young age. By this time, I had fallen so in love with music that I would just sing all the time. Professor Phillips had taught me quite a bit in his little storefront studio—breath technique, the scales, and a lot of songs. I soaked it all up. During this time, Mom started to find out about little competitions around town that I could enter. She would enter me into talent showcases at churches and community centers. Everybody in the neighborhood told me I could sing and I felt it too. This made my mother so proud.

Miss Hattie tried to convince my mother to talk to one of the music teachers in the Carnegie Building, Professor Robert Malone. He was a vocal coach for opera singers and he'd pass through the lobby every day. He had a music studio in the building. After seeing the man come in and out of the theater, week after week, one day Miss Hattie took things into her own hands. Mom was very shy, so it was a bit out of character for her to go up to a stranger and start talking. She was a classy lady, very proud. Anyway, on this particular day, Professor Malone was walking through the lobby, getting ready to leave the building. And Miss Hattie spotted him. I had gone to work with Mom that day, so I was sitting there, off to the side, staying out of the way. Before Mom could say a single word, Miss Hattie spoke up. She hollered out to the man:

"Her daughter's got a real nice voice."

He turned around, looked at us, and said, "Well, let me hear it."

Just like that.

Next thing I know, I'm auditioning for this highly respected and well-established professor of music. We went up to his studio, he ran a few scales, and I sang for him. I don't remember being nervous, but I was surprised by just how much confidence I had. I was only about seven years old at the time.

After the audition, Professor Malone brought me back downstairs and spoke to my mother.

"With the proper training, Gloria could sing professionally one day, if she wants to," he said.

Of course, Mom was concerned about the cost of the lessons with such an accomplished teacher, but that didn't stop her from sending me on.

She simply told me, "Get as much out of those lessons as you can because it's expensive and I don't know how long I can afford this."

Luckily, Professor Malone knew my mother didn't have the kind of money needed to pay his usual fee, so he offered to train me at sliced prices. I studied with him once a week and he taught me all the basics, building upon what I had already learned from Professor Phillips in his basement studio. I was so grateful and a very good student. I paid very close attention.

To this day, in my live performances and recording sessions, I draw strength from those lessons. I have found that some training, if it is intense, makes a big difference. It usually opens the door for more training. There's nothing like having a working knowledge of technique. You need it. It gives you so much confidence and control over what you're projecting.

I continued to study throughout my young adulthood. At one point, I even began operatic training with a wonderful opera singer, Marie Louisa, who smoked cigarettes like crazy but could shatter a window with just one note. I trained with Marie for nearly five years. My classical training has been the greatest asset to me in my professional career. No matter that I couldn't afford to study for years and years, the little bit I got, I held on to and put to good use.

Without my father around, Mom was working hard, doing all kinds of odd jobs. She did her best to get me everything I needed, but it was hard. When she wasn't working, she was at home with me. I remember these days as being very special—very quiet and special days. We enjoyed each other's company. After leaving my father, there weren't many men around the house. I don't remember Mom dating very much, which was fine by me. I loved it being just the two of us.

I was eight years old when Mom met Mr. Johnson. It was 1939. I believe he was from the neighborhood but I don't know how or where they met. He was a big, tall man with very serious looks. He courted my mother and would come by the house from time to time. He didn't say much to me, just a hello, or a good evening, every now and then. Well, one day, out of nowhere, he moved in. Mom and I never talked about his coming. She never mentioned it, never told me he was moving in. So, in a heartbeat, everything went from normal and ordinary to something very different. Mr. Johnson moved in and my life flipped upside down.

The foremost thought in my mind was that Mr. Johnson was picking up where my father left off. He was a huge man, very heavyset. He worked for a garbage collection company that went around to all the restaurants in lower Manhattan and collected their leftover food and garbage. Mr. Johnson paid the rent, bought our clothes and food, and took over the household. When he came on the scene, our fun ended as abruptly as ever. Imagine someone snatching an album off the record player smack dab in the middle of your favorite song, and at the best part: the screeching noise of the scratched and ruined record, the sound of the needle flying off the album—that was Mr. Johnson.

This man moved into our home and changed everything. He convinced my mother that I should be doing nothing but schoolwork. I couldn't play with Helen anymore and hardly ever went out. He didn't allow my mother to visit with Aunt Elsie either. He put a stop to their friendship (as if such a thing is really possible—they loved each other!). They would have to sneak around during the day while he was at work, in order to spend time together. We were held captive in our own home, following his strict orders while living under *our* roof. There were no more chats with Helen about boys and school, no more loud laughter shared between my mom and Aunt Elsie. No more bus rides, no smiles, no games, no jokes, no singing, no music, no nothing. Our fun ended and our family was torn apart. All I could do was go to school, come straight home, and do my homework. He also insisted that I know all the books of the Bible. He had a Bible fetish, as mean as he was. He demanded that I learn every book of the King James Bible by its title and in the correct order. I had to practice the books every single day. He made it part of my regular schoolwork. So when I finished doing my spelling, math, reading, music and history work, I would have to stand up and recite the books to him. If I didn't do it correctly, he would beat me. One wrong name, one wrong pronunciation, or a mixed-up order, Judges before Joshua, Mark before Matthew, meant a whipping.

"Genesis, Exodus, Leviti—Levit—"

"LEVITICUS!" He'd shout at me like I had committed some kind of awful crime.

"Start over, Gloria!"

"Genesis, Exodus, Leviticus, Numbers, Dot- Dot-eronomy . . ."

"Deuteronomy!"

"Speak up, Gloria! Do it again!"

"Genesis, Exodus, Leviticus, Numbers, Deuteronomy, Joshua, Judges . . ."

Mr. Johnson would tie up both of my hands with rope, and my feet, too, then proceed to beat on my naked body until he felt like stopping. With every slap and punch, I cried and cried and tried to escape him but couldn't. He had stripped me down to nothing. I was powerless . . . *and where in the world was my mother?* She never came near when Mr. Johnson would whip me. Somehow, she would vanish into doing something, *anything* to occupy her time and her mind, while I hollered, screamed, and begged him to stop. But the apartment was only one room, so there was no true escape. She saw what was going on, and what she didn't see, she heard.

Mom stood by and said nothing. Mr. Johnson would use any excuse to find fault in how we lived and enjoyed ourselves, any excuse for a beating. I was terribly affected by this. Not only was it a shock to my system, but mentally, I couldn't find a way to digest or make sense out of what was happening. I used to ask myself over and over:

Why did my mother pick these men? Surely, all men aren't violent, I thought.

Look at Professor Phillips, he's never hurt me. Look at Professor Malone, he was always kind. Who were these madmen that entered our lives and made it hell? Where did they come from? Did they all know each other? My God.

I didn't think I would live through this man's tirades. My schoolwork suffered. When I was in school and sitting in the classroom, I'd have bruises all over my body that hurt so bad, I couldn't focus on anything. I can't even begin to describe what it feels like to be hurting all over and trying to hide it at the same time. The shame was beyond belief. No one knew what was happening to me. My clothes hid most of the scars and I never let on. I sat, quietly, in terrible pain. It was unbearable.

Mr. Johnson would not allow me to leave the house without his permission. I could be sent on an errand to the store or the post office, but nothing recreational. And no matter where I went, he would follow me. He was ten steps behind me at all times. The kids on the block would ask:

"Is that your real daddy?"

The thought of this made me sick. I was so embarrassed and ashamed, I couldn't hold my head up or look people in the eye. Aunt Elsie and Helen were devastated by all of this. Sometimes when he would beat me, Aunt Elsie would come and shout from behind our door:

"You oughta be ashamed of yourself beating a child like that!"

She was completely undone by all of it. Mom was just as embarrassed and ashamed as I was. She couldn't face people. She even began to distance herself from Aunt Elsie. She had allowed a strange man to come into our lives and practically ruin us. I'm not sure if Aunt Elsie tried to talk sense into her or not. It was commonly considered bad business to interfere with a friend's personal affairs—that is, if you didn't want any bad blood between you. So, in the name of friendship, they kept quiet. But this was extreme. I'll never know why they didn't do more to try to stop this man. Now, I knew firsthand what my mother had gone through with my father. This was truly one of the most horrendous episodes of my young life.

I asked my mother, "Why does he have to hit me?"

"He's trying to discipline you, Gloria. That's all."

She said this, but her tone was unconvincing. I couldn't help but hold her partly responsible for what was happening. She was my mother. He was just a man off the street who she had dragged into our home.

Every night I would get on my knees and pray. I would ask God to stop this man. Stop him from brutalizing me. The beatings went on and on and on. Eventually, they became part of my daily routine. Every day he'd find something wrong with me, something to correct me on, some reason to beat my ass. I was a little girl whose body was trying to blossom and fill out but instead was marred with bruises and sores. And sadly, the real damage was inside, not out. I felt like shit. My personal development had been arrested because of this sick bastard and his insanity. Any glimmer of esteem or self-respect I might have been feeling, he knocked it away.

I was growing up and understanding less and less about my mother's choices. I just couldn't understand the hold this man had on her. My mother moved around quietly, not saying too much of anything. She had stopped working and I believe that's what Mr. Johnson held over her head. He paid all the bills. He clothed us, fed us, kept the roof over our heads. He used to lecture me about money matters. He wanted me to know the value of a dollar. And he would give me a weekly allowance, which hardly made up for the daily beatings. But I guess this was his way of being nice. Mom would still go and visit Harry and John at the hospital, still taking them little treats and gifts. She tried to continue with her life as if it were normal. She was living in a fog and I was living a nightmare.

I lost interest in everything. School became just a place to go to get away from home. Music appreciation class was the only class that held my interest. In fact, music was my only escape. I was distracted and distressed. I couldn't learn a thing. If I was smart, I didn't know it. If I was pretty, I didn't know. If I was funny, or bright, or witty—I didn't know it. I wasn't paying enough attention to myself, or what was going on around me, long enough to find out. Everything was a big blur and I couldn't see where I was going. Adolescence set in, and things got even more complicated.

I found ways to hook up with Helen outside the house. I confided in her. She would do her best to cheer me up or give me her nine-year-old advice to help me cope. Knowing she was there for me helped so much, because I didn't know where my mother had gone. It was as if my mother had disappeared. Her body was there, but her mind and spirit had flown off to another place. Mom sunk into a private darkness, and I couldn't reach her. Nobody could.

Hypnotized. That's what she appeared to be—hypnotized. This man had a hold on her that was beyond explanation.

We suffered separately.

And night after night, there I was in that tight space, suffocating and reciting:

Genesis.

Exodus.

Leviticus.

Numbers.

Deuteronomy.

Joshua.

Judges . . .

3

Amateur Nights

One day, Mr. Johnson decided that we should move, so we did. We moved into a larger apartment, a two-bedroom, at 111 West 135th Street, right near the Schomburg Center Library. Leaving the Phillips's building was very upsetting. Mom and I were both devastated, but she couldn't talk Mr. Johnson into letting us stay. That was our home. No matter how small, we had made it home. Our only friends were there, Helen and Aunt Elsie. And we didn't know what this man had in store for us. He had snatched us out of the only home we'd ever had and away from the only family we'd ever known. Had it not been for Mr. Johnson, I'm sure we would have stayed there for many years. Even though we were moving just a little further down the street, it was a frightening feeling. Without Aunt Elsie and Helen there, Mr. Johnson didn't have any eyes on him to bear witness to his madness.

Now, in this new place I was able to have my own room for the first time, but that didn't stop Mr. Johnson from coming in and out whenever he wanted. He would find his way into my room and beat the shit out of me, every day. I was at my wit's end. It had been years now of this nonsense and no relief in sight. I would pray for God to take him away from us:

Lord, he ain't got to die, but just take him away from here.

From time to time, I would see my father—off and on, you know. My mother would contact him to see if he could help out buying my school

things. I don't know why she bothered. She knew, as well as I did, that he wasn't going to do anything but whoop and holler about it and pretend that he didn't have any money—at least not any money to spend on me.

And I know my father had money. He didn't know I knew, but I knew. He still had his job as a longshoreman, working down on the docks. But in addition to that, he had about five apartments, in different buildings up in Harlem, where he sold liquor, food, and ladies. He was making grand theft dough.

He just didn't want to share any of it with his family.

But they went around and around like that for as long as I can remember—Mom trying to squeeze a dime out of him. Well, he'd have to recognize us as his family first, before he could even start thinking about sharing.

He took great pleasure in simply saying no.

Once, I spoke to my father about Mr. Johnson. When I told him about the beatings, I'll never forget his reaction: My father just sat there, looking up at the ceiling. He didn't utter a sound. He said nothing. Then, it became crystal clear, my father didn't give a damn about anybody but himself. I was completely alone. I really didn't feel like I had any parents. One had disappeared spiritually, the other one physically, and neither one was clear-headed enough to see their child needed help. I wasn't nothing but ten years old dealing with all of this. It was my battle to fight and I had to be the victor. Winning meant staying alive, living through the beatings, and overcoming the whole thing.

My father was just altogether strange *and* estranged. I never knew anything about the man. I never met anybody on my father's side of the family, not a brother, or a cousin, nobody that could say they grew up with him or was raised with him. I heard some people say that he was from the islands, somebody else said he was Trinidadian. All I know is he had a slight accent, but it could have been Caribbean, Creole, or Southern. I do remember that he never said my name right. He pronounced it Glo-ree-us, instead of Glo-ree-a. Knowing so little about him was really disturbing to me, and it took me a long time to come to terms with it. I felt like a part of me was missing, not knowing where I came from or who my people were.

During this time, there was a lady he had been keeping time with, Miss Pearl. He was a ladies' man and always had plenty of women. I remember all these women coming around him, calling my father "Daddy." They all called him that and I just hated it. But he and Miss Pearl were together, off and on, from the time I was five years old. When I got older, Miss Pearl shared a few things with me about my father. She told me that my father was a twin. She said his twin brother looked like a white man. Now, this sounded crazy because my father was jet-black. Miss Pearl kind of believed this had something to do with why he was so bitter. Because you know, he used to beat her damn near to death, too.

On more than one occasion, Miss Pearl wound up coming over to see my mother. I never understood that, but you know, my mother was just different. Odd. She accepted this woman coming to our house to complain about her former husband. Well, baby, one night Miss Pearl showed up and that woman's eyes were black and swollen and one of them was dangling damn near out the socket. It was just hanging there. She told my mother that J.D. had beaten her up. That's what they used to call my father, J.D. That was the first time I had ever seen a leech. The doctors had put a leech on her eye to help drain the blood. Well, it was a sight! My father had beaten her so bad. He almost knocked her eye out! And here she was coming to get help from my mother. Some of my mother's friends would often say to her:

"How can you take that woman into your home after she took your husband from you?"

My mother replied, very simply, "She needed help and I know how lowdown J.D. can be."

My mother, I tell you, was just a different kind of woman.

Our neighbor Addie Barkley looked after some of the neighborhood kids when their parents were at work or tied up. She was my baby-sitter around this time. She lived across the street from us on 135th Street. Addie also took care of her grandchildren. The oldest of them was her nineteen-year-old grandson. Well, he was grown compared to the rest of us, so I never understood why he always hung around. He would lurk around all the little girls, seeing who he could pick on next. He made us all uncomfortable.

When Addie wasn't looking, this boy turned to us for his enjoyment. He teased, grabbed, fondled us, which all led up to his final act—molestation.

He molested me when I was ten years old.

I don't recall the exact time or even the way it happened because something as horrible as this, you tend to block out. Anyway, he had his way with me when I was just a child. A baby, really. And he did it whenever it was convenient—when Addie had stepped out on the stoop for a minute, went to the toilet, or was in the kitchen talking on the phone. He would yank one of us girls up and have his way. We were all sexually molested by him.

It never occurred to me to tell anyone.

I didn't really understand what the boy had done to me, but I knew enough to know it was wrong. And I felt guilty about it, even though it wasn't my fault. I didn't think to tell my mother because I didn't want Mr. Johnson to find out. I thought if he knew, he would beat the hell out of me, blame me, persecute me. So I stayed silent. I just shut up about it.

Eventually, my mother noticed that I was having a discharge in my panties. That's how she found out. She was shocked out of her mind. She took me over to Harlem Hospital to get checked out. I'm sure she was praying all the way there, that it wasn't what she thought it was. Surely, a ten-year-old child isn't sexually active. Somebody's been messing with her. Someone had taken advantage of her little girl. When the doctor finished examining me, he told my mother directly.

"She's been tampered with."

My mother was horrified. She went completely off.

"Who did this!"

I had to tell her who it was. She was so upset, I was scared not to.

"Mrs. Barkley's grandson did it. He did it to me and he did it to all the other girls, too," I told her.

Mom told Addie Barkley about it, but I don't know how she reacted. Something this horrible usually finds its way under a rug, covered up. A thing that makes you want to scream out loud and never stop is quieted by other people's fears and embarrassment. There's the real shame. I was young, but smart enough to know that the damage he had done could not be undone. I was violated—mauled, grabbed, groped, "tampered with," as the doctor said. But nobody said raped and nobody said damaged.

By now, I felt like damaged goods, something you just throw out. Between the ass whippings by Mr. Johnson, which were still going on, and the random intrusions of this boy across the street, I felt worthless. Nothing made any sense.

This same boy was involved in a gang rape of a white woman. It was in all the papers. He and four other black boys grabbed a white woman off the streets and went to town on her. Of course, this was cause for public outrage and every journalist in New York had something to say about it. It was news. She was news. And they were all thrown in jail.

This white woman's rape was the only justice any of us little black girls sitting up in Miss Addie's house would ever get. Nobody knew about us. Not the papers. Not the police. Nobody but us and our mamas. And we all dealt with it in our own way. It never left me. Sex was a very hard thing for me to grasp from that age on into my adulthood. But more than sex, it was trust. I didn't know who to trust my body with. The feeling of ownership had been snatched away. And I had to work to get my body back.

My godparents, Harriet and Alphonso Robinson, lived nearby at 229 West 134th Street, between Seventh and Eighth Avenues. They owned the building. Harriet was a wealthy black woman who owned several brownstones in Harlem. One building was 224 West 134th Street, another one was right on the corner of 134th Street, and three blocks away was another one, at 137th Street, right off of Seventh Avenue. Harriet and my mother were close.

She used to call my mother Lady.

Harriet Robinson gave me my first black doll. My mother used to buy me all kinds of little dolls. I wanted a Didy doll and all of that, so Harriet said to my mother, "Lady, Gloria has to have a black doll." She brought me the prettiest little black doll I had ever seen. It was beautiful. I didn't even know they had them. Black dolls, of course, weren't common when I was coming up. I went crazy over this doll baby. She wore a beautiful dress and looked very expensive. I knew my godmother had spent a lot of money on the doll, because black dolls were nearly nonexistent in 1942. I cherished it. I truly did.

The Robinsons had a son around my same age, Alphonso, Jr. They desperately wanted him to become a minister. On Sundays, after church, they would make him stand in their living room and recite from the Bible like he was a preacher. They were power church members, high up in the A.M.E. Zion Church in Harlem. Alphonso would get up there and do the best he could. If he didn't do the recitation to their liking, they would take him in the back kitchen.

Now, if you've ever been in a basement apartment in a brownstone, the kitchens are usually very large. They're situated in the back of the building, leading out to the backyard. Most of them, at this time, had these huge sinks with the big bellies. The big-bellied sinks you would use to wash clothes in and all. Well, they would take that boy back there in that kitchen, strip him naked, hang him over that big-bellied sink, and beat the living shit out of him. Yes, they did. His father would beat him with a silver-buckled belt and his mother would stand beside him, to make sure he was doing it right. They beat Alphonso so bad. It was a shame. The Robinsons were serious underground people—involved in the community and politics, well-respected pillars of the community on the outside, and behind closed doors all hell and the devil was breaking loose. They wanted their son to be a preacher but nearly crucified him in the process.

I don't know if it was more helpful to know that I was not alone in this or if that made it even more frightening. I just didn't understand any of it. Abuse—you are never prepared for something so brutal.

I grew up around some mean and crazy people. They marched their asses into church every single Sunday, after being wicked all week.

Alphonso died a very young man strung out on dope. And I know it was because of his upbringing. Nobody suspected that he came from an abusive household, since his parents were wealthy and prominent people in the community. But, baby, I saw it with my own eyes. I don't know why I'm not a junkie or half crazy or in a nuthouse somewhere myself. I know I was spared, because it didn't have to be. It was really pitiful watching him grow up. He just couldn't get it together and only a few of us knew why. Alphonso ended up marrying a Korean girl and had a few kids. But that was a fiasco. He couldn't get his life together, but it wasn't his fault. He was not to blame for any of what happened to him.

I went to Jr. High #136, right in the neighborhood, and Helen went to a nearby Catholic junior high school. One of my classmates was Eartha Kitt, who later became a famous singer and actress. Actually, we attended elementary and junior high together, though we didn't know each other very well. I became good friends with Ramona Davis, who is Sammy Davis Jr.'s sister. If I remember correctly, Sammy Davis Jr., by this time, was already on his way to Hollywood, dancing and singing and making a name for himself. Ramona and I are still friends after all of these years. I was also close to their mother, who everybody called "Baby Sanchez." She was very well known up in Harlem. She used to work as a barmaid at some of the popular nightclubs.

Helen had started going out with a neighborhood boy, Ernie. And they called themselves "in love." She was twelve years old when she became pregnant. And I nearly had a fit! Honey, they would be in there hitting it, while her mother was at work. And chile, they humped and humped, and humped that baby right into the world. Helen was way ahead of the game as far as I was concerned because I hadn't paid boys much attention at that age. I was singing in the glee club at school and I had gotten a part-time job working after school, at Harlem Hospital, serving patients from 4 P.M. to 8 P.M. a couple of days a week. My mother had signed the papers for me, thinking this would be something constructive for me to do with my time. When Helen went into labor, they rushed her over, and I was right there in the room with her when little Ernestine came into the world. She was the most beautiful baby I had ever seen! But I was about to have a fit over Helen having this baby.

You would have thought there had been a death, instead of a birth, the way I carried on.

I screamed and hollered about it. The people in the hospital thought I had taken leave of my senses. I felt like I had lost my best friend.

"My friend is gone," I said. "Now, who am I going to play with?"

I didn't know what to do with myself. We were only twelve-year-old little girls. I did not know how to deal. Of course, things took care of themselves, like they always do. Helen and Ernie went on and got married and they stayed together for a long time. Helen and I both took care of little Ernestine. Ernie could hardly get near her, for bumping into me. I stayed over at their house constantly. We played with the baby like she was a little doll. Ernestine laughs about it now when I tell her how we carried on.

"It's a wonder y'all didn't kill me," she said.

Around this time, Mr. Johnson started getting sick. He was having severe stomach problems and couldn't keep any food down. My mom tried to fix soft foods for him, but nothing helped. He started losing a lot of weight. He left me alone for the first time. He didn't even have enough strength for evil. He laid around that house and suffered like a dog. He waited until the pain was unbearable before he went to see the doctor. Then, he was admitted into the hospital immediately. They had to operate on him right away. Three days later, he was dead. He had been walking around all of that time with liver cancer.

That was the first many of us had ever heard of cancer. I know that was the first time I had ever heard the word. It was the mid-forties and the disease just wasn't as widespread as it is today. Or maybe it was, but they didn't have a name for it.

My mother had a small funeral for him and that was that. Mr. Johnson was gone.

After his death, my mother became very withdrawn and somewhat indifferent toward me. She fell into a deep depression. So, I started staying out late and playing hooky from school. This was the way I coped with her coldness. I had to do something. I was afraid that she didn't love me anymore. I was so wrapped up in my own hurt feelings. I never considered what she must have been going through. I simply wanted what had been denied me these past five years, freedom. I wanted some freedom. I felt I had missed out on what the other kids had. I wanted to express myself, a chance to scream and holler, a chance to laugh out loud, have fun, and run wild. When you're caged up for so long, breaking free is a natural reaction. So, I started "acting out," as people called it then. Meanwhile, Mom was hurting. She could hardly speak. We didn't say much to each other in the weeks that followed Mr. Johnson's death. When we did talk, she'd be reprimanding, and I'd be defending—*Why had I stayed out past my curfew? Why hadn't I gone to school that day? Why was I cutting classes? Why? Why? Why?* Everything was "Why?" We rarely had any conversation. Things were bad between us and I wasn't helping matters. I was thirteen years old and thought I was grown.

I went to Washington Irving High School downtown in the Village. Well, high school and I didn't quite hit it off. I had lost interest in school, pure and simple. I started cutting class and hanging out. I remember a bunch of us would take the train up to the Apollo Theater and hang out in the balcony section, smoking cigarettes, talking and laughing, doing what teenagers do. The truancy officer got hip to us, so when we least expected it, he'd come up there and wipe the whole place out. Then we'd all hightail it back to school.

One time, I decided to cut class three days in a row. My mother found out, so she took me to the Court for Wayward Minors, at the suggestion of Miss Hattie Jones. Now, this is the same woman who introduced me to the fine arts and took me all over the city as a child—my guardian angel. (I tell you about these angels and how they switch up on you.) That's what they did back then. If you were acting up in school, they'd fix your behind. It's nothing like it is today. Baby, back then, they had an answer for everything. Talking about discipline. Mom didn't know what else to do with me. She just didn't have the energy to try to straighten things out. She knew the last few years had been rough on both of us, but she had gotten tired of my nonsense.

So we went down to the court. The judge heard my case. They asked my mother questions about my behavior and she told them, very plainly, that I had been ditching school on a regular basis. Well, baby, they sent me straight to the reformatory. The judge sentenced me to one year in reformatory school with two years probation. Just like that. I will never forget it. When the judge said I was to be put away in a state institution in upstate New York, Westfield State Farms, I thought of myself and of my brothers and said:

"Well, we're all in institutions now."

Very little was said about the judge's decision. We left the courthouse and went home. Not a word was spoken. Mom and I moved about in a very perfunctory fashion.

On the scheduled day, I packed my things and went away. As devastating as this experience was, being confined for a year, I believe with all my heart and soul that it strengthened me. It prepared me for the rest of my life. Your blessings often come in strange packages. This experience taught me how to truly hold on, to have faith and courage, and to rely on God for everything. It forced me to deal with my life and all that had happened. I was able to stop, take a breath, and put things together in my mind. All of the scattered pieces began coming together for me during that year. I had time to think. Up until then, I had never really been around anybody except my mother. That year at Westfield changed me forever. I decided then that my life would not be wasted. I would make something of myself. It was time to grow up. It felt like I went from thirteen years old to thirty. I really matured.

After I was released, I was put on probation for two years, not that I needed it because I had cleaned up my act and was determined to make something of my life. I returned to Washington Irving High School to complete my studies and was fortunate enough to graduate on time, in spite of everything. When I came home, my mother had moved from Harlem to the Bronx. She was living with another man, Mr. Miller. He held a regular, full-time job as a security guard but also worked as the superintendent of the building they lived in, so he could live rent-free. They lived together, along with his mother, in the small basement apartment of the building. Cramped was not the word for it. We were jammed up in that little apartment and it was anything but pleasant. I had almost given up where my mother and her choices of men were concerned. There wasn't much I could do about it.

Now, because Mr. Miller held a full-time job, he left the superintendent duties for my mother to do. She was in that big old building cleaning and scrubbing floors and stairwells, shoveling coal into the burner to heat all the apartments, just dogging herself out. I couldn't believe it. None of this work was fit for a woman. It was heavy, demanding, backbreaking work. I watched my mother's skin turn dull from the coal and her back slump from the labor.

Mom always had beautiful skin. She had an olive complexion that was smooth as silk, and here she was sacrificing herself for this man. Her skin looked sallow and tired all the time. Even her hair had gotten dry and brittle. He had broken her. This situation really got her down. Hell, she was down when she met him, so she didn't have far to fall. In addition to all of this, Mr. Miller's mother, who was about seventy years old or so, couldn't do for herself, so my mother had to care for her, too. They had her in there working like a slave. I hated every minute of it. I hated to see my mother cramped up there with Mr. Miller, and I said to myself, "I have got to do something! My life has to turn around. Things have got to get better for us." I was hell-bent on making some very definite changes in my life.

Mr. Miller and I never did hit it off, because I saw immediately that he was using my mother. He had found himself a pretty, young woman that cared so much for him, she would shovel coal for his ass—*he had it made*. Well, he never took well to me and tried to knock me down a few notches in front of my mother. Well, baby, this man didn't know what I had already been through. The nonsense he was serving up was nothing compared to what I had already experienced. So, I let him know right off the bat that he didn't scare me. I mean, enough is enough. He would love to say to my mother, "Gloria's not going to be nothing, 'cause she don't have what it takes to be something." Mom never confronted him about his comments. She would let it all go. And this man was all talk. He had so much to say. He would sometimes threaten to hit me, but he never tried it.

Once, after threatening me one time too many, I cut him short, in midsentence.

"If you ever put a hand on me or Mother, I'll find a way to kill you," I said.

I wasn't taking it anymore. My suffering ended when Mr. Johnson died, as far as I was concerned. I dared this man to raise a hand to me. After that, he left me alone. My presence began to scare him and make him nervous. Although my mother always denied it, I really do believe when they were alone, he would beat her. I could tell she was afraid of him by the way she would respond to him. Whatever he said, she would quickly agree. When he'd come around her, she'd jump. He took away her last bit of self-esteem and she had no confidence to speak of. I had a terrible, sinking feeling that this relationship would be her last straw, that it would eventually destroy her.

Late one evening, Mr. Miller had a bitter argument with my mother about something. I'm not sure what it was all about. Mom never told me. But, baby, after this big fight, she grabbed me and we left.

Just like that. Just like before.

We went back to Harlem, found an apartment on Lenox Avenue, right across the street from Harlem Hospital. The two of us moved in that day and never looked back. It was 1946.

I had given serious thought to studying medicine. Since I had experienced so much pain in my life, I felt that maybe I could heal others, maybe I could become a doctor or a scientist, something in the healing world. I began to think God put me on this path to heal others and the way to becoming a great healer was to experience some pain of my own. There had to be an explanation for all that had happened.

Around this time, I had gone back to serious study of vocal technique. After five years of concert training with Marie Louisa, I started working with Danny Small. Danny was a brilliant pianist and songwriter. He worked with a lot of the publishing companies and had written songs for everybody. He also coached a lot of singers, but he gave me special attention. My vocal quality and phrasing, I owe to Danny. As far as singing goes, the two of us sound exactly alike. Our tone and cadence was exactly the same. Danny worked for Happy GoDay, at GoDay Publishing Company. Happy GoDay always looked out for him even though he knew Danny was messing around on that stuff. His drug problem never interfered with his work. It was amazing. Danny wrote songs with an ease and confidence like no other. He was absolutely brilliant. And so creative, he could not be stopped. Danny gave me so much. I studied with him for several years and because of him, I sing today the way I sang way back then.

Danny and I were good friends, so from time to time we would hang out together up in Harlem. I was really too young to be hanging out anywhere, but I didn't think twice about strolling into Small's or Minton's when I was a teenager. As a matter of fact, it was at Minton's that I first met Billie Holiday. Danny and I walked in one night and Billie was seated at the bar. I had to be only fourteen or fifteen years old, but I looked older. Well, Danny knew everybody and everybody knew Danny. He introduced me to Billie and I nearly fainted. I was in total awe of her. I kept thinking to myself, *My God, she is so pretty.* I had seen her picture on the marquees of all the clubs, sporting her white gardenias in her hair and all that. Well, in person, she was simply gorgeous. She had a beautiful mink coat thrown about her shoulders, and she was wearing plenty of diamonds on her ears and her fingers. I remember she had a little Chihuahua in her purse. A real glamour girl. She was very warm to me, she smiled and shook my hand. I was so excited to meet her that I really felt like running out of the place to go tell the whole world that I had met Lady Day, but I smiled back and said, "Pleased to meet you, Miss Holiday." That was my first brush with greatness.

Mom was working for the Edelsons around this time. Dr. Murray Edelson and his wife, Gloria, were Jewish multimillionaires. They had two children, a son and a daughter, and Mom worked as their maid for years. The entire time Mom worked for them, she never had to buy me clothes. Their little girl would wear an outfit once, then throw it out. We were the same age and the same size. So, Mrs. Edelson would pass her daughter's things on to my mother. I remember being in school wearing Lord & Taylor and Saks Fifth Avenue dresses. All the clothes she refused to wear, I wore. The Edelsons were extremely kind to my mother. She and I used to go there on Sundays and sit down at the table with them and have dinner. I have one very vivid memory of eating dinner with them. One of the children, I believe it was their son, looked over to my mother as we all sat eating.

"Mary," he said, "would you get up and get me some milk?"

Before my mother could make a move, Dr. Edelson said:

"You get up and get your own milk. Mary is eating."

He insisted that my mother be given the proper respect at all times. They had a place in Manhattan, a house in Manhasset, New York, and property in Europe. Whenever they would get ready to take their vacation, Dr. Edelson would ask my mother:

"Mary, we'd like to take our vacation soon, how does your schedule look?"

They really did right by my mother.

I considered enrolling in Fordham University, which was right in Manhattan, on the West Side. And I thought I could work to save up the money for tuition. But just as these practical, commonsense thoughts would enter my mind, I'd remember what Professor Malone told my mother all those years ago:

"Gloria could sing professionally one day . . ."

I didn't even know how to go about singing for a living, but it was an idea that would not leave me alone.

Uptown was the place to be in those days. There was so much music going on. It was hard to escape. We lived several blocks away from the Apollo Theater on 125th Street, which by this time was known all over the world. And I had been seeing shows there since I was child. I remember the first time I ever walked into the Apollo. It was the biggest place I had ever seen. It was really amazing. And in Harlem, it was the biggest thing going.

The Apollo Amateur Night competition was turning out talent faster than lightning. All of the top headliners of the day, like Ella Fitzgerald, Billie Holiday, Pearl Bailey, and Billy Eckstine, had made names for themselves by winning the Apollo Amateur. Back then, the standards were very high and the Apollo was considered the testing ground for new talent. They had a full orchestra and the sound was out of sight. It was so great to live in a neighborhood surrounded by so much fame and success. We all felt there was something special about Harlem. There was always a feeling in the air that anything was possible.

I was fifteen years old when I got up the nerve to audition for the Apollo Amateur. I didn't tell a living soul. I thought about telling Helen, but I wanted to keep this one to myself. And I knew I couldn't tell my mother because she wouldn't have allowed me to go. I think you had to be at least eighteen to enter the competition. Well, I had that all figured out. I decided to lie about my age and go on down there. As shy as I was at that age, I really don't know where I got the nerve. It just came. And I followed the urging. I selected my music and rehearsed my song on the sly, then went down to the theater and signed up for an audition. I told them I was eighteen and I looked it. My figure was in full bloom, so I had no problem convincing them that I was of age. After making the cut, the contest officials gave me the rehearsal schedule and I went home and prepared.

On the day of the contest, I left the house and made up a story about where I was going. I told my mother I was going over to my girlfriend Cynthia's house. This meant, of course, that I had to tell Cynthia a little something about what was going on, just to cover my tracks. She was the only one who had a clue what I was up to, but promised not to tell. I went to her house to change my clothes. That afternoon, I left the house in bobby socks and hit the stage in silk stockings. I wore a little red dress with my new high heels. I strutted in that place like a grown woman, completely full of myself.

While I was backstage, Pigmeat Markham, the Apollo mascot and famous comedian whose job it was to tease and taunt the amateurs (and shoot your ass off stage if you got booed), starting making all kinds of threats. He came up to me, got all up in my face, and said:

"I'm going to get *you.*"

Well, even though I was nervous as hell and scared to death, I snapped back at him:

"Uh-uh. No you ain't."

While I sat there in the wings, I began thinking, maybe I should have told my friends, so they could have come down here to cheer me on. But it was too late to turn back now. I was an absolute wreck sitting there by myself. I decided that at the very least, I would get through my song without getting booed off stage.

I changed my name that day for the contest. It was all part of my master plan to keep this whole charade from my mother. So, I used an alias. I told the people my name was Bobby Wilson, so my mother wouldn't know it was me. (As if my mama wouldn't know my voice if she heard it!) You do so many crazy things when you're young. Just crazy. Well, baby, when they called my name, "Now let's have an Apollo welcome for our next amateur, Miss Bobby Wilson!" I like to died. I was extremely excited but more nervous than I had ever been in my entire life. And the only thing on my mind was getting through my song. When I stepped out on stage, I rubbed the "Tree of Hope," which sits upstage, and went over to speak to Ralph Cooper, "Coop," as they called him. He was the emcee and the producer of the Apollo Amateur. I looked out and saw that whole sea of people looking back at me and I remember thinking: *They're going to judge whether I'm good or not. This is it.* I didn't fully realize it then, but my whole life was getting ready to change. The new direction I had prayed for had come.

I strutted on that stage and strolled right into a brand-new life.

I sang "Don't Take Your Love from Me," which I used to hear all the time on the radio. It was one of my favorite songs. I especially loved the way Dinah Washington sang it. Well, I gave it my best shot. I sung my heart out. And when I finished, the audience went nuts. They applauded and applauded. I couldn't believe it. They really loved my singing. They whooped and hollered and carried on for me. The other amateurs performed and then we all came back out onstage to get the final results. I distinctly remember all of the amateurs that night being especially talented.

In fact, years and years later, my longtime manager, Duke Wade, ran into a guy who owns a lounge in Hartford, Connecticut, who said he was on the same night as me. He jokingly said:

"That damn Gloria Lynne ruined my chances. If she hadn't been there that night and been so damn good, maybe I could have had a chance at a career!"

Well, I was happy just to get through my song!

So, they lined us all up one by one and asked the audience to respond again to each individual performance. Well, when they got to me, the audience went berserk. Talk about excited! They clapped and stomped and cheered for me. I won. Miss Gloria Mai Wilson, alias Bobby Wilson, from the neighborhood, had just won the Apollo Amateur.

I won first prize—fifteen dollars and a weeklong engagement performing at the Apollo. I looked at Ralph Cooper and I couldn't believe I was standing there with that handsome man, who I had seen in the movies and heard on the radio. He smiled at me and said:

"Congratulations, Miss Wilson."

It was unbelievable: *I won first prize in Ralph Cooper's Amateur Night at the Apollo.*

It took awhile for it to really sink in. And when it did, a great feeling of satisfaction came over me. Fate had stepped in and played its part. There have been many great moments in my life, but this one is right on top.

4

Living Wages

*N*ow, everybody in the neighborhood knew the goings-on at the Apollo. Every Wednesday was the talk on the street: Who had been on the Amateur hour? Who had won? Was it somebody from the block? Everybody knew what was happening down there. And the show aired on WMAC. They had been airing the show live on the radio since '37. So, those that didn't go down to the theater would tune in. Before I could get home good, the whole neighborhood knew I had won the contest. Of course, my mother got wind of it. Baby, after she heard I had been down there and won, she showed up at the theater to get me! When I came out of the backstage door, she was standing right there. And there I was with a face full of makeup, silk stockings, high heels, and a tight red dress. She was mad as hell. The look on her face scared me to death. Winning didn't mean a thing at that moment. I was scrambling trying to figure out how I was going to explain this to her. She didn't say anything on the walk home. I had to try to wipe the grin off my face because I didn't want to upset her even more. But I was beside myself with excitement and couldn't wait to get ahold of Helen so I could share this with her. I knew she was somewhere having a conniption fit that I had won.

I swear, Mom didn't get excited about my big win until weeks later. I think deep down she was hurt. She had always entered me into singing contests and recitals, and here it was the biggest competition around, and

I didn't share it with her. I was afraid she would never forgive me for that. God knows she never forgot it. But the more people in the neighborhood talked and cheered me on, the more she softened.

Eventually, she came around and became extremely proud of it.

But I still wasn't convinced. Even with all the buzz around me and the encouragement I had received from the people in the neighborhood, I still wasn't convinced. I had medicine on my mind and thought, if I wasn't going to be a doctor, I could go to school to become a nurse. Well, all of that went right out the window the day I got a call from Frank Schiffman, the owner of the Apollo Theater.

Mr. Schiffman asked me to be the opening act for the show that they were preparing for that week. Now, this came months after my big win and I never expected it. Not really. Deep down, I probably wished it would happen. I was so excited to get his call, I didn't know what to do. I told him, "Yes! I'd be happy to open the show." This time, I told everybody I knew in the world!

As the opening act, I did one quick number with the band and it was over in about two minutes. So, if you didn't get there exactly at show time, you'd miss me. Some of the girls in my neighborhood talked about me, "She ain't singing at no Apollo. Her name's not even up there." Well, it was up there, it was just in small print. After my first week, Mr. Schiffman called on me many times to open at the Apollo. This was quite a feat, and a huge compliment, since most of the opening acts had established careers and some even had records out. I had neither, but I put on a good show and audiences came to love me.

Frank Schiffman had bought the Apollo Theater in 1934. In the twenties, he had also owned the Lafayette Theater and the Harlem Opera House. Both appealed mostly to white folks. However, the first musician Schiffman ever put to work in one of his theaters was Fats Waller in 1925. Around that time, a lot of the theaters in Harlem, which had been known for their live shows, vaudeville and all that, were victims of the Depression and had to be turned into movie houses. But the Apollo remained. As the others were falling, it was flourishing. Thanks to Ralph Cooper. Now, Coop came into the picture in the thirties, I believe. He began producing and hosting the Apollo Amateur around '34. Coop was something else, baby. He knew exactly what he was doing. He was a shrewd businessman and a fabulous entertainer in his own right. The Apollo is a landmark today because of the work Ralph Cooper put into it. The Schiffmans owned it, but Coop made it what it is. Who would have guessed that Amateur Night at the Apollo would still be going on today? I suspect Coop knew.

In his years as producer, he discovered people like Louis Jordan, The Orioles, as well as his sidekick, Pigmeat Markham. They made the famous skit "Here Comes De Judge." Coop wrote it for Pigmeat, who captured quite a bit of fame because of it. Sammy Davis Jr. made it famous on television on different variety shows. Ralph Cooper had starred in the early black films of the thirties and he was also the deejay at the Palm Café in Harlem. It was Coop who spotted Billie Holiday singing in the back room of the Hot Cha on 134th Street and Seventh Avenue, right near where I grew up. When he put that woman on the Apollo stage back in 1934, everybody said, "She's no amateur." Billie became legend that night. The audience loved her so much, she not only stopped the show but was forced to sing the same two numbers over and over again.

When Coop joined the Apollo management team, he opened all kinds of doors for black people. He made that stage available to anyone who had the desire to perform. He knew there was an abundance of black talent right there in the community. And there were plenty of black folks who would be more than willing to pay the price of the ticket. What began as a vaudeville house for mostly whites became a world-famous theater known exclusively for turning out phenomenal black talent. We have Ralph Cooper to thank for that. I appeared in his book on the Apollo years, called *Amateur Night at the Apollo*.

In those days, everybody told me I sounded like Sarah Vaughan and that I'd never make it sounding like her. I admired Sarah and loved what she did with a song, but during this particular period in the music, singular style was necessary for success. Though we were all coming from a common jazz root, there were no imitations. Though we may have covered some of the same standards or ballads, everybody had to make the music their own, through different arrangements, vocal style, interpretation, finesse, costume, performance. You had to come with the complete package. There were no two of a kind. That was unheard of. Originality was golden. But at this time, I wasn't even sure if I wanted to be in the music business. Some days I wake up, even now, and I'm not sure if I want to be in this business.

And I know as sure as I'm breathing, this business chose me, I didn't choose it.

Honest to God, every time I would try to stray away from it, it would come right back and grab me.

I loved to work and never turned down a job. When I finally committed to the business, I was sincere about it and worked very hard. I continued to work at the Apollo. Whenever Schiffman called, I would show. All of the acts would bring their charts and rehearse their music with the big band days before the actual performance. The Apollo had incredible musicians at that time. Art Blakey would play there with his band, Billy Eckstine, Earl Hines, Erskine Hawkins, Gene Ammons, Dizzy Gillespie, a lot of the guys who became huge names in jazz started out right there at the Apollo. They would play for the opening acts, the guest stars, and the amateurs. The Apollo Amateur was always on Wednesdays. Rehearsals were always on Thursdays, and the show opened on Fridays. Shows ran for seven days.

I remember telling Mr. Schiffman, "One day, my name's going to be up there, *big*, and you're going to pay me top dollar to perform here."

He just smiled in agreement. The Apollo always felt like home. It was very special to me, since I grew up in the neighborhood. I had a special connection to it. Mr. Schiffman's two sons, Jack and Bobby, worked around the theater. Eventually, Jack Schiffman took over running the Apollo. Jack ran things between '49 and '55. Jack and I have been friends since way back when. He wrote a book about the Apollo years, called *Uptown*.

The Baby Grand was the hot new nightclub on the block and I performed there pretty regularly. It was on 125th Street near St. Nicholas Avenue. The comedian Nipsey Russell was the emcee at that time. This was the most ongoing club in Harlem, besides Small's Paradise. But Small's came in and out; sometimes they'd have a steady flow and sometimes they didn't. They really didn't get hot until the fifties. There was also Minton's Playhouse on 118th between St. Nicholas and Seventh Avenue, where a lot of musicians hung out, like Miles Davis, John Coltrane, Charlie Parker, Dizzy Gillespie, and Thelonious Monk. Minton's was called the Black Jazz Capital of the World.

Musicians would come in from places like Chicago, Detroit, St. Louis, and New Orleans and make a beeline to Minton's. Fifty-second Street they called "The Street," but you had to prove yourself up in Harlem before going downtown to make money. And Minton's was the place. It was owned by a black man, Teddy Hill, and if you ask anybody who was around at the time, they'll tell you that bebop originated right there in that club. This was a time of tremendous creativity and innovation. Harlem was home to black musicians. Out-of-town musicians stayed up there at the Cecil Hotel, which was right near Minton's. And the deal was, if you couldn't hang with boys up at Minton's, there was no need for you to go any further. Just pack your bags and go on back where you came from. Later, white folks tried to take credit for discovering a lot of these musicians, but it simply isn't true. Uptown was the place to be, make no mistake about it.

The club scene really began to flourish in the forties. Clubs were popping up all over the neighborhood. The Harlem club scene was full of high-society black folks—doctors, lawyers, politicians, they were all there. Plenty of rich black folks were living in Harlem back then, and they would come down from Sugar Hill to 125th Street in gowns and furs and suits, in full regalia, to hear the music and see the shows. Now, these clubs weren't just corner bar rooms, they were fancy, elegant places. I remember Minton's used to have white linen tablecloths on every table and the clientele was top-drawer. Jazz had made an impact and everybody was coming uptown to hear good music. Bebop was the thing. People had never heard anything like it.

Billie Holiday was world-famous by this time. Then Ella appeared on the scene. They called her the "First Lady of Song," and the "Queen of Scat." Scatting was unheard of before Ella Fitzgerald. Musicians would describe her style as a doing with the voice what a horn would do if it could speak. She got out there and just laid everybody out. Then there was Dinah Washington and Sarah Vaughan and Carmen McRae. And just one after the other, female vocalists were coming on the scene, stirring things up. These were exciting times. There was a feeling like we were all on the brink of something big, bearing witness to something truly extraordinary. And we were.

Now, there were jazz clubs for vocalists and then others for instrumentalists. Musicians' hangouts were places like Minton's, of course, but downtown on Fifty-second Street there was DownBeat, Birdland, Kelly's Stable, 3 Deuces, and the Onyx. Well, the Baby Grand was the place for vocalists to be showcased. They had a real regular crowd. The place only seated about eighty people but it was a very charming room. It was owned by the Krulick brothers. They also owned Town Hill in Brooklyn. So, if you were booked at the Baby Grand, they would also contract you to work Town Hill, which was equally nice.

There was also the Brankers, which was up on 155th Street off of St. Nicholas, where I worked a lot. That's where I first met Kenny Burrell, the jazz guitarist, and we became good friends. Kenny was a big influence on my career. He was one of the people who was really in my corner. He wanted the best for me, to see me go far. He used to say:

"Gloria, you're a great singer."

He was very encouraging in those early years of my development as a vocalist. He taught me a lot of songs, a lot of music. Kenny is a brilliant musician and a very sweet man. Our days at Brankers were pretty special. The organist Ram Ramirez was with me then. He's another good friend who was with me from the beginning. Playing at Brankers, I made five dollars a night. And I didn't mind. Money was money, as far as I was concerned, even if it was just pocket change. I don't know what the musicians were paid, but we were all so thrilled to be performing, we didn't really think about the money.

Along with the nightclub scene, in the daytime, I had started going to auditions for off-Broadway and Broadway musicals. I began to get a reputation around Harlem as a really good singer, so finding jobs got easier. I did get a job once, performing in a musical Off-Broadway called *Chris Columbus Brown* down at the Henry Street Settlement, a thriving black theater on the lower East Side of Manhattan.

Harry Alleyne was my first boyfriend. In between my different club bookings, we found time to date and hang out together. He used to come to the clubs to see me perform. Harry was my first love. We started out as friends and started dating when I was around eighteen. He grew up right across the street from us. He was tall and handsome, a pretty boy, looked almost like a black Italian or black Cuban or something. His mother was Cuban, Louise Hernandez. She wasn't his biological mother but more like a foster mother.

Let me see, how did it go? Harry's father abandoned his natural mother, Bertina Alleyne, when he was about two years old. He never saw him again. Didn't know where he was. He was from Martinique and just dropped out of sight, right out of their lives. Bertina Alleyne was only about twenty years old when he left, then she died not long after that. She died very young, leaving Harry an orphan, basically. I only saw pictures of Harry's mother. She was a beautiful woman. Her maiden name was Boardley and she was from a Philadelphia-based family. After her death, Louise, who we all called Nana, took Harry in and raised him like her own child. He had a good mother. She loved Harry and raised him like she had birthed him.

Harry was something else. The women loved him. So, I had trouble with them. They were just about finished with me, because, by then, most of the people in the neighborhood knew who I was. After I hooked up with Harry, who was considered one of the finest dudes in the neighborhood, well, that just did it. It was too much for some people. The women had gotten jealous. But I didn't care. I just loved Harry. Harry was young but he had women twenty-five and thirty years old hitting on him. They dug him. And he could handle it. These women would give him money and keep him dressed in fine clothes. He was that kind of guy.

Harry never finished high school but had a brilliant mind. He was self-taught and a great reader of all kinds of books. I always called him a self-made man. He could hold his own in any social circle. When I asked him why he left high school before graduating, he said simply:

"I didn't fit in."

He said all of his school days were really awkward. He was teased and felt isolated among the other students. Harry was about six-six and reached that height very early on. Back then, if you were tall and looked older than the rest of the kids, it was assumed that you had been left back a grade, that you were stupid or inept. It wasn't considered natural, to be so tall at such a young age. There must be something wrong with you, so people thought. When Harry couldn't deal with being ostracized anymore, he left school.

Harry's buddies from the neighborhood, Teddy, Boo, Duke, Arthur, and Mickey, were inseparable. They did everything together. The street we lived on was pretty sane. People looked out for each other. During that time, the worst thing we heard about was somebody smoking pot or maybe somebody was spotted drunk, stumbling out of the Hot Cha, which was on the corner of 134th Street and Seventh Avenue, about three doors down from Small's Paradise. But there wasn't a lot of violence of any kind then. Police used to walk the beat and made a point of knowing the families, your names, your parents, the building you lived in.

Well, around 1950, the worst thing that could have happened, happened. Rumors started flying that there was a new drug hitting the streets. An influx of heroin was being sold in Harlem and some of the young people were getting hooked on it. Well, this came out of nowhere. We went from pot and a little bootleg liquor to needles and shooting up . . . this changed everything. The whole community was disturbed by it, but we couldn't stop it. Some people just refused to believe the rumors, until they saw kids on the corner in a heroin stupor, leaning on lampposts looking gutted-out, half dead.

It hit our streets like wildfire. On damn near every block there was a kid who had died from an overdose. It became customary to hear about a heroin-related death. If it didn't attack your family, you thanked God.

I saw some of my girlfriends from school get turned out on this drug. Harry began to separate himself from his best buddies because they started using. In the blink of an eye, we saw our childhood friends get wiped out. Harry and I would talk about this all the time. We were Harlem-born and bred, and we could not believe that our neighborhood was being flipped upside down like this.

It probably sounds naive, but in the forties when we were growing up this kind of thing just didn't happen. No one expected it and nobody saw it coming. People were poor, perhaps, unemployed, maybe, weekend drinkers, even gamblers, but drug addiction had not been so out in the open, until heroin hit the block.

Harry went into a state of shock when he saw one of his buddies trying to shoot up in a vein that was ragged from so much abuse. He thought the guy was going to die right in front of him.

He came home with this blank look, in total disbelief. He told me what had happened when he walked in the house, then he just put his head in my chest and cried. This scared him to death and he made the decision right then and there to stay far from that scene. And he did.

All of Harry's friends died early. Young. I could sense just how lonely Harry was feeling during this time. In order to stay out of that scene, he had to stay away from guys he had known and loved nearly all his life. He and Duke Palmer, his best friend, were the only ones left. They both refused to get mixed up in the vicious circle. Teddy, Boo, and Mickey all died from overdoses.

We were both nineteen when I got pregnant. And we didn't have a dime. There was no money to speak of. Harry did what he could to make ends meet. He had tried all kinds of jobs that just didn't work out for him. He was a painter and did a lot of work painting in the neighborhood around 134th Street. But he was excited about the baby and wanted to marry me. And I always thought he was my soul mate. My mother saw things differently. From the time I met Harry, Mom was bitterly against our relationship. In fact, whenever somebody showed interest in me, my mother would find a way to discourage them by telling them mean things about me. I don't know why she did it, other than maybe she was afraid of losing me. But she didn't succeed with Harry. He loved me and he let her know it. The more she tried to destroy our relationship, the closer Harry and I became. We decided we would get married even though we knew it wouldn't be easy. I will never forget the day I told my mother the news.

Mom thought I should give my baby up and constantly nagged me about it. I didn't understand her attitude. I believed getting married and having the baby was the right thing to do. But she didn't feel the same way. I was shocked when she started talking about abortion, which was so risky back then, not to mention illegal. She was so bothered by my wanting to be married, she would say almost anything to change my mind, no matter how mean or nasty.

To add to the confusion, she got my father involved. *Why?* I'll never know. This was the first time I had ever seen any unity between the two of them. Their responses were almost identical.

My mother said, "You don't have to marry a man because he gets you pregnant."

My father said, "I don't think you should marry this boy because you're pregnant. We can take care of the baby."

As far as I was concerned, neither one of them had ever showed me much love in my life. They couldn't be in a room together five minutes without fussing and fighting. They fought nonstop. I certainly didn't trust them to raise my child. I was not going to allow what happened to me to happen to my baby. Now, how they could gather together and gang up on me to keep me from my first chance at real happiness was beyond me.

Between the two of them, they were making my life a living hell. With all the bickering that was going on, I was just miserable.

"I am not having a bastard!" I told them. "I'm a bastard. My two brothers are bastards. I'm not going to bring another bastard into this family."

Besides, Harry wanted to marry me. There was no reason for me to try to raise this child alone. I was three months pregnant during all of the fighting. We got married, three months before my due date.

During my pregnancy, I had one maternity dress. I wore it during the day and washed it out at night. It was a black dress trimmed in white lace at the collar and cuffs. I felt bad about wearing the same dress every day, even if it was clean. By this time, Mom and I had moved into my god-parent's building at 229 West 134th Street. We lived in the basement apartment and they lived upstairs. There were a few other girls on the street who were pregnant at the time. And I remember, they had nice maternity dresses, bright and pretty for the summer months. I was ashamed of my appearance, so I didn't go out much. I would go out into our backyard and sit there most of the time. I was sad at a time when I should have been the happiest.

Because of all the turmoil going on at my mother's house, my father stepped in for the first time ever and offered Harry and me an apartment he had on 124th Street and Eighth Avenue. It was a four-story walkup, and the apartment was on the fourth floor. The daily trek up those four flights was rough, but it beat staying at my mother's. Right after we moved in, my health started acting up. I think everything had just caught up with me and I was physically and emotionally exhausted.

My mother would come by every day to see about me. We had our differences but she would always come through. In later years, she went out of her way to take care of me. She insisted that I move back in with her during my ninth month. I guess she figured I had been through enough. Harry's Mom, Louise, helped out in every way she could. She was one of the sweetest ladies in the world. She always treated me like her daughter. She'd always come around to smooth things out and make it a happy time for me and Harry.

Our wedding was the funniest little wedding in the world. I always wanted to get married in a church but that wasn't to be. Harry and I went down to city hall and got our marriage license, then, five days later, we got married in our basement apartment at 229 West 134th Street. I was good and pregnant and all dressed up with my belly sitting way out, standing there, saying, "I do."

My mother had gone and gotten this jack-legged preacher to marry us. I don't know where she got that man. She was known to go into anybody's church and join up. My mother took me into more storefront churches than I can even remember. If you just put a sign outside your front door that said "CHURCH," my mother would go. And even though my mother and father had worn me out and made me depressed about the marriage and the pregnancy, our wedding was a regular comedy. It was funny, funny, funny. The preacher was running around there trying to drink up all the wine. And he just didn't look like a preacher. I didn't trust him. But we went on with the ceremony. Helen and Aunt Elsie were there. There were just a handful of people from the neighborhood there.

Well, Harry and I were married, but it was hell from day one. Looked like they just put something on us and determined that we would not be. No matter what we did or what we tried, it was hard on us. I am convinced that all that commotion during my pregnancy had a negative effect on the experience I had during delivery. I was in labor for what seemed like days but was only hours. It was brutal. Thank God we both survived it. Our son, Richard, was born in the winter, six pounds, twelve ounces. He had some minor health problems. He was born with asthma and he was a very nervous baby. But we loved him and cared for him; he had no choice but to get better.

I nursed him. I had so much breast milk that the nurses would come to pump my breasts almost every hour. They shared my milk with some of the other mothers who had problems lactating and for babies who weren't well. I certainly didn't mind giving up the milk, because my breasts were big as Harlem. I had enough milk to nurse four or five babies. It was really rather ridiculous. When I got home, my mother showed me how to dry up the milk. Her old home remedies, if they didn't kill you, they'd cure you. She had me press each breast out on a hot stove, one at a time, and between the heat and the pain, the milk would begin to dry up.

It was an old backwoods remedy, but it worked.

Soon after my son was born, I lost the ability to walk. I don't know what caused the condition, but it was a temporary paralysis. I had extensive physical therapy to gain back the use of my legs.

Harry was crazy about Richard. He always called him "that sugar." And I called him P.J. On our way home from the hospital Richard's godfather and our good friend, Russell Woodard, carried him to the house, singing, "*Yes sir, that's my baby, no sir, don't mean maybe . . .*" It was a joyous occasion despite its complications.

Harry's birth mother had a grandfather who was still living, Edward Boardley. We all called him Gramps. He made it a point to stay close to Harry and me. I really loved Gramps. Things were always better if he was around. Now, Gramps had some kind of life. He had traveled all over the world as a chef and had cooked in some of the world's finest restaurants. For a black man in the thirties and forties that was, of course, a huge accomplishment. He had been the chef for the mayor of Philadelphia at one time in his career. His closeness to our family meant a lot to us. It gave Harry and me a sense of family, which is one of the things I loved so much about being with Harry. I had met so few relatives on my mother's side of the family and knew no one from my father's side. This tormented me for most of my young life. Everybody wants to know where they come from, and in my life, there were so many missing pieces. When Harry and I got together, it made me feel that although they were in-laws, his family was my family, a place where I belonged. My son could grow up with a real sense of family and be surrounded by people who loved him.

We also had Aunt Pearl, Harry's aunt. Sweet Aunt Pearl, Louise Hernandez's sister. When our son, Richard, was born Aunt Pearl would come every day to bring him fresh fruit and vegetables, and whatever else she thought we needed. She worked as a domestic and went to work every single day, even on Saturdays and Sundays, if they needed her. Aunt Pearl looked just like a full-blooded American Indian. Her skin was bronze-colored and her hair was jet-black. She must have been about forty years old at this time. She never married. Aunt Pearl had spent her entire life helping her sister raise Harry when he was a kid. She was a wonderful woman and a great help to me and Harry.

Now that I had my husband and my baby, the dream of college and studying medicine slowly slipped away. I had to make a living. Harry had his own construction business. He was working as a painter and decorator, but he was frustrated. In those days, black men didn't have much opportunity to really work in that field. They weren't allowed in the unions, so they made pennies on the dollar, half the money white men made doing the same job. And Harry could build things. He could have worked in construction or interior design. Truth be told, Harry was a fine artist, a talented painter, with an honest to God gift. Doing odd jobs in the Garment district and out in Brooklyn at the Naval Yard got on his nerves. He knew he was talented but he wasn't making the kind of money he wanted to make.

I was proud of Harry. He was not afraid of hard work and he could find work just about anywhere. He was out there hustling numbers in the Harlem streets for extra cash, which is how a lot of black men made money in those days. People played the numbers the same way they play Lotto today, except it was all done undercover.

Back then, the winning number was based on the horse races. They would take the last three digits of the total handle, the total amount of money spent that day at the races, and that was your winning number. People would go into the barbershops and record stores and fish joints, all kinds of secret spots to put money on a number. They'd write their number down on a piece of paper and hand it over to the numbers runner, and at the end of the day, the winners would collect. I remember Harry used to take Richard out in the baby carriage in the afternoons, and he would pick up people's numbers along the way. He would stroll down the street and people would stop and talk, while making sure to give him their number in between the conversation. Ladies would come up, saying, "Oh, hey, Harry, how's the baby doing? Oh, he's getting big. Five-two-seven, boxed. Tell Gloria we said hello." And they'd slip him the money on the sly.

Well, baby, he would come back in the house with the baby, and all those slips would be hidden up under the padding of Richard's baby buggy. It was hilarious. You just had to laugh. I tell you, all the things we had to do to make a dollar! It wasn't nothing but funny. The money Harry made from the numbers kept us with all the things we needed, so I didn't worry about it. I let Harry do his thing.

At one point, we moved in with our childhood friends, Dorothy Gonzalez and her husband, Eduardo. When money got too tight, we all pitched in together to make it work. Well, these were fun times. Dorothy was like a sister to me. We all called each other sister back then, because nobody knew who their people were or where they were from. There was so much migration to the North from Southern cities, people were scattered all over the place. Growing up on the same block was like blood.

We took an apartment together on 118th Street. It was a big old place and we had a ball in there. We were two new couples. Dorothy and I had our new husbands, our new babies, and each other. There were nothing but good times at 118th Street. Richard was a baby then and Dorothy had three girls: Bonita, who we called "Red," Angela, and Bootsie, who died at a very young age of obesity. We lived together for at least a year or so.

I continued to sing, doing the nightclub circuit up in Harlem. In 1950, I joined a group called the Metronomes. There were three guys and I was the only girl. I stayed with them for a minute, about six or seven months, then I joined an all-girl group, the Dorsey Sisters. Now, we had a lot of success together. There were five of us, and out of the five, four of us were named Gloria. Well, we had to change that. Somebody would call out, "Gloria," and all four of us would turn around. So, we made up different stage names for ourselves. I chose the name Diane for myself.

As a group act, we entered the Apollo Amateur and won. So, we split the fifteen-dollar prize and got our songs together to sing for the weeklong engagement. Lucky Millinder's band was playing that week. Lucky was a terrific bandleader, a real showman. He had a lot of style and flair . . . and a brilliant smile. He was known for his smile. His smile took up his whole face. Well, Lucky liked us. He thought we had a nice sound. So, he took us under his wing and asked us to go on tour with his band. That was Lucky's reputation. He always kept an ear out for young, new talent. He helped a lot of musicians' careers over the years.

The Dorsey Sisters looked good and sounded good. So, Lucky organized a radio show for us, which we did for the veterans overseas. Well, we thought this was the living end. We came running back to the neighborhood, bragging:

"Hey, y'all, we gonna be on the radio!"

Then Lucky did the unimaginable. He set us up on tour as the opening act for Ella Fitzgerald. We did a complete tour of the eastern seaboard. We hit the Apollo first, then continued on to the Howard in Washington, D.C., the Regal in Baltimore, and the Earle in Philadelphia. We were so excited at the chance to just meet her, let alone to open for her. She had won the Amateur Apollo just like us. She had worked with every popular musician of the day—Benny Carter, Duke Ellington, Dizzy Gillespie—and she took over Chick Webb's orchestra after he died.

Ella *was* swing music. She was as big as it gets. She had tremendous energy. It was really quite amazing to witness. We were young girls and completely in awe of this woman's talent. Ella was extraordinary. She had one of the most incredible instruments ever. She had a wide range and her elocution was perfect. She could deliver such clear, round tones, and you understood every single word out of her mouth. Ella really set the standard for a lot of us coming behind her. She was sweet and sophisticated, and completely dedicated to her music. And she was one of the nicest ladies I have ever met. Ella was nothing but sweet and kind. Anything nice you can name, that was Ella. Well, I was going by the name Diane then, and I remember our first meeting. She came over to me during one of our rehearsals and said:

"Diane, you're going to be a star."

Ella's words were reassuring for me. They came at a time when I was so unsure about the direction of my career. Her endorsement meant the world to me. By this time, she had recorded hit on top of hit. Everyone knew her by "A-Tisket A-Tasket" and "Lady Be Good." She had done all of the famous songbooks—Gershwin, Rodgers & Hart, Cole Porter, Duke Ellington, Jerome Kern and Harold Arlen, Johnny Mercer. Ella was considered one of the finest singers in the world. I considered myself very lucky to have met her and toured with her so early in my singing career.

I tried to stay close to Ella but she was always on the road. She traveled most of the year. She was never off. Just like the blues artist B. B. King. B.B. works 360 days on the job and the other five he's traveling *to* a job. You find a lot of artists like that from the old school. They're not happy unless they're doing what they do best. Their job is their vacation. And let's face it, work is a blessing, no matter how you cut it.

I remember once the Dorsey Sisters had to work a club out in New Jersey. We were on the same bill with the comedian Redd Foxx. Mom, Helen, Aunt Elsie, and a few others from the block came out to see the show. Redd Foxx was a headliner on the comedy circuit then. This is before he had teamed up with Slappy White. We went out there and did our opening numbers, then I stood in the wings to watch Redd's show.

I remember peeping out into the audience, looking for my mother. Well, when I spotted her, she was out there falling all over the place, hanging all off her chair, screaming and hollering and carrying on.

I was outdone!

I had never seen my mother act like that.

I said, "I know this man's not that funny that he's got my mother showing out." I was actually angry. I was very disturbed to see my
mother in that state. I couldn't believe it. I said, "Oh, no, not my mother.
This just can't be." Well, after the show was over, I went over to Redd
and said:

"Who the hell are *you*?" He looked at me like I was crazy. I told him:
"You've got my mother out there coming all out of herself. Just who the
hell *are* you?"

Redd was crazy; he said, "Aw, fuck your mother." Just like that. "You
just mad 'cuz I made your mama laugh, that's all."

He was right. I had never seen my mother act like that. Now, she
could make you holler, have you in stitches, laid all out on the floor, but
not her. She could keep a straight face. She always taught me to stand up
straight and walk tall and dress neat and all that. And here she was falling
all out in public at the man's concert. Well, from that day forward, I had
nothing but contempt for Mr. Redd Foxx. I held on to it for a long time.
I was desperate to hate him. And I let him know it.

Redd and I used to run into each other a lot when we were coming
up and I tried hard to hate him, but finally I had to let it go. He was just
too damn funny, a real sweetheart, really. We ended up touring together.
Back then, we would do sixteen cities back to back. Going on the road in
those days was always a trip. We traveled by bus or a lot of times we went
in separate cars, like a traveling caravan. It was tiring work but it's how
we all made our living.

Redd and I worked the Apollo a lot together. He liked to hang out
back in the dressing rooms, just cutting the fool. He'd be back there telling
lies and jokes and would just keep you laughing. I remember one day Redd
Foxx, Art Blakey, and Jimmy Smith were hanging out in my dressing room
and Harry walked in. Harry said:

"I want all you niggers out of this dressing room because y'all making
my wife hoarse. Now, she can't sing *and* laugh."

Well, Harry was right. I would be laughing so hard before my concert
that my voice would suffer because of it. Singers aren't supposed to be
doing all that laughing and carrying on before a show, but with those fools
around, you couldn't keep it together. As it turned out, Redd and I got
real close over the years. We became the very best of friends. After all the
time I tried to hate him, he ended up being like a big brother to me. I

could go to Redd for anything. He would give me money, anything I needed. He treated me just like a sister. Always.

The Dorsey Sisters continued touring, but it was taking a toll on all of us. I was away from Richard, which was difficult for me, and the other girls had family obligations. Being a part of a group is hard, hard work. And since I had started out on my own, as a solo act, I had to adjust to working around other people's schedules. It wasn't easy. You can't ever seem to get everybody on the same page at the same time. People would show up late to rehearsals or not show up at all. All kinds of things went on. For all the good we gained and lessons learned, the Dorsey Sisters broke up after about a year together. We broke up for boyfriend reasons, husband reasons, baby reasons. I was the only one who had a baby, then one of the other girls got pregnant midstream, and it got too hard to keep the momentum going.

The next group I joined was the Delltones. I gave them a whirl for a while. The group was named for its originator, Della Griffin. Della's still in the business. She's a very talented drummer and vocalist, a real sweet lady. The Delltones were another all-girl group. It was a good experience, but after a few short months, I decided to go it alone. The thing is, we were all so young then. You didn't know what was going to happen next. You couldn't make a commitment to much of anything at that age. The uncertainty in this business never goes away, but the younger you are, the more uncertain it is. Even with the success I was having, I wasn't sure how it would all turn out. Harry was working hard and my mother helped out a lot with the baby, but I wanted some guarantees. Little did I know, that's the one thing this business can't give you.

I started doing demonstration work down in Tin Pan Alley, in midtown, near Broadway. All of the music publishing houses were down there. The Brill Building was a popular spot where most of us singers would go to try to get work. A lot of lyricists and songwriters had small offices there. Record producers would make demos of songs that they wanted to pitch to big singers.

They'd say, "We need this demo for Ella, we need this one for Sarah, for Dinah . . ."

Then they'd send the demos to the stars to see if they wanted to perform their songs.

I had a very versatile voice, so I could do just about any voice they needed. A bunch of us singers would hit this area every day. We did what the cleaning ladies used to do. Say it was four or five cleaning ladies, they'd take two or three floors each, so they wouldn't interfere with each other. We did the same thing with the music publishers. We'd go floor to floor, knocking on doors.

"You need any singers today?"

They'd say, "Yeah. Can you read music?"

I'd answer back.

"Yes, I can."

I lied, lied, lied.

I couldn't read a note.

"Are you fast?"

I was. Sometimes if the music was difficult, I'd ask the piano player to run it down to me once, slow. They'd only do it for you once, then you had to get it. I made five dollars a song. In the fifties, this is how I made my living.

It's also how I got discovered.

I was excited about the money I was making and happily shared it with Harry. He was still working as a painter and doing different odd jobs. And here I was making a name for myself on the singing circuit, making more money than him. Well, this was hard for him to handle. Even though he was supportive of me and would come to all my shows and sit right up front, underneath it all, he wasn't comfortable with the situation. It made him feel less than a man.

I couldn't let that stop me. I felt the money I was bringing in was for all of us.

"God has blessed us," I told Harry. "He didn't say who was going to make more money than who. We're a family."

5

Big Deals

In 1957, I met Harry Belock and Raymond Scott. I was making my usual rounds down at the Brill Building and they were scouting talent for their new label, Everest Records. They had gone around to different music publishers, listening to demo tapes, to find a new voice. In their search, they ran across a demo I had done. They really liked my voice, so they called me up. Raymond Scott said they were looking for a singer to work on some music they wanted to produce. So, I sat down with him and his partner, Harry Belock, and discussed their plans to build a sound board and do some recording. Harry was the money man and Raymond was the creative guy. They were talking in such technical terms that I didn't fully understand all of the mechanics of what they were proposing, but they were going to pay me five hundred dollars, and I understood that. So, I agreed immediately. Five hundred dollars was more money than I had ever made on one job. Five hundred dollars in the fifties was plenty of money.

Raymond Scott was a former bandleader and pianist. He performed a lot in the late thirties and in the forties. By the time we met, he was working mostly in pop music as a composer, arranger, and recording engineer. I believe he even had his own television show at one time. He invited me and my friend Kenny Burrell to his home in Manhassett, New York, to begin working on the music. He had a beautiful house. It was a mansion, really. Raymond was an electronics genius. He had a fully equipped recording studio in his house. I remember seeing all kinds of equipment. He even had an apparatus that allowed him to make contact with certain types of aircraft. He was a great recording engineer. And a really fine artist. Raymond had a way of making you feel comfortable and at ease. He was always interested in your input. And he was very interested in my vocal ability. He used to say, "Gloria, you have such sincerity and power." He thought I could really tell a story with my voice. We laid out some of the songs and played around with different arrangements. I worked on the vocals and Kenny did the guitar accompaniment. Well, Raymond fell in love with our sound, so he decided, right then, that we should do an album together.

While we created new arrangements for the upcoming album, we also created Gloria Lynne. I had been using, as a stage name, my married name, Alleyne, but people had such a hard time pronouncing it. They would say "Al-yen-nay" or "Ally-nay," so I took a derivation of the last name, and came up with Lynn, which I used for a very short time. Then Raymond Scott suggested that I add an "e" on the end of "Lynn," for flair. I think someone else told me, in numerology, Lynne had a stronger vibration than Lynn. And crazy as it sounds, I'm superstitious to this day about that little "e," because it seems like once I added it, my fortune changed. Good things really started to happen. So, I get a little panicked when people spell it incorrectly.

Our months of collaboration resulted in my first album, *Miss Gloria Lynne*. We recorded the album for Everest Records on November 1, 1958. I couldn't have asked for a better debut. Raymond handpicked these musicians and every last one of them was a star in his own right. I was a virtual unknown, playing with musicians who had huge careers, big names in jazz. It was an all-star band. We had Harry "Sweets" Edison on trumpet, who had played with Count Basie's big band, and Buddy Rich. He had toured with Pearl Bailey, Louis Bellson, and Frank Sinatra. "Wild" Bill Davis played organ for us. He was one of the few jazz organists of the day. A bad, bad key man. He was a native New Yorker, too. "Wild" Bill grew up in Queens. And of course Kenny Burrell had played with everybody. He toured with Dizzy for a while and with the phenomenal pianist Oscar Peterson when Oscar's regular guitarist, Herb Ellis, took a leave from the trio. Honestly, I had a fabulous band. I couldn't have asked for anything more. We had Milt Hinton on bass; George Duvivier; Tom Bryant; Eddie

Costa on vibes; Sam Taylor on tenor sax; and "Philly" Jo Jones on drums, who was, and I believe, still is, considered one of the greatest drummers in the world. He had worked with Gil Evans, Miles Davis, Dexter Gordon, and Tadd Dameron. Everybody knew "Philly" Jo. The album couldn't miss. It was a huge, huge debut for me. *Miss Gloria Lynne* was a very big deal. And I also found that the wonderful thing about having worked all the nightclubs and bar rooms up in Harlem was, when my album was released, people were ready for it. They knew me.

We recorded some wonderful songs on the album. A lot of the songs were standards and had been made popular by other well-known vocalists, so we really had to do some great arrangements to add something fresh to the music. With your debut album, you establish your style. You're judged on what you're bringing to the table. And although it's great to be compared to Sarah and Dinah and Billie, every vocalist wants to make her own mark. The critics are going to compare you anyway, but you want to give the public something fresh that's got your signature on it. I worked very hard on each song.

And I really trusted Raymond Scott. He had some very definite ideas for the album and we worked well together. We did our rendition of "April in Paris" on the record and "Perdido," which I had great success with in nightclubs. It's also a song you can sing slow, medium, or upstairs. It's a flexible little tune. We recorded "Bye Bye Blackbird," "I Can't Give You Anything but Love," "I Don't Know Why," "They Didn't Believe Me," "Without a Song," "Just Squeeze Me," and "Little Fingers." "Little Fingers" is a lullaby that the late great Nat King Cole made famous. I chose it to add some variety to the album. "Stormy Monday" was my idea as well. I remember growing up as a teenager and hearing Billy Eckstine sing "Stormy Monday" down at the Apollo on Saturday nights with Earl Hines's band, and I loved it. In fact, I loved Eckstine. Who didn't? He was our heartthrob back in the day. He was stunningly gorgeous. Amazingly charming. Truly. So, I added "Stormy Monday" to remind me of what I was swinging to as a teenager. Now, "June Night" was the biggest surprise yet. It was the one song I was a little reluctant to sing for whatever reason, but it turned out to be the big hit single from the album. "All Day Long" was Kenny Burrell's composition. And after a discussion we had in a cab, I pushed him to include it on the album and I wrote the lyrics to it right then and there.

Miss Gloria Lynne is so special to me. It was a wonderful collaboration of dedicated artists. And I will always love Raymond Scott for putting it all together. He's one of the greatest people I've ever worked with.

Miss Gloria Lynne got the attention of a lot of music people. Nat Hentoff and Leonard Feather, the music critics, gave it a "thumbs-up." I began to get bookings all over Manhattan and at some of the popular downtown clubs, like Café Society, Birdland, and the Village Gate. And I worked the East Side, especially at Basin Street East, where I later recorded a live album. I remember once, Miles Davis showed up at Basin Street East to hear me sing. After the set, he came over and said, in that gruff, hoarse voice of his:

"You know, these white folks don't know what you're doing. They don't even understand it."

He told me how much he liked my voice, which was a high compliment because Miles didn't like much. With the release of *Miss Gloria Lynne*, my career shifted into high gear. I got plenty of public exposure. Now, I was working like a mule, but I was loving the work.

My career was on the upswing, but my home life was on a serious decline. Harry was acting up. He had started running around with other women. Well, he was fine, so the women gave me a fit. They wouldn't leave him alone. I knew it but I didn't want to deal with it. Not right then. My career was on the move and I wasn't ready to face the fact that things between us were falling apart.

Everything was new. Being a mother. Being a wife. Being a professional singer. I was learning all the ropes, all at once. We were trying to make the marriage work, but there were so many pressures, so many frustrations. And when my measure of success came—when I say success I mean $500 and $1,000 dollars a week—Harry got downright belligerent. That money is equivalent to, maybe, $4,000 a week today. And even though our bills were paid and we worried less about money, Harry had to be "the man." He wanted to be the one to support the family. Instead of seeing it as a blessing, he took it as a personal affront, as if he wasn't doing what he was supposed to be doing, as the head of the household. We had never experienced that kind of money before. It was a point of contention between us, but we tried to get along. His mother, Louise, knew things were hard on us. She would hear us fussing and fighting all the time, because when things got really rough, Harry would go back to his mother's house and stay. But no matter what the argument was about, Louise always took my side. That woman was so good to me. She was the best mother-in-law in the world. Nobody had a mother-in-law as good as mine. She was a comfort to be around and she'd do anything for you. You didn't even have to ask.

Soon after my first album was released, Raymond Scott and Harry Belock decided to turn Everest Records over to a California-based business-man, Bernard Solomon. Although I knew about their plans to sell the company, I did not know what to expect from the new owner. Raymond was great to work with because he was an artist and was sensitive to the needs of an artist. He understood the creative process. Harry Belock I didn't know as well, but never had any problems with him. But the new owner, Bernie Solomon, was an entirely different story. He was all business. It was all about the money, baby.

I was locked in at Everest. I had a seven-year deal. So, Bernie Solomon couldn't change that, but the changes he did make affected me tremendously. After he came on board, I realized, for the first time, that I knew very little about the business side of the business. I had jumped in with both feet and never stopped to ask: *How deep is the water?* If there were flaws in my contract with Everest, they could have been staring me in the face and I wouldn't have noticed. I was young and naive and didn't ask the right questions. For my lack of knowledge and experience, Bernie Solomon got album after album out of me without paying me what I was worth.

Even though my name was out there and I was able to get work in clubs, it became very apparent to me that Bernie Solomon had cashed in.

It was strange, because in the very beginning, Solomon treated me well. When I would go out to California on tour, I'd have carte blanche. I'd stay in the best hotels, ride in limos, the whole deal. He had it laid out for me. But that's just it. Many record execs will pay you, they just won't pay you what you deserve. And before you know it, you owe them money. If you're not careful, they'll keep you indebted to them. It's a very tricky business. First of all, in those days, there was no clear-cut way of tracking record sales. You believed you sold what the record company told you you sold. If your name was out there and you were able to get steady work performing, you just assumed everything was cool.

I felt I was kept in the dark most of the time.

Ordinarily, artists are charged for 100 percent of the production costs, which can include everything from the cost of studio time, on down to the cost of the gown you wore to an interview to promote the record, and the limo you rode in to get there. So, by the time you go to the record company to get money, the answer is always the same, "There's no money . . . you owe *us* money." While you're out on the town, enjoying the high life, every red cent of those costs is being charged to your account, that and other costs that you may or may not know about. Things tend to get very gray when you're dealing with record executives.

Soon after the success of the *Miss Gloria Lynne* album, Solomon asked me to move to California. I considered it. I went home and asked my mother what she thought and she told me, very plainly:

"I do not want to live in California."

She had this thing about California. "Something out there's just not right."

She had gotten into her groove of Harlem living, free of all of the restrictions she had been living under with my father and Mr. Johnson, and she wasn't ready to give all of that up. I could hardly blame her, because deep down, I wasn't ready to leave home either. New York City was my stomping ground. I was working regularly and making a living.

Jazz was still hot and heavy in New York. First it was swing, then it was bop, then the cool jazz thing—Miles Davis and John Coltrane's sound, then it moved into what they started calling "free jazz," Charles Mingus and Ornette Coleman's groove. But for vocalists, it didn't matter quite as much what mode jazz was in as long as the public enjoyed your music and your execution of the songs. Like Duke Ellington used to say, "If it sounds good, it is good." During those years, some of the most gorgeous music in the world was written. And the term "standard" meant that the song would linger on for time immemorial. It would never lose its popularity, which, in turn, could mean longevity for a singer's career.

New York was faithful to jazz. There were still dozens of rooms that welcomed vocalists and dozens of bands that would play for you. New York and jazz went hand in hand. Jazz was the thing. Throughout the forties and fifties, if you were a tourist, you could get in a taxi and say, "Take me to the Street." And they knew what you were talking about. Fifty-second Street was jumping, the Village was happening, Harlem was still hot. And here was Bernie Solomon asking me to leave and come out to California. I turned him down. I told him I'd prefer to stay on the East Coast but continue to tour, occasionally, on the West Coast. I told him I didn't want to relocate my son and my mother.

Well, this bothered him, and after that, I noticed a complete turnaround in Solomon. His whole attitude toward me changed. He became cold and indifferent. He took it all personally, I guess. I never completely understood his reaction. But this is definitely when things between us turned foul.

In 1959, I met Duke Wade. We met at the Apollo Theater when I was performing there, along with some other acts Duke had booked.

Duke had a good reputation in the business. He was one of the few black booking agents at that time. Duke worked with a lot of female vocalists, like Ruth Brown, Etta Jones, and Betty Carter, and he was Ray Charles's road manager. He was also part of the so-called major agency fold. Duke was a rare breed. I believe he has single-handedly booked more bands, singers, and groups than some of the major booking agencies.

A lot of black artists reached out to him for engagements at nightclubs, theaters, and concert venues. When we met, he booked and managed the Club Baron in Harlem on 132nd and Lenox Avenue. Duke worked with all the top black artists of the day: Ray Charles, Billy Eckstine, Betty Carter, Etta Jones, Jerry Butler, George Benson, Jimmie McGriff, Ruth Brown, Ray Schinery, Gene Ammons, Lionel Hampton, Arthur Prysock, Freddie Hubbard, Marlena Shaw, Millie Jackson, Herman Foster, Sam and Dave. Down through the years, Duke has kept me working. I was really excited about our collaboration, because with the release of *Miss Gloria Lynne*, I could rely on Duke to book me on a steady basis.

Things at home hadn't improved. The more I worked, the more distant Harry became. He moved out, eventually, and went back to his mother's. Our breakup was sad and disappointing and everything else that breakups are, but we both loved each other and accepted the fact that we couldn't live together. I was hurt, but I can't say that I didn't see it coming.

I was making enough, by now, to move all of us, me, Mom, and Richard, to a really nice place, in a new apartment complex on Lenox Avenue and 132nd Street, The Lenox Terrace. It was absolutely beautiful. There were a lot of people in show business living there in the sixties. Nipsey

Russell, the comedian, was one of our neighbors, and the singer Linda Hopkins. Mary and Ron Gilliam lived there—Mary was Nancy Wilson's sister-in-law. We had a two-bedroom with a large kitchen and plenty of closets. It was the finest place Mom and I had ever lived. She was really happy there. In fact, later on, when I wanted to buy a house, it took all kinds of convincing for me to get her out of there. The Lenox Terrace, for me, represents the height of my success as a young singer. I could afford to do things for my family that I didn't think possible. The financial pressures of the past were gone, which was a real blessing. I could afford to send Richard to the best schools and ensure that he got a good education.

Around this time, Mom and I decided to pull my brothers, Harry and John, out of the mental institution. They were about eighteen and nineteen years old at the time. When they came home, we realized they hadn't been learning anything in all these years. They didn't know how to read. They didn't know how to write. They didn't know A from B. We taught them both all the basics. They had been in the institution all that time just existing. It was a shame. So Mom made sure they were up to speed. They were grown men and they needed to be able to cope in society. The institution did get them jobs and places to live. I was happy to have them back with us.

Things changed, of course, when my brothers came home. Well, first, my baby brother Harry didn't want to live with us. He wanted to live on his own. So, the institution had set up temporary housing for them, until they could place them elsewhere. Harry was always the independent one, even though he was the youngest. John had his own place, too, but he spent plenty of time at home with me and Mom. Well, honey, John in that apartment was a story in itself.

My son, Richard, must have been around seven years old at the time and wasn't accustomed to John's ways. Once, I remember, Richard was in the bathroom and John needed to get in there. So John, being who he is, just busted on in, knocked Richard in the head, and went on about his business. Well, Richard came running out of the bathroom, crying.

"He hit me."

I had to nip that in the bud. After I calmed Richard down, I told John:

"Come here. I want to talk to you."

I knew I had to get to John's level and really make him understand that he couldn't push Richard around. I knew he didn't mean any harm, but we had to try to restrain him, because John was just wild. Sweet as he could be, but reckless.

"John, listen," I told him. "Just because y'all were incarcerated because of your condition, that doesn't mean I don't have the condition. I just escaped it. Now, the next time you put your hands on Richard, I am going to go into the kitchen, boil up some hot water, and drown you in it."

Well, this scared the shit out of him. But that's how I had to handle John. And to this day, he minds what I say. Naturally, I hated to have to go to that place, but if we were all going to make it out of there alive, that's what I had to do.

I remember, during this time, I was pretty recognizable in Harlem. Everybody knew me on the club circuit. Well, when we were living in Lenox Terrace, people used to call my mother and tell her, "Yeah, you better come on down here and get Gloria, because she's around here using dope." And I'd be sitting right there in the living room. People were very mean. As much as I loved Harlem, I didn't have any well-wishers there. At least, I didn't feel like I did. The more successful I became, the less people liked it. I soon fell out of love with the neighborhood.

Here we were living in this luxurious apartment complex but we were constantly seeing people get evicted from the slum buildings on the other side of the street. My mother always felt bad about it. Sometimes, she would actually go outside and ask if there was anything she could do. She always gave money.

John loved to hear me sing and he would beg my mother to let him go to my concerts. Well, one time I was performing in Atlantic City and John said:

"I don't know why I can't go to Atlantic City. My sister's down there."

So my mother thought about it and said, "John, do you think you can get there on the bus by yourself?"

He said he could, so she called up my friend Willa Mae's husband, Mr. Barnes. She asked him if he would meet John at the bus stop and take him to see my show.

Now, Barnes was a handsome man. He was bald long before it was in, and it looked good on him. He was a yogi, so his body was strong and muscular. He was a good-looking man and he loved straw hats. Barnes always wore these nice straw hats. Mom explained to John that Barnes would be there waiting for him when he got off the bus. She gave him a description of Barnes so he could find him. Well, John had this jacket he used to like to wear. He had bought it for himself because we tried to shop for him, but he never liked what we selected for him.

So John said, one day, "I'm tired of people buying my clothes."

And he went down to a men's shop, somewhere in Harlem, and came back with this loud-ass, checkered jacket. The checks on that thing were wide as I don't know what, black and white checks. Baby, it gave gingham a whole new meaning. And it looked funny on him. Mom hated the jacket and told John she better not ever catch him in it. She threatened to throw it out, but she never did. Well, the day he got on that bus to Atlantic City, John had somehow slid out the house with the jacket on, without my mother seeing him.

When John reached Atlantic City, he got off the bus, and I guess he thought that Barnes was going to be standing right there in front of the bus doors the very second the bus pulled in. When John didn't see him, he panicked. He went straight to the telephone.

"He's not here! That man's not here to get me!"

And my mother asked him, "Well, did you look for him? He should be there."

John had a fit. He was so upset. He was easy to excite, you know. He started hollering at my mother.

"You said he would be here!"

Mom said, "Well, John, I'll try to call him and I'll describe you to him, so he can find you."

"Well, you can describe me if you want to," John said, "because I got that jacket on!"

All I heard was my mother calling him a black bastard over and over again. My mother, I swear, was so uppity. She did not enjoy being embarrassed. Now, she was a country woman, but you couldn't bring that back into her face at any point and time. She did not want to be reminded of where she came from. So, the idea that Barnes would have to see John in that jacket just sent her into a tizzy. John was hollering on one end of the phone. She was hollering out all kinds of "black bastards" on the other end. It was a mess.

Barnes finally found John, and I guess John called himself upset with Barnes for not being there, right in front of that bus. But John never gave the man more than thirty seconds to appear. He just went flying straight to the phone when he didn't see him. Anyway, Barnes walked John to his car and drove him to the club where I was performing. Well, John, being spiteful, sat on the man's straw hat and ruined it. When I heard this, I told John:

"I'm not taking you anyplace else. That's it."

My mother was upset, but I really felt bad. Barnes was my friend's husband and it wasn't a nice thing to do. And everybody knew Barnes loved his straw hats.

I had to stop letting John come to my shows. Before the end of the night, you could bet that John was going to get into something. I used to joke with him and tell him he really should have gone into promotion or public relations because he had a knack for getting whatever he wanted out of people. He would go up to people and say:

"I'm Gloria Lynne's brother. Can I have your number?"

Now, why people would give him the number I don't understand, but John would do this every time I had a show. He'd get home and have a whole pocketful of cocktail napkins with numbers on them.

"John," I tried to tell him, "people don't want to be bothered with that when they come out to a show." He just ignored me and kept right on collecting his numbers.

There was another time, John showed out at home. My mother was home one evening, entertaining her male company. I was getting ready for a gig that night and John had decided that he would be nice and leave the house, so Mom could entertain her gentleman caller.

Now, when John and Harry were in that institution, the people didn't show them anything about hygiene or how to care for themselves. I don't know what those people called themselves doing in that place. Anyway, Mom had to teach them both about all of that. So Mom told John once:

"If you ever run out of deodorant, use baking soda under your arms."

On this particular night, John had gone and taken his shower and gotten dressed to go out. Mom was in the living room with her friend, when John stuck his head out into the living room and said:

"Mama, I'll be going now. I'm getting ready to leave . . . and, uh, after I took my shower, I put that baking soda under my arms like you told me."

He was saying this in front of company, and my mother was furious. I heard this long pause and I knew she was getting ready to go off! I was back there in my room, cracking up. It was the funniest thing in the world. Because, John talks real loud. He speaks up, you know. And there he was shouting out, in plain English:

"I put that baking soda under my arms like you told me."

My mother almost had a heart attack. Now, for someone else, this would have been no big deal. But my mother had such uppity ways that a little thing like this was enough to make her crazy. When John stepped out of the living room, she hit the roof.

"You black bastard! Why did the Lord make it so I had to raise you black bastards?"

She was ranting and raving about John *and* Harry, and Harry was nowhere around. Oh, it was a scene. I don't know what my mother's gentleman friend must have thought. I guess he thought he had walked straight into a nuthouse.

Back then, the Lenox Terrace offered all of the amenities—they'd bring your car around for you, sign for your packages, there was a twenty-four-hour doorman. They offered all of the services. Well, John never got used to the doorman. He wouldn't let the man open it for him. John would come flying through the doors at Lenox Terrace! He would tear into the building like a wild man and damn near break the doorman's arms, he flung that door open so hard. By the time John was a teenager, the guards at the mental institution told us, it took eight men to hold him. So, they gave him small duties to perform around the place, because they didn't want him to go off. John was strong as a bull. One day, John came tearing through the lobby of our building, and the doorman called up to the apartment.

"Mrs. Wilson," he said, "I don't mean no harm, but your son, John, needs to wait for me to open the door. That's what I'm here for."

My mother didn't like that at all. She was so angry with John. She told him:

"John, that man downstairs . . ."

"What man?"

"The man downstairs who opens the door. John, that's what he's supposed to do."

"I can open the door for myself."

Three days later, as God would have it, John ran clean through the glass door.

"I knew it was going to happen," the doorman said.

Baby, John walked through that door, tore the people's door up, glass was everywhere, and he just kept stepping. He didn't have a scratch on him. Well, they called my mother to tell her about the damage he had done.

"John!" she said. "The people said you broke the front door down."

"They ought to make that glass stronger," he said. "You gonna blame me because the glass ain't strong?"

I tell you, my mother and John had a time together.

But John has always been very giving. So much so that I worry about him. He'll take the clothes off his back and give them to somebody, saying:

"My friend needed it."

He's as grown as grown gets now, but I still worry about him. As a young man in his twenties, we really had to watch out for him.

There was one incident where John got mixed up with these guys in the neighborhood. Now, John never drove a car, never had a license, but they put him in this car with them, to watch out while they went and robbed this place. Of course, they got busted. My mother panicked. They called us from the police precinct and told us John had gotten arrested and Mom nearly passed out. The guys responsible for the robbery told the cops that John was driving the getaway car. Well, John has never set foot in front of a steering wheel.

"How can they blame John for that?" my mother said. "He can't drive."

But this thing was serious, so we had to get John some help. I asked around and a musician friend of mine, Mickey Bass, recommended an attorney, Harold Lovett. He was Miles Davis's attorney.

When the court date came, I tried to explain to John that he didn't have to say anything, that Harold was hired to speak on his behalf.

"You don't have to say nothing, John," I told him. "Just sit there and be quiet. It will all work out."

Harold Lovett spoke to the judge and told him about John's mental condition.

"There's no way he could have driven the getaway car because this man doesn't know how to drive," he said.

Well, the judge made a remark in response to that, then John jumped up there and just tore the courthouse up. He ran up to the judge's bench, crying and carrying on:

"I didn't do anything! I don't know what this is all about! I didn't drive that car! They used me!"

John got off, but Harold Lovett told me when it was all over:

"If I had known your brother was going to do that, I never would have taken this case."

Well, what could we do? John is John.

Since the time of their release from the hospital, we have tried to ensure that both of my brothers have proper housing. Harry always wanted to live on his own and he's been very successful at it. John, on the other hand, has experienced more difficulty. He has lived mostly in adult care homes, where there's a full-time nurse living on the premises along with a few other mentally-handicapped adults, with conditions similar to John's. Finding a good, reliable, well-maintained home is often difficult.

Once, we thought we had found the perfect spot for John. It was a nice house, run by a woman in upstate New York. There were maybe six other patients living in the house. The state usually assists you in finding a home and can offer complete information about each owner or caretaker. Anyway, this particular home came well recommended, and from what we could tell it was well maintained. After several months there, John was complaining that things in the house weren't too pleasant. I decided to drive out to the home, unannounced, to see what was up. What I walked into wasn't only unpleasant, it was an outrage. The woman running the home had these retarded adults living in squalor. The place was filthy. None of them had their own rooms, as we had been promised. They were sleeping on sofas and were barely getting enough to eat. Come to find out, the woman was running a crack den. She was selling drugs in and out of the house and hadn't given a thought about cleaning, maintenance, the patients' welfare, or anything. She was able to get a government subsidy for keeping the adults in her home, but what she knew or cared to know about working with handicapped people didn't amount to a hill of beans.

So, finally, John and I tried to get the social service people out there to check things out. We reported her but it was weeks before anybody bothered to show up. Finally, when the state officials came out to follow up on our complaints, the woman would not let them in.

This was the break we needed.

"Get down on your knees and thank God," I told John. "Things will be straightened out now."

They ended up shutting the home down. They had a laundry list of violations, not to mention the possessing and trafficking of crack cocaine. John was really disturbed by the entire episode. It was discouraging for him, because he wanted to make it on his own and live in a stable environment. After that, he asked if he could live on his own. I thought it was just terrible that he had to go through all of this, so we buckled down and went out to find him a better home. We found a beautiful apartment in a senior citizens complex in upstate New York, which worked out really well for him.

Harry never really went through anything quite as traumatic as that, probably because he had a mean streak, so people usually left him alone. He got into a bad situation, once, with the police in his neighborhood. Harry was always a good dancer. He loved to dance. At one time, he decided to give dance lessons at his house. Now, the neighbors never bothered him or complained about him, until he began offering dance classes to their children. The kids would come by on weekends and Harry would teach them out in his garage. I believe he would have the garage door up, since it was the summer. So, he was in plain view of the neighborhood. Some of the parents knew Harry was mentally handicapped, and I guess they didn't like the idea of him being close to their children. All of a sudden, one Saturday afternoon, the police came by Harry's house and busted him. I got a call that Harry had been arrested and, without missing a beat, I called up another lawyer buddy.

Here we go again, I thought. I knew my brother hadn't done anything improper, but that was the charge, that there were "improprieties or suspected improprieties going on in the home." It didn't take but a minute for the charges to be dropped because they had no proof. And some of the children who danced with John came forward and said he was just a nice man showing them how to dance.

But he was a black man in an all-white neighborhood and that was enough for them to take my brother to jail.

Both of my brothers have done well for themselves, in spite of their condition. John retired from his job after twenty-nine years and Harry is ready to retire after thirty-one years on the job. Both of them held the same jobs that they were given after leaving the institution as teenagers.

They're both living on their own and doing well. They've led very stable lives, thank God.

The fifties were a good time for my family. We fell into a regular routine of living. I was working steady and Mom started looking like her old self again. She was happier than she had been in a long while. And Richard brought a lot of happiness into her life. They were extremely close. You couldn't get between the two of them. They were so tight. But Richard was running Mom ragged. She was getting older and he thought he was grown, even though he was only about ten or so. Well, we talked about it and decided that instead of letting him go to the neighborhood middle school we would place him in military school. Richard said he wanted to go, and he was always a smart kid, so he applied and got in. He attended St. Patrick's Military School in Harriman, New York.

Although he wasn't prey for the city streets, what was going on up there at the private school was an entirely different matter. Richard didn't talk about it much, but I could sense that he was having a time up there with all those white kids. There were only two black students in the whole school, and the other boy was older than Richard, so when he graduated, Richard was all alone. I had terrible dreams the whole time Richard was away. When I'd tell Mom about it, she would say:

"Stop worrying. The boy is fine."

I knew he would get a better education, but at what cost?

The school administration requested that all the parents send the guys their own toiletries on a regular basis. I used to send Richard all brand-name stuff, Ponds lotion and Dial soap. Once, when I went to visit Richard, I noticed that he didn't have any of the things I sent to him.

"What happened to the care package I sent you?" I asked.

"Mom, the school officials take all that stuff when you send it."

I couldn't believe what I was hearing. And trying to fight those military bastards was a battle beyond belief. They were using all kinds of tactics against those boys in the name of discipline and authority. Whenever I called Richard to check on him, there was always something that had gone down to upset him.

"I'm on my way up," I'd tell him. "If whitey gets to you, just beat the hell out of him till I get there."

No mother wants to hear about someone messing over their child, I don't care who you are. Relief is not the word for what I felt when he graduated, but I still believe those people really got in his head. It had an adverse effect on him. When he came back to the city, he attended Eron High School, for a while, but then graduated from the School for Young Professionals in Manhattan.

Mom and I went back to spending a lot of time together. It was like old times. She came to hear me sing, wherever I was performing. I remember doing a show at the Apollo one evening. Duke Wade was there, Art Blakey and his manager were sitting there, and a few other dudes. Around this time, Duke was acting as my manager and had begun to book me on different jobs. Well, baby, Mom walked in there with me and I thought those men were going to have a heart attack. Art Blakey swung around in his chair, and his manager followed right behind him.

"Who is that!" Duke asked.

"That's my mother."

"Your mother!" they all shouted.

They couldn't believe it.

Mom was always pretty. She was *fine*. Men would bump heads when she came down the street. They would knock me down trying to get to her.

"Look now," I told Duke. "Don't you start no mess with my mama."

These were fun times. Mom was enjoying all the limelight I was experiencing. In her own way, that is, because you know, Mom was very reserved. She never showed too much of herself. And she would never go with any man younger than her, so those guys didn't have a chance. But she had to notice these young dudes hitting on her.

Because they *were* hitting, honey.

Men loved her. You know that old blues song that says something about:

"My meat man was a sweet man, brought me chicken every day, said woman you so good, you ain't got pay."

Well, my mother had all that. She was something else. We always had a house full of people. Because Mom could cook like a demon. She had that Louisiana thing in her. She grew up on Cajun food—gumbo, jambalaya, shrimp creole, crawfish. I mean, she could make food taste so good, you'd hurt yourself trying to get to it. She made biscuits that were so big and pretty, they didn't even look real.

I mean, she was a mean cook.

Men just loved being around her. Mom would make desserts so good, you'd go damn near into shock. She had this one dude that worked for the slaughterhouse. He would come around just to bring her meat. He was a funny man, always laughing and making jokes. He would sit up in the kitchen and beat on the pots, making rhythms.

He drank a lot.

Well, my mother would indulge him in all his antics. She would sit through all of that nervous giggling and banging and carrying on, then finally, she would ask him:

"All right. What did you bring me?"

He'd get to pulling out pork roasts and porterhouse steaks. Whatever she wanted, he brought her. She would put all the meat up in the freezer, then she'd turn to him and say:

"OK. Time for you to go now."

I saw my mother do that I don't know how many times. I don't know what was with her. She was weak when she was weak, but when she was strong, watch out! Different men came to visit and when she wanted them to leave, she would pick them up with one hand, at the nape of the neck, and place them outside our front gate. When we lived in the brownstone at 229 West 134th Street, I saw her do this a million times. I remember it so clearly. She would just pick these big dudes up with one hand and drop them out in front of the gate, onto the sidewalk.

I'll tell you something else that happened at 229 West 134th Street. When the kids were really small, Richard and Helen's little Ernestine used to play together all the time. Mom used to let them play out in the back-yard because she could keep an eye on them back there. Well, one day they were out there playing. Little "Red" was with them, too, my friend Dorothy's little girl. We noticed them staring down into the ground. They were just looking in the same spot and digging around in the ground. All three of them were fixated on something and we didn't know what they were up to. And you know, when kids get quiet, they're usually up to no good. So, Mom hollered out there:

"What y'all doing?"

Then she went out there to see. Here comes the crazy part.

"We're playing with these little people," the kids said. We went out there to see what they were talking about. My mother, who wasn't scared of any kind of creature, reached down into the ground and picked up one of the smallest, oddest little creatures any of us had ever seen. They looked like miniature humans. They were about the size of a salt shaker and they had eyes, ears, legs, everything. Mom held one in her hand and I just about gagged. The kids weren't scared of them either. But it was a creepy scene. Anyway, none of us could figure it out. So, Mom decided to call the undertaker who was a friend of hers. Now, the way that block was laid out, it went: brownstone, brownstone, undertaker. They called him Blue and he was a big ol' dude. He came down there and said:

"What's up?"

Well, he took one look at these creatures and that man looked like he was about to faint. That's when my mother got scared. She hadn't been afraid until this big dude started stumbling and stuttering.

"Uh, I don't know uh," Blue said, "I need a drink."

This thing scared him damn near to death.

"Y'all better call the board of health," he finally said.

So, Mom went inside and put one of those things in a jar. I couldn't believe she was touching the thing. And when she held it in her hand, it looked back at her, just as alert, like "how dare you." It did everything but speak. The rest of the creatures had squirmed around and buried themselves back into the dirt. The woman from the board of health couldn't make out what Mom was talking about over the phone, so they finally sent some guys out there to check it out. The men came in the backyard, took one look, and said:

"We'll be back."

Well, baby, they came back with all this headgear on, driving in one of those big, funny-looking white trucks. They had on masks and every part of their bodies was covered up. They went out back and scanned the whole yard. They took away the little creature that Mom had put in a jar. Then they told my mother:

"Now, Miss, you can't talk about this."

My mother said: "The hell I can't. This is my house."

But she wanted that mess out of her yard, so she went along with them until they had cleared everything out.

Something is truly amiss with this building.

Right now, today, 229 West 134th is still standing but nearly all the buildings on that block have been knocked down or boarded up. But believe me, this story is true, I couldn't have made this up if I tried, and I have eyewitnesses. Richard was there. And Ernestine was there. They're both grown now, but they never forgot that day.

None of us did.

Around 1951, 229 West 134th caught fire. We were burned out of there in the dead of winter, with nothing but our nightclothes on. The *Daily News* came out to report on the fire, it was so huge. They even had a picture of us in the paper. I was standing there with my face all swollen up from crying. That building was full of memories.

Bernie Solomon was still running things like a tyrant at Everest. Nonetheless, I continued going into the studio to work on new songs for my next album, *Day In Day Out*. And *Miss Gloria Lynne* was still selling well.

To promote the upcoming album, Duke booked me to do two shows at the Apollo. My friend Helen was with me. She had started traveling with me at this point. Now, Frank Sinatra was *the* hottest name in the music business at this time. And he had just started his record label, Reprise. He didn't come to the Apollo to see my show, but he sent two of his guys down there. I saw them lurking around the backstage area. Something about them made me nervous, but I just went on with my show. When I finished the first set, they came over to me and said they wanted me to come with them. Well, I didn't know who they were or what they were talking about. So I refused.

"I have another show to do," I told them, "and if you would, kindly leave me alone."

They wouldn't take no for an answer. So I went and got Mr. Schiffman. I told him:

"These men are demanding that I go with them right now."

Mr. Schiffman looked at them and said:

"What's the problem? She has another show to do. And who are you?" They wouldn't tell him. They just turned and said:

"We'll wait."

Helen and I were scared to death. I had never seen them before and I didn't know what to think. After my second set was over, I was walking out of the dressing room and they said, very firmly:

"Get in the car."

Now, I had a guy who used to travel with me, Percy Fuller, who my mother had hired as my personal masseur. I used to get massages after all of my shows. She believed in that. She wanted me to keep my body healthy. Well, Percy saw these guys take me and Helen out to their car, so he followed us. They drove us downtown somewhere and we went into a dark building. They held us for hours in a small room, and they would not tell us who they were or what they wanted. I tried to get information out of them and they wouldn't budge.

All they said was, "We have to hold you."

And I was screaming at them, "Hold us, for what?"

I kept asking what the hell was going on. Finally, one of them said, "Mr. Sinatra needs to speak with Bernie Solomon about an agreement they made, involving you. That's all we know."

Evidently, Bernie Solomon had made some kind of deal with Sinatra that he hadn't told me about, but it involved me doing some recording on Sinatra's label, Reprise. My guess is Bernie probably got the better of the deal and Sinatra didn't like it, so he threatened him by kidnapping me. I didn't know what to do. I was mad as hell. Helen was a nervous wreck. We were both sweating bullets and couldn't think of a way out of there. It had been hours and they would not let us go.

"My mother's expecting me to come home," I told them. "She's going to know something's wrong if I don't show."

They didn't say a word. Now, they didn't hurt us or threaten to do us any harm. If we had asked, they would have given us whatever we wanted. We just couldn't leave. Helen was near tears and I was desperately trying to talk us out of the mess. It was one thing that they had *me*, but I felt responsible for Helen's welfare. She had nothing to do with Bernie Solomon or Sinatra or any of this nonsense, but there she was mixed up in the middle of everything. She was so scared, she couldn't speak. And I did everything I could to reassure her. But those guys were so big and rough, they looked like they could break us both in two, and I know that's what worried Helen the most. Somehow I knew they weren't going to harm us physically. Finally, Percy, who had been parked outside all this time, decided to come up and see what was going on. Percy was a big, huge dude. He was tall, with very definite looks. Well, baby, Percy knocked on that door and shouted, with his big deep voice: "What y'all doing in there?"

Those guys took one look at him. "You can go now," they said.

"Thank you," we said.

It was the strangest night of my life. And poor Helen was a total wreck. She had gotten so nervous, she pissed in her pants. I talked about her bad when we got out of there. I said, "Girl, look at you! You peed in your pants."

Of course, she didn't find it funny. But I was trying to make light of the situation. And little did she know, and I never did tell her, that I had pissed on myself, too. The whole time, I was just as pissy as she was. It was a mess. Once again, I had to thank God for Helen. If I had been alone, there's no telling what may have gone down. Every time I was in a fix, there was Helen, right by my side. Bernie Solomon never did speak to me about the incident or let me in on what it was really all about.

I still don't know.

Percy and I dropped Helen home first. We had to get her home as soon as possible because her family didn't know what had happened to her. Her daughter Ernestine was old enough to remember this fiasco. She was about twelve or thirteen when it happened. And Helen had, by this time, left Ernie and married another guy, Kenneth Carey, and they had bought a house out on Long Island. After eleven years of having only one child, Helen had started a whole new family with Kenny and gave him four more babies. There was Junior, Bernard, Geralyn, who was named for me, and one baby who we called T.T. who passed away as an infant. Four kids after eleven years! I never expected Helen to have any more children after Ernestine. But, she was still young, and she was a wonderful mother. I was like an aunt to all of Helen's kids, so the last thing I wanted to do was put their mama in danger. In all of our years on the road together, that night had to be the most frightening.

I heard from my father every once in a while. When I performed up in Harlem, particularly at the Apollo, he would come by to see my shows. But he never made his presence known. People would see him, then come back and tell me:

"Your father's downstairs in the audience."

He never came up to the dressing room to speak to me or congratulate me on a show. His interest in my career was an in-and-out kind of thing. Once, in the beginning of my career, I had gone down to meet with a theatrical agent, for the very first time. The agent was Fritz Pollard, who I believe was a former football player. Anyway, he gave me a breakdown of what I would need to get started, you know, music, gowns, and all. He thought I had talent and that he could book me on jobs. So, I decided to go to my father to ask him to support me on this.

"Well, how much is all of this going to cost?" he asked. I suggested that he come down to Pollard's office with me and let him explain everything. My father sat there in the man's office and told him he would finance the whole thing. Of course, that was just him talking because he never spent a dime on me. And this time was no different. He didn't do shit. He never followed through with his promises and we never discussed it. I wasn't fool enough to ever ask again.

I remember once, my mother and I were short on money. This was back when we were living at 229 West 134th Street. We didn't have our rent money, which was eleven dollars and fifty cents by the week. We didn't have it and we needed it, so I decided to go to my father's place and ask him for it. I walked from 134th Street all the way down to 118th Street, where he was living at the time. I told him what our situation was and he refused to give it to me.

"You should always have your rent," he said.

I turned around and started for home. As I was walking I stopped into a drugstore on the corner to make a phone call. While I was making my call, I looked down on the floor of the phone booth and I saw some money, all balled up, like it had just fallen out someone's pocket. I reached down to get it and sure enough, it was twelve dollars. I had found the rent money. I went home and told my mother what happened at my father's and she said:

"Well, where did this money come from?" I told her I found it and she looked at me kind of strange, but my mother was a little psychic, so she knew I was telling the truth.

It's a funny thing. The whole time I lived in my father's house, as much as he beat my mother, he never once hit me. He didn't hit me until I was grown. I remember I got a phone call from him, and he asked me for some money.

"Hey, Gloria, you got fifty dollars? Well, I'm coming over there to get it."

So he did. He came over to our apartment in Lenox Terrace. I told my mother he had called asking for fifty dollars. She didn't say anything. And even though he was a mean, mean man, he was still my father. And I loved him. I had the money and had no problem giving it to him. He came into the place and barely spoke to anybody. I handed him the fifty dollars. He snatched it from me, then out of the blue, he hauled off and slapped me in the face.

"You think you're so much," he said.

Then he left.

6

***

Queens & Kings

$\mathcal{N}$ineteen fifty-nine was a hell of a year. News was coming out of Detroit that Berry Gordy III, an R&B songwriter, was starting the first black-owned record company, Motown. Music journalists were writing story after story about Billie Holiday's battle with addiction. There were hints that she was in a state of decline, which was sad, sad news. And sprinklings of stories about race riots and demonstrations down South were starting to make national news. We were entering a new decade, and an uneasy feeling was setting in.

My dealings with Everest brought back some of the original doubts I'd had about the music business. Although I was excited about the success of *Miss Gloria Lynne*, fear crept in. I began to question whether or not I had what it took to really make it. It became very clear to me that, as an artist, I was not getting my fair share. The only way I was making money was through live performances. It was strange because I looked up one day and realized I was working in an industry that I knew very little about. There were a lot of singers out there who were at the top of their game and I wondered: *How do I get there?*

Dinah Washington was named the "Queen of the Blues." She picked up where Bessie Smith and Ida Cox left off. By this time, she had a whole string of hits—"Salty Papa Blues," "Bad Case of the Blues," and "This Bitter Earth" were big hits for her. And "What a Diff'rence a Day Makes" won a Grammy for Best Rhythm & Blues Recording. Dinah reigned in the fifties. Her audience was every single black household in America. Everybody loved Dinah. She could wrap her voice around a lyric and bellow out the blues enough to make folks holler. And one day, clear out of the blue, she called me.

"Gloria, I want you to stand in for me tonight at the Village Vanguard. Can you do it?"

Well, first of all, I could not believe Dinah Washington had called my house, so it took a half second for that to sink in. Then, my mind started racing trying to figure out why she was asking *me*—how did she find me? Maybe she had heard my album, maybe she had seen one of my shows. Well, I replied, nervously:

"Yes. I can do it."

Not that anyone with any sense would ever dare say no to Dinah Washington. She had a reputation for being hard core. I heard that she put the fear of God into the people around her. But this is what I came to know and love about Dinah: She didn't take no shit from nobody.

"I want you to come over to my house," she said. "I want to meet you."

She lived in a fabulous building in the Sugar Hill section of Harlem, at 345 West 145th Street. It was a brand-new apartment building, the Bowery Bank Building, it was called. The Bowery Bank was on the main floor and these new luxury apartments were above it. Dinah lived on the fourteenth floor, the top floor. On the way up there, it occurred to me that I hadn't even asked her why, when, what. Nothing. I just said:

"Yes."

Her place was laid to the bone. It was one of the most spacious and beautiful apartments I had ever seen. The foyer alone was bigger than most apartments I had been in. Everything from furniture to fixtures—it was all gorgeous. When she opened the door, she looked at me with those eyes, smiled, and said:

"Come on in."

She was very gracious. I made myself comfortable while she took care of some business with a few associates who were already there when I arrived. I realized, in the years to come, Dinah was always handling her business.

"I got some business to take care of" was her familiar refrain.

Dinah didn't play. She didn't have to. Everybody treated her like a queen and those that didn't were out the door.

I sat there about an hour, my head ready to split open. The windows in the living room faced St. Nicholas Avenue, which was a busy, good-looking street in that day. I stared out of the window, trying to gain my composure, but the anticipation was just too much. My day had started out so ordinary—doing laundry, cleaning my apartment. Regular stuff, now *this*. All of the rumors and gossip I had heard about Dinah took turns taunting me—that she was an extremely difficult woman, impossible to work with, a bitch. All of this I had to put in its proper perspective, because this same "impossible" woman had just paid me the highest compliment a singer could pay another singer.

Dinah finished her business and escorted me to her wardrobe. She had three very large mahogany closets carved out in the apartment, built big enough for two or three people to sit in. "We're about the same size. I want you to pick out something for your performance tonight," she said.

I couldn't believe it.

She was actually offering me her clothes! I never expected her to be so generous, especially to a complete stranger. We didn't know each other, but it didn't matter to her. As far as Dinah was concerned, we were peers.

I stood there, spellbound, my eyes open wide with amazement at all of the beautiful gowns and furs she owned. "Go ahead, pick out a couple of gowns," she said. "I want you to look nice tonight. You never know who's going to be out there."

I couldn't make up my mind between the beaded or the sequined, the fur-trimmed or the diamond-studded. It was all so fabulous. Dinah was a real glamour girl, all class and serious business. Here was a woman known to have matching wigs for her gowns. The same color and all. I remember once, in an interview, a woman questioned her about why she was wearing a blond wig, and Dinah's answer was:

"Because I can."

That was Dinah, honey.

Well, I was thrilled by her offer, and thanked God for it, because I certainly didn't own anything that could compare. Not even close.

Dinah wanted me to stroll in the Vanguard in grand style. That afternoon, I left her place light-headed and happy with a couple of gowns and a mink in my arms. Dinah had taken care of everything. By the time the cab pulled up to the Vanguard door, and I strolled out of there in my pale green silk chiffon gown and my mink thrown about my shoulders, the management had already been notified. They were expecting me.

Her band, the Wynton Kelly Trio, was very warm to me. They welcomed me like old friends and they weren't but kids themselves. I think Wynton was only about nineteen years old when he started playing for Dinah. Her trio was incredibly talented.

They had to be, if they were working with Dinah.

That night, I'm sure it must have crossed their minds, "Who is *this* standing in for Dinah?" Everyone knew, if Dinah Washington had sent you, you must be good. In the years to come, I got plenty of work on Dinah's word alone.

When the announcement was made that Dinah would not be performing, the crowd balked. They had their minds and their money fixed on seeing Dinah Washington. Going on in her place was rough. It took everything I had to step out on that bandstand. She was right to give me all of the outer accoutrements because inside I was a wreck.

I was very nervous, but we made it through. Wynton Kelly struck up the band and it was business as usual. I pushed on past my anxiety and gave it my best.

For Dinah's sake.

It was the least I could do after all she had done for me. When I hit the first note of the first tune, I felt my body relax.

And for the first time in my life, I felt like a celebrity.

I had never known that feeling before and Dinah gave it to me. By the end of the show, the crowd was on their feet. When I took my final bow, I thought of Dinah. I will never forget her kindness, her friendship. To think, this woman, this *superstar*, had gowned me, given me her fur coat, and set me before her public, the *right* way. Dinah had sent me on that job and primed me for success. That's how much Dinah Washington thought of me.

After the show was over and the crowd was leaving, a rich-looking, silver-haired gentleman walked over and introduced himself. It was Joe Glaser, the president of ABC, Associated Booking Corporation. Of course, I had heard of him. Everybody in the business knew Joe Glaser. His company did the booking for all the major acts of the day. I mean, everybody—

Louis Armstrong, Barbra Streisand, Pearl Bailey, Billy Eckstine, *and* Dinah Washington. He told me how much he enjoyed my performance, then he left the club.

You never know who's going to be out there.

Dinah's words suddenly flew back to memory. To this very day, I believe Dinah arranged the entire event, although she never admitted to it. The very next day, I received another phone call. This time, it was Joe Glaser.

Joe Glaser was a real agent. King of the agents, they used to call him. He was always concerned about your welfare, really and truly interested in whether you were happy or not. He was a good agent in a cutthroat business. Joe Glaser was the kind of businessman that would take time to answer all of his calls and sign all of his correspondence, personally. Each and every letter. A real hands-on, face-to-face kind of guy. You never got the run-around if you called the office to speak to Joe. If he was in, he would speak to you. By the forties, Glaser was already a veteran in the music business. He was known for discovering and cultivating black talent. That was his thing. Before establishing ABC he headed the Rockwell-O'Keefe Agency's "colored-band department." Louis Armstrong was one of his clients, along with Hot Lips Page, Willie Bryant, Andy Kirk, Claude Hopkins, and Lionel Hampton. Lionel was the one to introduce him to Dinah, I believe. After my first meeting at ABC, I signed, and stayed with the agency for years, all because of Joe Glaser. I trusted him from the moment I met him. He was more than just a booking agent. He ran that company like a champ. He knew all of his artists, on a first-name basis, and genuinely gave a damn about your welfare. I know he kept me working for years. Once I got with ABC, bookings were not a problem. I made my rounds at all of the clubs, in every major city.

Duke Wade and I were still friends and we continued to work together, but after my signing with ABC, Duke went through the agency to hire me for different jobs. The funny thing is, as long as Duke and I have been together, we don't have any paper between us. I've never signed a thing with Duke. We always had an understanding: If there was work, we'd work, if there wasn't, then hey, we'll catch up with each other later. We've always been that kind of cool with one another.

Joe Glaser felt I wasn't getting enough from Everest because I was out there touring and performing, back to back, on jobs he had booked me on. And Glaser knew if I had been getting paid well I would not have needed to work so hard out on the road. Doing hit-and-run gigs—hitting one town one night, then jumping in the car to get to another town before sundown the next. It was hard, hard work. Looking back on it, I realize that I should not have been relying, exclusively, on club dates to pay my bills. I mean, I was no longer an amateur. I had an album out, my name was out there. But this was the grim reality for a lot of black artists, most of us were scuffling on the road to make ends meet, hit record or no hit record. It didn't matter, because only the record companies made real money.

In the days before integration, black music was lumped into one big category called "race music." Our music was played only on black radio stations and promoted to all-black audiences. There were very few mainstream black artists in the fifties. You had people like Nat King Cole, who was a beautiful balladeer and one of the first blacks to have his own television show, but he was a rarity. Even someone as big as Dinah, during segregation, had to cover songs that white singers made popular, in order for these songs to be released in the black market. Segregation laws made it so that even music was divided along race lines. If you were black you were expected to listen to a black singer and if you were white you had to tune in to a white singer, even if they were singing the same song. When dances at big ballrooms were the "in" thing, they would put a rope down the middle of the floor to separate the races.

Well, if the music got good enough, of course, that little piece of rope would be up underneath somebody's feet.

White folks were afraid that their children would get too turned on by black folks if they listened to their music. It was a period of a lot of fear. As a result, black artists suffered. We had a tight niche in which to maneuver, meaning there were definite limitations on the amount of money, exposure, advertising, and promotion we could get for our records. Now, the black community loved the music we were putting out. A lot of these songs became ghetto anthems. The music represented the sentiment and emotion of the community. It was passionate and real. So, that made it very significant. The music became an expression of black pride in a time when black people had very few rights. However, record companies had their own agenda. They paid us pennies on the dollar while they made grand theft dough on the so-called race market. You can believe that.

Meanwhile, I heard the same song and dance from Bernie Solomon. "There's no money, Gloria." And to add insult to injury, he treated me like I was asking for something that wasn't mine, like I was begging. I eventually hired lawyers to try to get my residuals from Everest. They'd come back with the same answer. "There's no money there." My record was playing on the radio. I heard "June Night" just playing and playing, while I broke my back on the road to make a few dollars. I'd see my name on the music polls and on the charts, but it meant nothing.

Trying to follow record sales was futile.

If you challenged the record company about how many records you'd sold, you wouldn't get the facts. And you couldn't believe what you read in the industry papers, because they were often full of lies. It was not uncommon for record companies to report false record sales to magazines like *Downbeat* or *Metronome*, in order to pump the record up, to make it look bigger than it actually was. Listen, ambiguity is this industry's middle name.

The artist was the last to know everything. Once, Joe Glaser booked me on a job at a club in Boston called Storyville. He told me the owner, George Wein, had requested me personally. When I went to do the show, the producers of the concert told me to be sure to sing my "new hit song." Well, I didn't know what song they were talking about. It turned out that they were referring to "June Night," from the *Miss Gloria Lynne* album. It took complete strangers to tell me that I had a hit song on the album. And instead of being excited by the news, I became that much more disgusted with Everest, because a hit song meant hit residuals. If it was a hit, that meant people were buying it, so where was the money?

George Wein, who was also in charge of the popular Newport Jazz Festival, was so excited to have me at his club, he paid me five hundred dollars to perform a weeklong engagement with all expenses paid, which was a very nice deal in the fifties. Meanwhile, at Everest I was being told that I wasn't owed any money and that I was lucky to be recording. I was told, "You owe *us* money." By the time the record company finished recovering your production costs, giving away freebies, deducting returns, and subtracting any handouts, limousines, or hotel rooms they might have paid for, you, the artist, were in the hole. You'd be talking about suing them and they'd come back with, "We ought to be suing you!" Making music was a complicated and confusing affair.

In spite of the financial frustrations, artistically I enjoyed the Everest years. All of my recording sessions were a blast. We used to record out on Long Island and there was a lot of land surrounding the studio. Sometimes, in the winter, the musicians and I would go outside and have snowball fights in between sessions. It was always a good time recording. And we produced so much music. Every time I turned around, I was recording a new album. I was very fortunate because songwriters would bring me material they wanted me to sing and I worked with some really great arrangers who gave me beautiful new arrangements of old standards.

I did some great albums with Ernie Wilkins. He had done a lot of arrangements for Count Basie, Carmen McRae, and Harry James. We did my album, *Go Go Go!* together and it was fantastic. I had approached Count Basie about conducting but he was too busy, so Ernie went and pulled all of the members of Basie's band together and they did the album with me. The album cover read: *Gloria Lynne with Ernie Wilkins and His Orchestra.* It was Basie's band minus Basie. It was another great record for us. And the sound was incredible. The music critic Nat Hentoff wrote:

"It's a measure of Gloria's own power that she is not only not overwhelmed by this band but becomes its leader, soaring over it."

What a compliment. As a singer, with all of that beautiful orchestral sound supporting you, you just can't go wrong. The days of orchestras and big bands are definitely missed. No matter how many machines they invent to simulate the sound, ain't nothing like the real thing.

We did some great albums at Everest, like *Day In Day Out, After Hours, A Touch of Tenderness* with LeRoy Holmes conducting, *This Little Boy of Mine, He Needs Me, Glorious Gloria Lynne,* and *Gloria Blue.*

I also did a couple of successful live albums in the sixties, including *Gloria Lynne at the Las Vegas Thunderbird,* where I'm wearing the same pastel green gown Dinah Washington let me borrow for my Village Vanguard debut. She thought it looked so good on me, she let me have it. That live concert is one of the most memorable. Because we were on the West Coast, all of the stars came out to the show. Vegas is like that. It's a really exciting place to do a show, though it's hard work. The night we recorded the album, back in the winter of 1962, I sang in the wee, wee hours of the night. We did several shows in one night and the crowd just kept coming. I remember doing a show as late as four in the morning. The whole place was packed full of celebrities and entertainers. And when I started singing, there was a complete quiet in the room. Then after I finished each song, the applause was just overwhelming. That was an incredible feeling. On that particular live album, nothing was deleted. Ordinarily, live albums are remixed and edited, but *Gloria Lynne at the Las Vegas Thunderbird* was untouched.

Herman Foster did all of the arrangements and conducted the band. That night, we were all just out of sight. I sang a lot of the all-time favorites, like "What Kind of Fool Am I," "But Beautiful," "This Could Be the Start of Something Big," "In Love in Vain," "I'll Buy You a Star," and "End of a Love Affair." And looking back, I sang several tunes that I'm still singing in my live shows today—"Sunday, Monday and Always," "So This Is Love," and "Something Wonderful." Those songs never get old.

I remember while I was performing in Vegas, B. B. King invited me and my band to his house for dinner. He had a beautiful place out there. And he had the most fantastic cook in the world. This woman's cooking was almost as good as my mama's. They laid out a feast for us. The food was so good, I can still taste it. It was such a gracious thing for B.B. to do. Because, everybody knows that B.B. stays busy, but he opened up his home to us and made us all feel so welcome. B.B. is a blues legend and his musical contribution can't be denied, but more than that, he's a wonderful human being. He is one of the kindest people I've ever met. I've known him so long, I don't remember how or where we met, but when I'm around him I know I'm home.

I remember once, recording live at the Village Gate and my husband, Harry, was there. The club was packed, and the Village Gate was a huge place. I started singing the ballad "For You." Well, right in the middle of the song, when I sang the lyric, ". . . for you . . ." Harry hollered out—he had a big, booming voice—"For who?" And sure enough, when the album was released, his voice cut through that crowd just as clear. You'll hear him on there, shouting: "For who?" Harry was something else.

I also recorded a live album at my regular stomping ground, Basin Street East, that was a big seller for me. That album had quite a few standards on it, songs that had been sung by every great jazz singer—"Mack the Knife," "I Got Rhythm," "I Get a Kick Out of You," "Autumn Leaves," and "Wouldn't It Be Loverly." I did new arrangements of each song and the audience just ate it up. Those live albums really helped establish my sound in the minds of record buyers and radio disc jockeys, who were so instrumental in getting you mass exposure. Larry McCormick was a big radio personality back in the sixties. He used to introduce me at some of my live shows, so we knew each other well. On the album, he wrote: "You name the song and Gloria Lynne makes you like it a little bit better." Artistically, I cherish my early years of recording because we made so much good music and people loved it.

Joe Glaser was still booking me at this time, but he chose not to get involved in my contractual affairs with Everest. And I learned that you can't fight people who have more money than you. You're fighting a lost cause. I had lawyers come back to me, as they were flying off on their vacations to the Bahamas or some damn place, and tell me Everest had no money of mine. They ate lawyers for lunch. Lawyers would go in there fighting like a bulldog, and they'd come out pussycats. This is the only business in the world where you *earn* your money, then you have to hire a lawyer to go *get* your money.

Now, Joe Glaser was scared to death of Dinah. She was one of his top moneymakers and Dinah didn't take no mess. She was a pioneer in this business. She didn't take nothing off those white folks. She didn't have to. Joe Glaser could be, when necessary, aggressive and hot-tempered, but Dinah could tame his ass right on down.

I remember once I was in the ABC office and Joe got a phone call from a furrier. It was Dinah. She had been buying some furs and told the people to send the bill to ABC, attention, Joe Glaser. The furrier was calling to verify the transaction and get his approval. Well, Joe hit the roof. He started screaming:

"What's that bitch buying now?"

Well, Dinah overheard him. About fifteen minutes later, Dinah showed up at the office, which was on Fifth Avenue, 745 Fifth Avenue. She used to carry a little pearl-handled pistol around with her. She sat down in Glaser's office, crossed her legs, pulled that pistol out of her pocketbook, looked that man dead in the eyes, and said:

"If you ever call me a bitch again, I'll kill you."

Then she got up and left. Joe Glaser was scared to death of her. They fought all the time, but they really did love each other. He gave her what-ever she needed. And that which she didn't need. He treated Dinah just like what they called her, a queen. She acted like a queen and demanded that you treat her like one. I never met anybody like Dinah in my life. And I don't think I could have ever made it in this business without the stamp of Dinah Washington. She paved the way for a lot of black women.

Joe Glaser had all the confidence in the world in me, so he would send me to almost any big name club, anywhere in the country. Our relationship was one of trust from the very start. Within two years of my working with ABC, Glaser booked me at Carnegie Hall. In 1962, I performed in an afternoon concert, the "Ninth Annual Festival of Negro Music and Drama," presented by WLIB. It was a four-part concert. The first segment was classical choral music sung by the Chancel Choir of the Salem Meth-odist Church and the Senior Choir of the Concord Baptist Church in Brooklyn. The second segment was called "The Concert Stage," with opera solos. The libretto was written and read by Langston Hughes. And the third segment was all jazz. They called it "The Jazz Scene," and it featured myself, the Billy Taylor Trio, Al Sears and Orchestra, Brook Benton, Clark Terry and the Bob Brookmeyer Quintet, the Montgomery Brothers, and Ronnie Mitchell. For a young singer like myself, I was so impressed with the other acts, I had to really concentrate to perform my songs. It was truly amazing to grace that legendary stage.

The concert ended with "The Gospel Train." It was really a beautiful concert. I don't care if you perform at Carnegie Hall only once in your life, it is an unforgettable experience. I was fortunate enough to perform there several times in my career. About four years after this first concert, I did another performance with Mongo Santamaria and Dick Gregory, who was doing political comedy at that time, and Billy Taylor was the master of ceremonies.

I never will forget the time Joe Glaser sent me to replace Billie Holiday. This was my first horror experience in the business. Billie was in the hos-pital and had to cancel her bookings at the last minute. So, Joe Glaser called me and said, "Gloria, just go on out there and do the show. Don't worry about it. Just go on out there. They'll love you."

He flew me to Los Angeles and I had to go on for Billie at the Pink Pussycat. When I arrived at the club, the owner was not expecting me. He didn't know who I was. Joe Glaser had sent me out there without calling the club's manager to tell him that Billie couldn't make it. Well, the man pitched a bitch. He went off. He had a sold-out crowd that night. It was going to be full of stars, Marlon Brando, Ava Gardner, Elizabeth Taylor, all of these Hollywood people had reserved seats to see Billie Holiday. I thought this man was going to have a heart attack right in front of my face. He was so upset. And I couldn't believe that Joe had put me in this position. I was still a relatively new name on the circuit. The West Coast didn't know me nearly as well as the East.

Anyway, I introduced myself to the band. This was my first time working with the jazz arranger Marty Paich. I went over the list of songs with the guys and went back in the dressing room and changed into my gown. Well, baby, the people balked. They had paid their money to see Billie and they got me. I gave them my very best and they enjoyed it, but I guess if I had paid to see Billie Holiday and got some other woman, I would've been upset, too. Billie Holiday was the most famous black female singer in the world at that time.

She was Lady Day.

But I made it through the night. The crowd liked me and in the end everything turned out just fine. But my nerves were shot. And I could have killed Joe Glaser, sweet as he was, I could have killed him dead.

And let me just say this about Billie—she had more talent *high* than most folks can muster sober. Billie was incredible. A true pioneer. And an original. There was only one Lady Day. In some ways, she was like a savior to all of us singers. She was the first black woman to make such a huge breakthrough in the business. We all looked up to her.

Billie made plenty of money for a black woman in that day. She was a shrewd businesswoman, the importance of which can't be stressed enough, because so many black artists were being pimped back then. So, when you heard about one that actually got what she deserved, it was encouraging news. As early as the forties, Billie was pulling in $3,000 a week plus a percentage of the bar takings at a lot of clubs. In New York, she put the DownBeat club on the map. They used to advertise, "Never a Cover Charge." Well, people didn't care what they had to pay, as long as they got a glimpse of Billie.

When Barry Josephson opened Café Society back in '38, he christened the club by inviting Billie to perform opening night. Café Society became a landmark nightclub for jazz artists. All of the top headliners performed there. And it was one of the first clubs in New York to instigate an integrated policy for both artists and customers. Because things were very separate during this time. Black folks patronized the clubs in Harlem, white folks stayed downtown. However, if white folks felt like strolling up to Harlem, they could, but there was nothing but trouble to be had if black folks tried to stroll downtown too regularly. They didn't mind the black musicians on Fifty-second Street, because that's who they were coming to see. A lot of the black musicians loved to play Harlem because they were among their own, but also because they felt like they had to water down their sound when they played downtown to make it more palatable for the white audiences.

Café Society was a high-class club. It was one of the most beautiful clubs in town. Billy Strayhorn, the pianist, composer, and arranger for Duke Ellington, made a name for himself at Café Society, as well as pianist Hazel Scott, one of the few female jazz instrumentalists on the scene.

Back in that day, the press wouldn't as much as put a black performer's picture in the paper. This was the era of journalists Hedda Hopper and Walter Winchell. It was nothing like it is today. Now you see big billboards with black faces. That was unheard of when I was coming up. If people didn't come to see you perform live or buy your records, they didn't know what you looked like. Most papers didn't even pay any attention to what was happening on the jazz scene. They deliberately ignored it.

Duke Ellington was actually one of the first to speak out about racial politics in the jazz world. He was the first to call his music "Negro music." He spoke out in published interviews, which was truly remarkable in the forties and fifties. And Duke was one of America's premier bandleaders and composers, but a lot of the credit he deserved he didn't receive until after his death. His influence on the development of black music is immeasurable.

Miles Davis was once quoted as saying, "I think all the musicians should get together on one certain day and get down on their knees and thank Duke."

So, I say all that to say—for Billie Holiday, a black *woman*, to come along and command center stage was extraordinary.

Billie was one of the few vocalists who performed regularly on Fifty-second Street. Most of the clubs on the street were really venues for jazz musicians, the instrumentalists Charlie Parker, Miles Davis, John Coltrane,

Thelonious Monk, Dizzy Gillespie. They were little, tiny rooms with small bandstands that could hardly fit all those musicians and instruments. They were small in size but big in reputation and everybody flocked to them. Most of my regular engagements were at clubs on the East Side like Basin Street East, at Café Society uptown, or at the Village Gate downtown. Billie, on the other hand, was a main attraction for any club in New York worth its weight. She christened many a club. Her name alone could guarantee a steady flow of customers. Even if she had just performed there once, that was enough to make people patronize the club.

Billie was world famous by the times the fifties rolled around. And unfortunately, her personal problems made more news than her tremendous talent. That upsets me to this day. Every time you turned around there was a story about Billie's drug habit or her being hospitalized, but you never heard anything about what she had contributed to jazz and the American music scene. I remember hearing about Billie Holiday when I was very young coming up in Harlem. And meeting her that time at Minton's. She started out right up in Harlem singing at the Hot Cha, Small's Paradise, Alhambra Bar and Grill. When John Hammond, a record producer, got wind of her, she was sent straight to the recording studio. Her first recording was with the famous bandleader Benny Goodman for Columbia Records. And from that point on, she made history.

All of the singers who came behind her looked up to her. We were all trying to be as glamorous, as sexy, as bad as Billie.

Billie's death was like a sacrifice. It seemed like she had been taken so the rest of us could live. Every woman that opened her mouth to sing a song in that day paid homage to Billie. She was our idol. We loved and adored her. Billie was the queen bee. She was our big sister and we didn't know what we were going to do without her. When the news of her death hit the streets, everybody was torn apart.

When someone that phenomenal leaves here, there really is a great chasm, because no one can fill the space. No one can take the place of Billie. We learned by her example, the good and the bad. She was an incredible talent, a great songwriter, a shrewd businesswoman, and a very nice lady. Dinah told me once, when she was starting out in Chicago, at Garrick Stage Lounge, she would go to Billie's shows and just study her— her vocal style, her way of dressing, her gestures, everything.

There was nothing like hearing Billie put away a song. "God Bless the Child," "Lover Man," "Good Morning Heartache," and "Come Rain or Come Shine" can hardly be sung today without bringing Billie to mind.

We also looked at her story and vowed not to let that be our story. We knew how brilliant and multitalented she was, but she had problems. I told myself then, there is no problem so great in my life that will throw me to drugs or alcohol. She centered me as an artist.

But in those days, they put everybody in the same boat. If you were an entertainer, particularly a black entertainer, you were always "suspected of." Billie passed away a few months after the release of *Miss Gloria Lynne*, in the summer of '59.

I was the new face coming up behind Dinah Washington, Sarah Vaughan, and Carmen McRae. As my popularity grew, they would throw gigs my way. If one of them had been double-booked or tied up and couldn't make a gig, they'd say, "Call Gloria."

I had a great deal of respect for them. I hadn't accomplished half of what they had accomplished, and to get their endorsement, so early in my career, meant everything to me. The black women of the jazz era were very tight. We had a camaraderie, a sisterhood. We always helped each other. There wasn't any cutthroat competition going on in those days. Each of us was genuinely impressed by the others' voice or style or level of performance. We learned from each other. But we appreciated the fact that we were all individuals, with a different set of experiences, which colored our interpretation of music and our overall performance. And the bottom line is: originality breeds confidence. If you realize that what you have is unique and special, no one can take that away from you. What's for you is yours.

I didn't mind hard work, and people came to know that about me. If there was work to be had and money to be made, I would show up. Carmen McRae would recommend me sight unseen. If I remember correctly, she referred me on a few jobs, before we actually met face to face. She would ask club owners:

"Have you heard Gloria Lynne? Have you heard her sing?"

Whenever she wasn't able to perform, she would call me. I worked a lot on Carmen's recommendation. She was a great singer and a really great lady. Carmen was a survivor. She was a native New Yorker. She started out as the intermission pianist and vocalist at Minton's. In between gigs, she worked as a clerk-typist in downtown Manhattan offices. Her break came when Irene Wilson, the ex-wife of jazz pianist Teddy Wilson, discovered her in a club. By 1944, she was working with legendary musicians like Benny Carter, Count Basie, and the Mercer Ellington Band. By the mid-fifties Carmen had made it to the top. And that's where she remained.

She did well in the business, in spite of the critics' constant comparisons of her and Sarah Vaughan. People told her she would never make it in the business sounding like Sarah. Well, Carmen never let that stop her. She persevered. She had a wonderful career and made a ton of records. The comparisons eased up over the years when Carmen began to really carve a niche for herself and build up a faithful following.

I was performing at Birdland, on Fifty-second Street, which was run by Morris Levy, when I first met Sarah Vaughan. The industry called her the "Divine One" and all her friends called her "Sassy." She was a very sweet lady. Very quiet and reserved. But didn't nobody mess with her either. We hit it off right away. Sarah always offered me her help and guidance. At one point in our friendship, I was in between personal managers and she recommended her husband, C. B. Atkins. I used him for a minute, but he just wasn't any good at it. A nice man, but not a good man for the music business. He even messed Sarah around trying to manage her. C.B. had also been married to the singer Esther Phillips.

They used to say Sarah wasn't human, because of her incredible voice. Well, I remember, Sarah told me one time:

"Watch the humans."

I didn't catch her meaning. And this thing really tripped me up. I ran home and told my mother, "Mom, Sarah Vaughan told me to watch the humans!"

"Oh, she's just saying to look out for all those raggedy people," my mother said, "you know, nasty, lowdown people."

That stuck with me a long time. Sarah was something. And she never spoke above a whisper. The only time you would ever hear Sarah get any kind of loud was when she was singing, or if you messed with her, then she would be very cool with you. They said she was mean to the bone, but I never saw that side of her. Then again, I didn't give her reason.

Billy Eckstine, who was very close to Sarah and was her mentor in a lot of ways, said about her vocal style, "You'll love it, if you hear it."

When Sarah came on the scene, all the musicians went crazy. They all loved her phrasing and vocal emphasis. She always said that she didn't give a lot of thought to her style, but she just followed what the horn players were doing.

All the guys used to say, "Sassy's one of the fellas."

Sarah could drink beer, smoke cigarettes, hang out all night, then grace the stage in a gorgeous gown, fresh as a rose. No matter how much partying she did, her voice remained untouched, golden. She always joked about her presence onstage, saying:

"I come onstage looking like Lena Horne and leave looking like Sarah Vaughan."

By definition, Sarah Vaughan's voice was operatic, but she knew how to manipulate it and make it whatever she wanted it to be. Without a doubt, her voice was truly one of the most beautiful ever.

She came out of Newark, New Jersey, straight out of the A.M.E. Zion church. But very few people even remember now that Sarah was an accomplished pianist and organist. Down through the years, some people have even suggested that Sarah initially set out to be a concert pianist, not a jazz singer. But the world of instrumentalists was, and still is, dominated by men. Women were expected to stand there, look pretty, and sing, not play. So Sarah entered the Apollo Amateur, sang "Body and Soul," and won. And like Billie, Sarah's star rose that very night. Billy Eckstine spotted her and immediately asked her to join him as a lead vocalist for Earl Hines's big band. When he formed his own band, which included Charlie Parker, Dizzy Gillespie, and Gene Ammons, he loved her enough to ask her to join him again.

Eckstine always said about Sarah, "She came equipped."

As great as Sarah was, she had gone through her share of craziness in the industry. I remember one of the well-known music critics of the day had written an editorial about jazz called "And What Ever Happened to Jazz?" Now this was when jazz was really hot, so I don't know where he was coming from with this. But anyway, in the article he slammed our music, saying that nothing new was happening in jazz, and called Sarah Vaughan "a tinny, shallow flash in the pan."

By this time, Sarah had trotted the globe. Everybody knew her music. She was an international superstar. Sarah had made a ton of records for Mercury, EmArcy, and Columbia Records. Anything she sang sounded good—"Lover Man," "Cherokee," "Body and Soul." It didn't matter with Sarah. Her voice was just that great. But people would just say anything and write anything, just like they do today. I think there was a lot of envy involved. Jazz was created by and dominated by black folks and the whole world had embraced the music. It was fresh, provocative, creative, ingenious music and no one had ever heard anything like it. And America, where it all originated, was too blinded by its opinions of black people to give the music and the artists the credit we deserved. And there were plenty of white folks in the jazz world, but honestly, the black performers dominated the whole scene. All you had to do was take a look around.

Sonny Rollins used to say, "Jazz is in the genes."

As artists, you learned to disregard a lot of what was written in the papers. It was an endless trail of nonsense. You could read and read and still not find anything new or interesting. But a lot of critics and journalists of that era stood by, waiting for jazz to fall on its ass. Then, you had white writers like Leonard Feather and Nat Hentoff who loved the music and appreciated it—but they gave them hell for writing good things about us. Leonard Feather was also a songwriter who wrote several big hits for Dinah Washington. He made it very clear that his love for jazz was not to be denied.

Back in the day, the South Side of Chicago had a whole strip of jazz clubs, so all the singers would hit them, regularly. I did a run there several times, at a couple of clubs. There was Club DeLisa, Rhum Boogie, Silhouette Club, the Regal Theater, and the Southern Lounge. The situation in Chicago was much like that in New York—black patrons stayed on the South Side, white folks went to the clubs downtown. And nobody crossed the line.

Once, while I was on tour in Chicago, I met up with Mahalia Jackson. She began singing, like a lot of us, right in the church choir. Her father was a Baptist preacher in New Orleans. After leaving the South, she made Chicago her home. That's where she gained a lot of recognition, as a featured singer at the South Side Greater Baptist Church. And God knows, she worked hard to make a way for herself. When she moved to Chicago, she worked as a domestic, a maid, a laundress, anything to make ends meet. Like me, she dreamed of becoming a nurse. She claimed she used to listen to Bessie Smith records while scrubbing floors to pass the time. "The blues are fine for listenin'," she would say, "but I never would sing them. I sing God's music because it makes me feel free. It gives me hope."

We had met a few times before on the entertainment circuit and I always loved and admired her. Mahalia was a real inspiration to me when I was growing up. And she was my mother's favorite gospel singer.

At the same time I was in Chicago, the Congressional Black Caucus was having a fundraiser. This was in the early sixties. Now, Mahalia could get you to do anything in the world. She was so sweet. She could get you to jump right out the window and you'd do it with a smile on your face, because Mahalia had asked you. One morning, she called me at my hotel; she said, "Baby, I know they got you working all night long." Back then, we would do three shows in a night. Every nightclub you went into, you did three shows. "Well, you know, Dr. King is in town. And we want to raise money. Now, we've got the gospel part of the show and we're going to make it easy. We're going to do the jazz part first, then come on with the gospel. That's where you come in, darling."

I listened, then in the next beat, I said, "Mahalia, what time do you want me to be there?"

"I know you're tired, baby, I can hear it in your voice," she said. She was the sweetest lady in the world.

"What time, Mahalia?" I said.

She told me when and where to show up and I made it over there. Nobody could ever find it in their hearts to turn down Mahalia Jackson. She had tremendous power and could move a room like no one else. Mahalia would sing the Lord's Prayer and folks would be about ready to fall out. And she didn't need a lot of fanfare. She'd sing a cappella or with only a piano or organ accompaniment. She was known to say onstage, "Don't need any microphone. Just open the windows and the doors. And let the sound pour out." She was so full of the Spirit that her voice transcended everything. She had such soul and depth. Her voice just soared. Mahalia was a true contralto with amazing presence. They called her the "Queen of Gospel Song."

Now, as great a voice as she had, people in the music industry wondered why Mahalia didn't cross over into secular music, why she didn't sing jazz or blues. She would say, "Gospel music preceded jazz, affected jazz, gave it inspiration and new forms. But jazz did not affect gospel. That inspiration came from the Lord." She would only sing music that moved her. "I'm Going to Move on Up a Little Higher," "Didn't It Rain," and "The Upper Room" were her signature songs. She was one of the pioneers of gospel music, and one of the first to achieve commercial success in nonsecular music. Mahalia sold millions of records throughout her career. She packed houses the same as any popular jazz or blues singer of the day. She was an international star. Carnegie Hall she packed on four separate occasions. And she sang for four American presidents—Truman, Eisenhower, Kennedy, and Johnson. So in many ways, Mahalia did cross over. She introduced gospel music to the American and European masses.

That evening, I performed a few songs for the fundraiser, along with a few other jazz vocalists, and the music was so good. I ended up staying for the entire event. Well, when the gospel segment began, Mahalia walked that stage, clapped her hands together, and you could hear a pin drop . . . I can see her now . . . back and forth . . . back and forth . . . and she sang and sang—a sound like the coming of the Lord.

Mahalia was a powerhouse. She was a strong, forthright woman and some kind of wonderful. That day she raised $64,000 dollars. Now, I'll tell you what, she may have been singing gospel, but do you think her record company could steal a penny from her? Oh, honey, she'd start to grinning and laughing under her breath, and smiling that sweet smile, but Mahalia had an undercurrent that could roll through there and destroy everybody. She made her money. They paid her. They didn't want that woman to go off. She'd look like she was about to explode.

After the concert, I met Dr. King for the first time. He paid me the most wonderful compliment. I never will forget it.

"*What* a great lady," he said.

Standing there before me on that stage, he looked me straight in the eye, held my hand and said, very sincerely, "*What* a great lady."

I will never forget him.

When people used to talk to me during the civil rights movement about marching and freedom fighting, I would say, now, first of all, you have to understand that I have bad feet. My daddy used to squeeze those too small shoes on my feet, just to keep from giving my mother the money to buy me a new pair. I had rows of corns and bunions on my feet at a very young age. I've never been too big on walking.

My mother said I talked before I walked.

But I'll tell you this, I wouldn't mind getting out and crawling if the purpose was right. I don't have to be the fastest person out there walking and marching. I can take my time and get there at my own pace. But if it's for a purpose, I will do it. Dr. King did amazing things for black people in this country. In fact, the work he did benefited the whole world. He was an example of true leadership. And if ever there was an opportunity for me to contribute my time or my talent to his cause, I would do it. I am really disturbed now when I see all of these politicians and leaders out there pumping themselves up. People don't know who to believe in anymore.

When Dr. King was assassinated it cut through us all. It was a dark day.

I remember being invited for the first time to the White House for a press conference. John F. Kennedy was in office and he was one of the first presidents to truly reach out to the black community. I was contacted by his associate press secretary, Andrew Hatcher, and was extended the invitation.

I took my hairdresser and good friend Natalie Haskell with me. We used to call her the "Queen of the Weave." Natalie was really talented. She could do miraculous things with hair. And she was doing everybody's hair back then, James Brown, Dakota Staton. I think I even met James Brown through Natalie at one point. We were both waiting for her to get busy on our heads. She often traveled with me and helped me buy gowns for my shows and all that. Natalie learned everything she could about her industry. She was always attending a seminar and getting new information on the latest styles. She was really a terrific girl and a great friend to me and my mother. So we went together to the press conference. Oh, baby, we were so excited you would have thought we were on our way to see Jesus. We got all decked out.

When I arrived for the cocktail hour, I found out that President Kennedy and the first lady, Jacqueline, grooved to my music. Come to find out, they were big fans of mine and that was one of the reasons I had been invited. They told me they had all my albums. I was flattered but very surprised. I couldn't believe they were really fans.

Well, I knew it was the God's honest truth when I was invited back to sing at an outdoor music festival organized by the President. He contacted me personally and asked me to play on the bill. This was, of course, a tremendous honor, which I never will forget. It was a summertime festival and it looked like the whole nation had turned out. I had never sung for that many people before in my life. There were hundreds of thousands of people at this concert. It was a magnificent, really beautiful experience. Truly indescribable.

Andrew Hatcher, JFK's press secretary, became a good friend and ally. He was one of the first black men to have such a prestigious position in the White House. Andrew was very active in the civil rights movement and later helped establish 100 Black Men of America, Inc., an organization that is still thriving today.

Once, while on tour in Atlanta, Georgia, my band and I ran into problems at our hotel. We arrived at the hotel around three o'clock in the morning. When we gave our names to confirm the reservation, we were told, "You have no reservations here." Now, it was the sixties, but some people just weren't feeling the civil rights movement.

Integration, my ass, I guess they were saying.

Well, we realized that the South was lagging far behind the rest of the country, but Jim Crow laws of "Colored Only" and "White Only" were no longer in effect down there, so we could not understand what these people were trying to pull. Nevertheless, we didn't want any trouble. We were all dead tired from driving all day, performing all night, and we needed some sleep. The hotel attendant insisted that our reservation was nonexistent. I tried to think of the most influential and powerful person I knew who wouldn't mind a three A.M. phone call. I decided to call Andrew Hatcher. He responded immediately. Andrew told us to leave there and go straight to the Peachtree Marriott. They would have rooms for us. So we followed his advice, checked into the Marriott, and went on about our business. I heard later that we were the first black patrons to ever stay there. That was a landmark evening, but we were too tired to take notice.

Touring in the South, you always took precautions. Over the years, we had all heard such horror stories about black singers and musicians getting into trouble with racist cops and club owners. When Billie Holiday wrote and recorded "Strange Fruit," which described a lynched black body hanging from a poplar tree, it struck a chord in all of us, because being in New York or Chicago or Philly, you could sometimes lose sight of the real turmoil the country was in during the civil rights era. Not that it wasn't there. It was just more covert. In the big cities, you were turned away from performing in certain clubs, or you were paid a lot less than white artists, but in the South, you were spit at, beaten, or even killed. Every time I performed in the South, which wasn't often because my following was in the larger cities, I remembered my mother saying: "Leave the South where it is."

After I had been at ABC for a while, Joe Glaser asked, "Where do you live?" I told him my mother and I were living in Lenox Terrace and he said to me, point-blank, "All my artists have homes." Well, of course they did. I'm sure they had homes and homes and homes. Joe Glaser only represented the very top acts in the country. He had everybody—Satchmo, Sarah, Streisand, Eckstine, everybody. I didn't consider myself on par with them. I wasn't as big a name as any of them, but Joe insisted.

"Go find yourself a home. I'll have my bankers appraise it."

I was a little nervous about this house business. I had never owned a home and hadn't given the idea any serious consideration. I talked to Harry about it. We were still good friends, even though we weren't together anymore. And he made me feel more comfortable about it, because I didn't know a thing about a house. Buying one or otherwise.

And to tell you the truth, me and my mother thought we had arrived when we moved into Lenox Terrace. We had made it our home, and I had never lived anywhere other than Harlem.

However, the idea of being able to put my mother in a beautiful house would be worth the effort, I felt. And honestly, as hard as I was working, I had gotten tired of Harlem. Lenox Terrace was a very nice building, but the block was an entirely different story. One side of the street looked good and the other side of the street looked like a bomb hit it. Years had gone by and the city hadn't done a damn thing about fixing up the area. They just let it go. And nobody cared. There were empty lots full of garbage and abandoned, boarded-up buildings scattered throughout the block.

Harlem was hit hard by drugs and you could see the effects everywhere. There was crime and violence in the area, drugs, all kinds of illegal activity. It was not the same place it had been when I was growing up. Over the years, things had gotten progressively worse and I had gotten tired of the whole thing. Richard would come home from military school for the weekend and he had to deal with all kinds of nonsense. I really didn't like the idea of living in Harlem when Richard became a teenager. There were just too many things going on, too many dangers. So, when Joe Glaser said go get a house, I gave it some serious thought.

But first I moved into an apartment of my own, without my mother.

My mother and I had reached another impasse. We were having it out over every little thing and it got to be too much. I was under a lot of pressure, performing and working on my career. I needed some space of my own, so I started looking for a new place. I looked on the upper East Side in Manhattan and saw a one-bedroom I really liked, on Seventy-ninth Street. The rental agent showed me the apartment but Mom was pessimistic about it.

"You'll never be able to get that apartment," she said.

After seeing it, the agent took me into her office, then proceeded to tell me the place had already been taken and she had only shown it to me out of courtesy. "Are there any other apartments available in the building?" I asked.

"No" was the answer.

A flat, resounding no.

Well, something about the rental agent didn't set well with me, so I did some investigating. We all knew that real estate agents tried to keep blacks out of certain neighborhoods. They did it then, and they do it now. And it's always very subtle and underhanded.

I mean, you can't argue with: "There are no more apartments available. I don't know when one will become available."

I called up one of my good white girlfriends, Ellen Mousari, and told her what was going on. Actually, she was Ellen Bernstein then. Her married name was Mousari. She went over to the building. It was at 333 East Seventy-ninth Street. It turned out, Ellen was shown the very same apartment, by the very same rental agent, and was quickly asked, "When would you like to move in?"

Ellen came outside and told me what had happened. So I got Joe Glaser on the phone. This thing really got to me.

"Just hold on," Joe said.

He called over to the building's management office and within fifteen minutes I got the apartment. I moved in later that week.

This time away from my mother was absolutely necessary. We both needed breathing room. The upper East Side was a much nicer environment for Richard. I didn't worry about him as much when he came home on weekends. It was also more convenient getting to my jobs, since getting a late-night cab to take you to Harlem has been, and I guess will always be, a trip.

Still, this was a not-so-cool time for me. Not many people knew it, except for Helen, of course. She was my confidante. She knew what kind of pressure I was under. I wasn't feeling like myself physically, and with Harry and me separated, emotionally I wasn't too together either.

I had gone to the doctor on several occasions complaining about this and that. It was always something. Each time I visited his office, I was given a new prescription. Before you knew it, I was taking a pill for everything. A red one to get up. A green one to see. A black one to smell. A purple one to walk. Prescription drugs, baby, they're a killer. I was walking around in a haze, strung out on drugs my doctor had prescribed. And who questions the doctor? If he gave them to me, they must be all right. That's what I thought, until I could hardly think at all. I was completely incoherent. I really don't know how I worked or did anything.

Helen kept a close eye on me, and one day, she just got sick of the whole thing and threw every single pill down the toilet.

"Enough is enough," she said.

And that was the end of that phase. It had lasted a couple of months. But I trusted Helen more than life itself and I knew if she had done that, she was doing it for my own good.

Besides, I was too out of it to even fight her about it. Thank God she did it. She probably saved my life.

I worked very hard to get my life back under control and my head together. To this day, I'm hard-pressed to take a pill of any kind. If my family sees me taking as much as an aspirin, they say:

"Oh, she must really be sick."

That episode scared me so bad. I never wanted to see another pill.

Meanwhile, one of my singles, "Impossible," had made the Top 20 R&B chart and "You Don't Have to Be a Tower of Strength" had made Billboard's Top 100. Though progress was being made, in fits and starts, Everest did not have my back. It was still a game of hit and miss. Hit singles meant cash dollars for Everest and very little for me.

The money it would take to get out of the contract with Everest would take a lifetime of earnings. I had no other choice but to deal with things the best way I could. During these years, I was working hard to cultivate my own sound, carve a niche, and gain a following. All of which I had to do on my own with no help from Everest.

And I wasn't alone.

All the black people I knew in the business were singing the record company blues. No one was getting paid properly. Everybody was complaining about getting no royalties. In most cases, not only would you receive no royalties, you wouldn't even get a royalty statement that outlined your zero balance or your negative situation. These companies were not ashamed of the fact that they were ripping you off. They did it in front of God and his whole kingdom. They simply didn't care and they knew you didn't have the money or the power to fight them on it. I remember once calling the union, AFTRA (American Federation of Television and Radio Artists), to get them to arbitrate on my behalf. They came back with nothing. I even called the Internal Revenue Service and what they told me shocked the hell out of me:

"There is nothing we could do because taxes have been paid on your earnings." *What earnings!*

People like Ruth Brown have been real champions in this regard. Ruth fought for all of our rights. She was another pioneer. She pulled the rug out from under their asses in regal fashion. Because we all know, there would be no Atlantic Records without a Ruth Brown. Ruth Brown *was* Atlantic Records. She put them on the map and made them millions upon millions with her hit songs, "Lucky Lips" and "This Little Girl's Gone Rockin'." Ruth and I met on the singing circuit and became friends. She kept an apartment up in Harlem, though she was on the road most of the time. Now, Ruth went through her share of ups and downs in the business, but she always continued the fight to recoup what was hers from rip-off record companies. She is a talented lady. And she has earned every ounce of credit and acknowledgment that she's gotten late in her career.

After decades of fighting, she and other singers, like Bonnie Raitt, along with a group of attorneys, were able to get several record companies to donate thousands of dollars to help fund and create the Rhythm & Blues Foundation. Now, they honor several artists each year with the Pioneer Award, acknowledging their longevity in the business and their contribution to the music industry. They also provide financial assistance to those that need it. Along with the Pioneer Award, each honoree is given a monetary award.

After the Rhythm & Blues Foundation was established, record companies began to make charitable contributions to the organization. Whether they wanted to or not, it became the "correct" thing to do. It began as a lawsuit between Ruth Brown and Atlantic Records, but resulted in this thriving organization. It was designed, essentially, to right the wrongs of the past, to help legendary artists in the music industry. Dedicated attorneys forced certain companies, particularly Atlantic Records, who had ripped off so many black artists, to make contributions, then other companies followed suit. It set a trend in the industry.

I am very proud of the women of the jazz era. We were fighters, and God knows, we all paid some hefty dues. Della Reese was another strong force in the industry. She paid her dues and somebody else's dues. That woman drove trucks and taxis and everything else to make it. I remember when I first saw Della perform, I thought she was so striking, just a great lady. I always admired her. I remember when Della had a little studio apartment on Central Park West. Everything in it was so pretty, it looked like a little dollhouse. Della came from Detroit and started out as a singer. She had roots in the church and toured with Mahalia Jackson as a teenager. She had her own group, the Meditation Singers, who took gospel on the road. Della was the vocalist for the Erskine Hawkins Orchestra and had two very big hits in the fifties, "Don't You Know" and "And That Reminds Me." In the late sixties, she had her own television show, *The Della Reese Show*, which was a major accomplishment for a black woman. She later appeared on popular TV shows like *Sanford and Son*, with Redd Foxx, and *Picket Fences*. Now she has a successful dramatic series, *Touched by an Angel*. When I see Della now I think of all those years of hard work. She deserves every bit of her success. She had it coming.

There is something to be said for the black women in the business who have persevered and broken every imaginable barrier. Nothing came easy.

7

$\mathcal{N}$ineteen sixty-three was a landmark year. Dr. King led thousands to the Lincoln Memorial with his March on Washington, where he gave his phenomenal "I Have a Dream" speech. Muhammad Ali was *Time* magazine's Man of the Year. People were still up in arms over Vietnam, but we all got the shock of our lives when the President was assassinated in Dallas. JFK was dead. Medgar Evers, the civil rights leader and officer of the NAACP, was shot and killed getting out of his car. And this was just the beginning of a whole string of assassinations to come. Things had been building up for a while, but in '63 things came to a head.

The writer and activist LeRoi Jones published *Blues People*—the first book to argue that jazz is essentially the music of black people. This marked the beginning of the music wars—jazz competed with R&B, soul music competed with standard blues, and more and more music forms were being introduced, which meant competition was getting fierce.

By '63, Motown, the wealthiest black-owned corporation in the country, was dominating the airwaves. They employed talented songwriters like Holland-Dozier-Holland and Ashford & Simpson. Their solo vocalists were all climbing the charts: Stevie Wonder, Mary Wells, Junior Walker, Marvin Gaye. And the all-male and all-female groups were making a comeback. They had the Four Tops, who were a class act, the Supremes, the Vandellas, the Temptations. People said Motown made such a hit because they were the first to produce black music that appealed to middle-class, white suburbanites. Times were truly changing.

This was the year I won the Playboy Jazz Award. It was sponsored by *Playboy* magazine, and Hugh Hefner presented me the award at a huge gala in New York. I believe you were selected by music critics, magazine journalists, record company execs, and other people in the media. It was largely an industry award much like the other magazine polls at *Downbeat*, *Metronome*, and *Billboard*, who ranked music—the artist and their albums. These awards were also popularity contests. And it worked both ways—if fans bought your albums, it gained the attention of the industry and if the industry granted you the award, it grabbed the attention of the fans. There was loads of press coverage at the Playboy Award ceremony, which was great for me because it established my name among the top jazz vocalists of the day.

Over the years, I've performed at their clubs in Chicago and in California. They sponsor the Playboy Jazz Festival every year, and have been a great supporter of jazz music down through the years.

This was also the same year "I Wish You Love" was released.

My producers loved the song so much, they decided to release it as a single, before the album was even completed. So, when the album was released, *Gloria, Marty & Strings*, the single was already a huge hit and the album followed suit. Marty Paich was the arranger on the album. He was really dynamic and added so much to the whole record. It was a string album, so the sound was just great. You rarely hear albums with strings anymore. None of the record companies want to pay for it. *Gloria, Marty & Strings* was released late in the year, and charted early in 1964 in the national listings.

None of us knew what a huge success "I Wish You Love" would be. It had wings of its own. I had no idea, back then, that it would become my signature song, but people still associate me with the song and it's always requested at my live concerts. I didn't make a dime on it, but it gave me plenty of exposure. I became very recognizable after "I Wish You Love" became a hit. Suddenly, everyone knew my name.

I was invited to appear on *The Ed Sullivan Show*. His variety show was the most popular TV show of the day. It aired on CBS. Careers were made on *The Ed Sullivan Show*. He'd have all kinds of guests on, from athletes to dancers to singers, everybody. And some of the biggest stars in the world made guest appearances on the show, like Frank Sinatra, Judy Garland, Sammy Davis Jr., and James Brown. He is even given credit for skyrocketing Elvis Presley's career. After only one appearance on the show, the world lost its mind over Elvis.

I remember being thrilled to death about going on the show. The other guests that evening were Robert Goulet and the actress Mae West. I met Ed Sullivan before the show, did a quick rehearsal with the band, the producers showed me my spot, and when airtime hit, 8 P.M. on Sunday evening, I stood there in my pretty dress and sang "I Wish You Love." It was sublime. There I was, a young singer on the circuit, singing in front of the entire country. I mean, this was the big time.

When the Beatles made their first appearance on the show American audiences went wild over those British boys. I'm not even sure if many Americans knew who they were at the time, but after their performance, their careers were set. And I must say, I was content with getting union-scale pay for my performance, which must have been a hundred dollars or so back then, until I found out that the Beatles were paid umpteen thousands of dollars.

That's the way it was.

And if the truth be told, all of those white boys had stolen from black artists. You ask Chuck Berry and Little Richard who the kings of rock and roll are, they'll tell you. Some of the white groups were proud to admit that their musical influences were black. Sam Phillips of Sun Records, after discovering Elvis, said he'd always dreamed of finding a white recording artist who could rock and roll like the black stars.

However, the American media was not trying to hear that. They wanted their music heroes to be white. They pumped those boys with enough hype to pack football stadiums. They made tons of money ripping off poor black artists that have yet to receive their proper respect in this business. And this is not news. Everybody knows, by now, what went down.

I hadn't forgotten my conversation with Joe Glaser about the house business. When I was ready to buy, I asked for his help. He gave me the name of a realtor, some locations to consider, and all the brass tacks to buying a home. And even though my mother and I were at odds, as hard as we had worked, it was time we had a nice home to live in.

I was ready to settle down.

My first house was in Englewood Cliffs, New Jersey, at 495 Woodland Avenue. It was a very special place. I ended up on the same block with all of these superstars in the music business. Dinah Washington had a home on one corner, Sarah Vaughan was down on the other, Dizzy Gillespie and his wife, Lorraine, were two doors down, and across the street was Clyde Otis, one of the few black A&R (Artist & Repertoire) men in the business.

The neighborhood was gorgeous. The homes were expansive, and quite expensive. Most of the people that lived in the area were well-to-do. I bought a thirteen-room, tri-level home with a basement and a subbasement. I had over a hundred-some-odd trees in my backyard. It was a really beautiful place. I later put in a pool and added some other upgrades. I still spent most of my time on the road, so the biggest kick I got out of the house was seeing my mother in it. I felt that I had finally been able to give her what she deserved.

She, on the other hand, was not excited about the house even a little bit. She tried, but she was a Harlem lady. She loved Harlem, never wanted to leave it.

"You're trying to get away from where you come from," she used to tell me.

"I am simply trying to better my life."

This mentality just killed me. I couldn't get with it. And she wasn't the only one who felt that way. I remember when I went down into the rental office at Lenox Terrace to finalize our move, one of the office workers said, loud enough so I could hear:

"As soon as they get big, they move."

This really disgusted me, because I had worked too hard to have to defend wanting a better life. I didn't feel that I owed anyone any explanations, nor did I feel obligated to stay in a neighborhood that had become unsafe for my kid. But my mother would repeat this to me all the time:

"You can't get away from where you come from."

It wasn't as if I was ashamed of my upbringing, it was what it was, but there was no reason in the world to stay stuck and refuse to move forward. I wanted a nice place to live just like any other right-minded person.

We entertained a lot. We always had a house full of people. Dizzy Gillespie used to come over and swim in our pool. He and my mother would play cards all into the night. They were crazy about each other. She couldn't wait to beat him at Tonk.

"Is Dizzy off the road yet?" she used to ask.

She would wear him out, beat him bad, and take all his money. They were a regular mess together. My friend Helen was another one who was crazy about Dizzy. She loved him to death. In fact, I think part of the reason she married her second husband, Kenny, was because he looked something like Dizzy.

It was a celebrity neighborhood, so we had a lot of high-profile people to come by and visit. Muhammad Ali used to stop by every once in a while. He and I had some very interesting conversations together. Actually, I had the pleasure of knowing Muhammad Ali and Joe Louis. Joe was very cool. He had a way about him that stopped you in your tracks and made you pay attention. He was a charmer. And he loved show business people. Joe used to come out and hang with us after shows. He used to call me "Chairman" and he called my friend and personal secretary, Bertha Coultier, "Sec." And, of course, he was the "Brown Bomber."

During this period, we had so many black heroes. I mean, we whooped and hollered whenever Joe Louis or Ali beat somebody in the ring, or when Jackie Robinson or Willie Mays hit a home run. It was a victory for the entire black race. People were proud in the sixties. Everybody's conversations circled around civil rights, the movement, the struggle, the government, the Vietnam War. This was our kitchen-table conversation. That's just what time it was.

And everybody loved my mother.

She would cook for them and talk all into the night. One day, Muhammad was over and Mom had cooked all this food, a pork roast, I think it was, with all the fixings, and she asked him:

"You gonna eat some of this?"

He said, "No, you know, my religion—" He had just joined the Black Muslims and changed his name from Cassius Clay to Muhammad Ali.

"Well, seems to me your mama fed you pork," Mom said, "and that's how you became champion of the world. All that pork is up in you. That's what makes you strong. How you think you became champion of the world?"

She went on and on about it and wouldn't let him rest. She figured he wasn't nothing but a big ol' Kentucky boy, so surely he knew his way around the kitchen table. Muhammad had been boxing since he was twelve years old, and by this time, he had beat everybody's behind from Alabama to Zaire. Now, I'm not going to say whether or not he ate the pork, because I know the Muslims are serious about their beliefs, so, let's just say, *he ate the dinner.*

Muhammad used to come by and talk politics with us. He had given the government plenty of grief himself. They didn't expect that from a country boy. He was supposed to be a boxer, not an intellectual. But Muhammad is a brilliant man. He has always approached his life and career without fear. He didn't mind taking a stand on the issues of the day, on his religious or personal convictions, even if it meant becoming less popular in the eyes of the masses. And for those of us in sports and entertainment, that is really saying something. Your paycheck often depends on your popularity. That has never changed. Nowadays, people don't stand for a damn thing other than themselves.

My mother was especially fond of him. She loved to hear him talk . . . *but who didn't?* Muhammad could turn a phrase. He was very serious about civil rights and didn't think twice about marching right next to Dr. King, Malcolm X, or any other black leader if it was about racial equality and justice for black people in America. He is a beautiful man.

I remember Muhammad telling me once:

"Gloria, the way you sing, if you were a white girl you'd be on the moon by now."

When Dick Gregory came by our house, the FBI came right behind him. They had spread themselves out all over the yard and in the garden, ducking in the bush. My mother went out on the back porch and hollered out:

"Listen, y'all can come on in if you want. No need in you laying out here, messing up my grass. This boy's going to be here for a minute."

They were on his ass in the sixties. They followed him everywhere. Followed him right out to Englewood. They didn't know who they were up against, because Dick is a formidable man, very intelligent and highly motivated. But this was during the time when J. Edgar Hoover, the head of the FBI, was taking names and asking questions later. He was completely against the efforts of Dr. King, and considered anyone associated with the movement to be a subversive. This was a time when everybody and their mama was being put on a "list" for one reason or another. And artists and athletes were some of Hoover's prime targets.

Regardless, the civil rights movement was a very special period in time for black people. I can't remember a time when we were more unified, focused, and supportive of one another. There was a real spirit of community and the feeling that we were all moving in the same direction with the same goals in mind. Dick was relentless, and the man still hasn't quit. He is still an important black political figure.

Unfortunately, the only way the government could think to control the power and influence of black leaders was to use scare tactics and threats. Dick was "wanted" by the FBI because he was one of the front-runners of the movement. J. Edgar Hoover had a "hate list" (meaning, hit list), and he developed special measures to "neutralize" Dick and a few others.

What can you say?

It was a very deep period.

Honestly, I was always so busy out on the road, I never stood still long enough to really get involved. I certainly aligned myself with the views of Dr. King and many of the other black leaders, but my contributions came in the form of my artistry. I performed at different benefits and fundraisers for the cause. There were plenty of artists and athletes that took the time to march right alongside King. Others expressed themselves through their music. And nothing told it like it was like Marvin Gaye's "What's Going On?" They called it protest music, but we called it the truth. It was an interesting but frightening time for all of us.

From day to day, you didn't know what was going to happen. You would hear about people losing their jobs, being wiretapped, and even killed for all sorts of crazy reasons. White folks were scared to death that the hands of power were turning from white to black. There was tension so thick, you could cut it.

My mother had a way about her, and all of these men loved coming by to talk to her. Now, she wasn't exactly a witch, but she was very intuitive, psychic really. I'll tell you how my mother was: I could go around the block and talk about my mother, and when I came back she could tell me every word I'd said. It was scary. She was a very deep lady. So, they enjoyed getting her insights on the issues of the day. And God knows there were more issues than there were jobs. People were up in arms about something every minute of the day.

Because I was traveling so much, I followed another bit of Joe Glaser's advice: I hired a live-in maid to help with the cleaning and maintenance of the house.

Baby, that was a fiasco.

My mother had cleaned our two-bedroom apartment over in Lenox Terrace, but I knew she couldn't handle all the work that the house needed.

What I didn't know was what kind of grief she was giving the maid.

I came home one day, after being on the road for about two weeks, and the maid came to me in confidence.

"I hate to tell you this," she said, "but I haven't done a thing around this house. Your mother won't let me work. When I try to clean a room, she follows behind me and wants to talk. She won't even let me make her a cup of coffee. I bring her the coffee, she says it's rabbit piss. It ain't strong enough for her. I am very sorry, but you've been paying me for nothing."

I couldn't believe it. I knew my mother could be a trip, but this was too much. I tried to talk to her about it, but she refused to listen.

For whatever reason, Mom could not get comfortable in that house. She tried, but every day she wanted to go to Harlem. So, when I was home, I would take her.

Baby, my mother in that house is a story in itself. She used to walk around in her old housecoats, no matter what nice things I bought her. She wore them every day with her stockings rolled down to her knees and old house slippers. As pretty as she was, Mom would go around with a head rag on and just look a mess, walking around in a mansion. She was country, you know. Delivery people would come to the door and she would answer looking just like that. They'd ask for the lady of the house.

"You're looking at her. What do you want?" she'd say.

And I suppose, she was right. She was the lady of the house, no matter what she looked like. But if I said anything, I mean, anything at all, about her dress, it would be the worst fight and argument you ever had in your life! I bought her a mink coat and that thing just laid there, looking at her. She only wore it once. It was at times like these when she'd hit me with:

"You can't get away from where you come from."

I had no other choice but to let her alone about it. Black folks are funny when it comes to money. Some people cannot accept living well. They don't like it and they don't want you to like it. There's something about wealth that makes some people very uncomfortable. I don't understand it.

I wanted my mother to be happy. Too many years had gone by that were unhappy. So, I thought what I accomplished in my career could make up for all of the hardships. But she seemed hell-bent on holding on to the past. She wouldn't let it go. Thinking back, I believe my mother was really a depressed woman. If she were around today, there would be help for her—medicine, treatments, therapy. She was mistreated most of her life. She had it hard. It was difficult for me, always seeing her in pain. I wanted my mother to be happy. So, I tried everything—gifts, good times, money. I had to learn, finally, that I could not take responsibility for her happiness. If she wanted it, she'd have to allow it into her life.

It wasn't for a lack of company that Mom turned her nose up at that house. Every day, there was a constant flow of people. I think Mom liked a lot of company—it kept her mind off things. I would be out on the road and come back home and the bar would be drip-dry, not an ounce of liquor left, after I had just fully stocked it weeks before. People felt very comfortable just stopping by, to say hey to Mom, swim in the pool, eat dinner, whatever.

I had a friend, Stormy Redcross, who used to be one of my drivers. Now, I've had a lot of cars and I've always kept a license, but I've never cared much for driving, probably because I was always on the road. Well, Stormy used to stop by often to see my mother and she would always bring her a box of candy. It didn't matter what kind of candy it was, as long as it was a box. Stormy was a real popular girl, very pretty, stunning, really. She loved to sit and talk to my mother.

She'd say, "Mazie, I brought you some candy."

Everybody called Mom Mazie.

Richard named her that as a kid, when he couldn't say Mary, he said Mazie. And the name stuck.

Anyway, Mom would say, "Oh, yes, Stormy, I *know* you brought me some candy."

See, Stormy would bring my mother the candy but she wouldn't leave that house until she herself had eaten every piece. Mom never even got as much as a taste or a lick of that candy. Stormy would eat it all. It was hilarious.

Mom would just say, "Uh-huh, yeah, Stormy, I know you brought me some candy."

On Richard's eighteenth birthday, Mama went out and bought him a Cadillac. I was so mad I didn't know what to do.

I hit the roof.

I could not believe she bought that child a Cadillac. He was only eighteen! When I confronted her about it, she said:

"This is my only grand."

She spoiled him rotten all his life. Now, I fully understood that he was her only grandson, but I said:

"This boy does not need a Cadillac. Get him a normal car like the other kids have."

I pitched a bitch. We went back and forth on this thing for weeks, until one morning, she said:

"Come on. Let's go out."

I didn't know where she was taking me. She didn't say much but jumped in my car and gave me the directions on where to go. We ended up at the Mercedes-Benz dealership in Englewood. Turns out, she had already been there and talked to one of the salesmen about a car for me. She looked at me and said:

"Go head. Pick out your car."

I couldn't believe it. I was so tickled. I picked out a 230SL, a two-seater. I never will forget that car. It was $8,500 dollars in 1963. After we had done all of the paperwork, Mom turned to me and said:

"Now I don't want to hear nothing else about what I bought my grandson."

I never asked her where she got the money to pay for the car because Mom was so tight with a dollar she could have used money she had saved up from 1945, for all I knew. I always took care of her and gave her money to get around, but she didn't spend what she didn't have to. And the Benz, I think, was her way of thanking me for all I had done.

We went everywhere in that car.

And we went to Harlem every day.

But, no matter what I did, Mom didn't want to be in that house. I came to accept that. For years, she kept telling me I wasn't ready for a house, that I didn't need a house. And looking back, maybe she was right. What I didn't know was my money didn't add up to that house. As well as I was doing, it wasn't enough. I remember, when I first got to Englewood, I had been there about six or seven months, and one day, I took a look around and it occurred to me, I was living in the midst of multimillionaires.

My money just wasn't that long.

Living in a home like that has a certain lifestyle attached to it. You have to keep up. People would come by the house to socialize and eat and drink. We had to keep the refrigerator full and the bar fully stocked. My food bill was over a thousand dollars a month. In the sixties, that was a lot of money on food. We had barbecues and cocktail parties and card parties, the whole deal.

But the money wasn't there.

Like we used to say, you can't fight city hall. I didn't have the funds to keep up the lifestyle.

I was working like a dog trying to live like a queen.

8

———❀———

Rocky Road

$\mathcal{T}$oward the end of my seven-year contract with Everest, I moved over to Mercury Records, which was based out of Chicago. I needed to reposition myself in the industry because "I Wish You Love" was no longer a hit on the jazz side. In fact, it was no longer considered jazz.

Well, I had a hell of a time because the R&B people didn't know me and the jazz people I had outgrown. Making the transition was difficult. Though I have a deep respect and love of jazz music, I have never been interested in categories. Music is music to me. I am more interested in the quality of the music. When I'm singing, I am not conscious of whether what I am singing falls into pop or jazz or R&B. My interpretation of the song is purely intuitive. I don't think any good singer stands there saying, "OK, this song is jazz so I have to sing it like this," or "this is R&B so I better do it like this." You let the music guide you. But while you're performing, this kind of analysis is not necessarily taking place. Different forms of music cross lines at some point. You can sing a jazz song with some pop licks or vice versa. The only music that can claim some level of exclusivity is opera. When you hear an opera, you know exactly what it is. But the rest of the genres tend to blend.

In 1964, King Curtis came to me with a song.

"Gloria, I wrote this song for you," he said.

The song was "Soul Serenade." Now, technically this is a blues song so I told King:

"Are you sure you want *me* to sing this song?"

He wouldn't even entertain the thought of my not singing the song. So he said to me:

"Gloria, this song is for you."

Blues or no blues, I did it. The song was released on Mercury (Fontana). It was also the title cut. Hal Mooney was the producer and conductor on the record. The *Soul Serenade* album included "That's My Desire," "Baby, Won't You Please Come Home," "If I Love You," "Don't Go to Strangers," "Watermelon Man," which I wrote the lyrics to, with music by Herbie Hancock, "Teach Me Tonight," "People Will Say We're in Love," "All Alone," "I'll Be Around," "Joey, Joey, Joey," and "It Could Happen to You."

This album was another notch in my belt, letting the industry know what I was capable of producing. It was well received by the public. And the critics loved it, too. Joe Segal wrote in the album's liner notes:

"While most of today's singers twist and turn lyrics and melody into unrecognizable gibberish, Miss Lynne follows her self-directed path of straight-forwardness and honesty in music. The original song is always apparent, with the initial intent of the composer always honored. . . . I find her professionalism and simple, direct and musical approach to this most difficult field of creative endeavor highly satisfying."

Now, every time I perform live, I take the time to pay tribute to King Curtis. I credit him with the success of that album. He heard something in my voice that even I didn't know was there. And this is the kind of growth I wanted. I always wanted to stretch myself as a vocalist and see how far I could go.

For two years, between 1964 and 1966, I worked double duty with Everest and Mercury Records. While Everest was releasing my single "Don't Take Your Love from Me," the Fontana label (a division of Mercury that was initially developed as my own production company) released "Be Anything (Be Mine)."

It was around this time that I met two super-talented songwriters who would later become two of my best friends—Buddy Scott and Jimmy Radcliffe. It was around 1965, and I was asked to share the bill with Arthur Prysock at the Apollo.

Now, Buddy and Jimmy were full of fire back then. I mean, you would be in the middle of a recording session and they'd just bust in there and ask you if you wanted to hear one of their tunes. They didn't bother with any formalities. They came with the talent and figured that was enough.

And they'd catch you wherever they could. If they heard a singer they liked, they'd come into your dressing room after a show and let you hear their songs. That evening at the Apollo, they said they had a song for me, "Love Child." Well, Buddy was standing there, singing a few bars for me, then suddenly, all the lights went out in the place. We thought it was just a problem in the theater. We had no idea, until a little later, that there was a blackout all over New York City. So Buddy went and got some candles from somewhere, and without missing a beat he kept singing this song in my ear. I told them:

"I think y'all need to come on by my house, so we can finish this."

And they did. I really loved their music and always appreciated their interest in my voice. When I learned "Love Child" I fell in love with it, and I knew then that Buddy, Jimmy, and I had formed a lifelong collaboration. If I recall, when I finally performed "Love Child" on stage it was at the Village Gate. None of us knew how the audience would receive the song, but we took a chance. Well, when I began singing the room was completely quiet. There wasn't a sound coming from the audience. And when I finished the song, the same thing. A hush. Well, Buddy told me later that he was a nervous wreck the whole time I was up there, and he looked over to Jimmy and said:

"Jimmy, we bombed. We bombed, man."

Jimmy didn't say anything.

Then all of a sudden, from out of the blue, this thunderous applause came. People jumped to their feet and screamed and shouted. That night, two grown men cried real tears. By the time I came offstage, Jimmy and Buddy were fit to be tied. They were thrilled to death and so was I.

I have never taken my audience for granted. And I credit black people for making me. Joe Glaser used to tell me all the time, "Gloria, your audience is almost completely black. We have to get white audiences interested in you." I told him that was fine but I knew if black folks like you, *they like you.* And when they love you, they show you. The toughest audience in the world is black people. You have to come with it, baby. So,

I've always appreciated looking out and seeing a sea of my people out there supporting me. That ain't nothing but a good feeling.

My release *Lonely and Sentimental* on Everest was a monster hit. The album was arranged and orchestrated by Melba Liston, who was also a fantastic horn player. She was one of a handful of women horn players. Melba played in two of the best big bands around—Dizzy Gillespie's and Count Basie's. She was extremely talented. We recorded "Love, I Found You," which is still a favorite of my fans (and of mine, too) and was written by my good friend and mentor Danny Small. This song was so hot that in Philly it was being called the new Philadelphia national anthem. "Man of Mine" was also his composition. "We Never Kissed" was Melba's original tune. And we did "For All We Know," "Little Girl Blue," "Sentimental Melody," "In Other Words," " 'Tis Autumn," "Hands Across the Table," "Blue and Sentimental," "Am I Blue," and "Then I'll Be Tired of You."

Melba was very meticulous about the album. It was recorded in three separate sessions. I was backed by eleven strings, five saxophones, two trombones, and an all-star rhythm section for the first session. Then I came back in and sang with nine strings, five brass, four saxophones, and three guys on rhythm. The final session we did some sides with just trumpet, trombone, and a couple of saxes and a few guys in the rhythm section. It was a beautiful album. I always loved working with strings. There's nothing like that sound.

After I released my final album for Everest, which was *Gloria, Marty & Strings*, I was signed to an exclusive seven-year deal with Mercury. This was a little ironic considering *I Wish You Love*, my biggest hit ever with Everest, was on that last album. Irving Green was president at that time. I had met Irving years before, because he came to all of my performances. He would always ask me:

"Is that contract up yet? We want you over at Mercury."

He never let up and he won in the end. Irving Green pulled me out of the clutches of Bernie Solomon. Quincy Jones was working at the New York offices of Mercury then. He started out with them doing arrangements for Dinah Washington. Dinah just loved him. She told everybody about this new young kid on the block who was really going places. By the time I came on board, he was an executive, a vice president, in A&R.

Quincy Jones actually helped Melba Liston on some of the arrangements on my album *Lonely and Sentimental*. She and Quincy were very
close at the time. Now, I didn't have anything to do with writing the
credits, which were printed on the album sleeve, but I think it put a bad
taste in Quincy's mouth that he wasn't credited as one of the arrangers on
the album. It was obviously an oversight, because Quincy was in the studio
working on the album right alongside Melba.

The album sold well. The critics loved it. Leonard Feather wrote the
liner notes. All of those songs were very successful, and Quincy definitely
deserved credit for the work he did. To this day, I don't know how this
oversight occurred.

But I do know, from that day forward, Quincy lost interest in me as
an artist. And he let me know it.

Mercury offered me a base salary of $25,000 per year. Whether I was
hot, whether I sold, if the whole wide world was buying my records, I
would never get royalties. I accepted it because I needed the money. Simple
as that. It was steady, reliable income, unlike the sporadic pay I had been
getting from Everest. I figured, with Mercury, I wouldn't have to chase my
money down, like I had been doing for the past seven years. And I have
to say, I was excited about getting the twenty-five grand, until I found out
that they were paying secretaries that much, which really burst my bubble.

I believed Mercury was established enough to benefit an artist like
myself but young and vibrant enough to help develop and nurture my
career. They seemed to be on the cutting edge, with a real interest in the
jazz/pop scene. They also had a smaller label that was devoted to jazz only,
the EmArcy label. At this time, I was singing jazz, pop, and R&B music.
I was really trying to cross over, since the sound of music was changing.
By the mid-sixties a lot of jazz vocalists were experiencing a bit of a fade-
out. You could still get gigs at the well-known jazz clubs like the Village
Vanguard and the Blue Note, but the club scene followed what was happening in music. Change was everywhere.

If you hadn't reached the very, very top, it became increasingly difficult
to stay afloat in jazz. Record companies were doing away with their main-
stays, in order to trap lightning in a bottle, which in their minds was R&B,
soul, and the Motown sound. Bebop and jazz were now considered passé,
the music of intellectuals.

It seemed to me that all of these new categories were created to generate money, period. The money men didn't care that R&B had its roots in traditional blues and gospel, or that swing, bebop, cool jazz, or whatever you want to call it, was not something to be thrown out. All great music should be preserved. It's a continuum—there is no beginning, middle, or end to it. We have all been inspired by someone that came before. One sound builds on the other. And all of us build on the past, whether we're conscious of it or not. This would be impossible if music was discarded like old news. If music had no roots, we would be stuck in a place where we are constantly re-creating the wheel. The idea that a certain type of music has to be disposed of in order to make room for the new is just crazy. So, as an artist during this time, you had to figure out a way to maneuver in this environment of change.

It was hard as hell working in an atmosphere of "what's hot, what's not." Because we loved our music, we never thought it would be dismissed. Jazz has a kind of spontaneity to it, so the sound is always fresh and new. But commercial radio stations were only interested in hits, and at this time, hits were coming out of Detroit, and then, of course, the British invaded.

There were severe consequences in staying on the jazz scene, which was becoming less popular among the masses. It was tricky because going commercial often meant you'd be unsatisfied, artistically. For vocalists especially, part of being a commercial success meant you had to give the people what they wanted, how they wanted it, and when they wanted it. As far as record companies were concerned, you were only as good as the number of records you sold.

Betty Carter once said, "Quality is in the old stuff, but who wants it?" She was a renegade. A real die-hard jazz singer. Betty devoted herself to jazz music and stayed with it all the way to the end. Choosing to sing jazz, and jazz alone, meant less money and less exposure, less support all the way around. A lot of record companies, as well as nightclubs and lounges, abandoned jazz altogether. So as the sixties progressed, work for a lot of jazz artists began to dry up.

I realized: A good secretary can make as much as a jazz artist.

Many musicians went on tour in places like Europe and Japan in order to make money. There were several top jazz musicians, in fact, that became expatriates because of the commercialization of the music industry during this time. Talented musicians like Dexter Gordon and Kenny Clarke moved to Paris to distance themselves from what was happening.

Fifty-second Street was slowly demolished over time, to make room for big hotels and skyscrapers. If you walk down that street today, there is absolutely nothing there to remind you that it was the land where geniuses roamed.

All of the historians say that jazz is the only music that America can claim. It originated in the United States. I find this very curious because, if this is the truth, the country has a very bizarre way of expressing its appreciation for the music and its artists.

I was talking to a good friend of mine, who was recently nominated for a Grammy Award. She mentioned how interesting it is that at the Grammys, America's premier music award, jazz artists are given their awards in the middle of the afternoon, before the show is televised.

As if they're saying, "Take your award and get the hell out of here before the important artists get here."

It's ridiculous. We have never gotten the kind of respect we deserve. And we've never been paid right. But they say jazz is America's only original art form.

Maybe if black folks hadn't had a hand in it, it would be viewed differently. If the majority of innovators in jazz had been white, perhaps the reaction, the money, and the glory would be different. But those musicians, the real trailblazers, were black men, and the vocalists who became legends of the jazz era were black women. Now, you can play around with the facts, but you can't change truth. And the truth is that jazz is one of the greatest music forms ever created. We should all feel blessed that there was a Duke Ellington and a Charlie Parker, a Billie Holiday and a Sarah Vaughan.

Irving Green believed I had crossover appeal. He knew I could sing pop, R&B, and jazz. The EmArcy label was already releasing some great jazz artists' music in the mid-fifties. They had Clifford Brown and Max Roach, Cannonball Adderly, Nina Simone, Sarah Vaughan, and Dinah Washington. Sarah actually worked both labels. Her contract required that she record jazz for the subsidiary and pop for the parent company.

I was generally pleased with the work I was doing for Mercury. I had success with my album *Love and a Woman*, which was produced and arranged by renowned conductor Hal Mooney. The album was full of ballads and beautiful love songs like "Sunday Kind of Love," "I Love You for Sentimental Reasons," "I'm Just a Woman in Love," and "Til There Was You." It went over well with my fans. It was a romantic album, very mushy.

Everybody loved it, my peers and the critics. Del Shields, who was a pop-ular radio personality in the sixties, said:

"Miss Gloria Lynne is singing love songs for those in love; the roman-ticists who search for love, the dreamers who dream of love, and for the music lovers who simply like songs of love."

One thing I remember about recording *Love and a Woman* was a party that Mercury gave me at the Village Gate. Some of the songs on that album are live recordings from that evening. Before my performance, there was a big cocktail party for the press and music company execs. It was really fabulous. Well, I'm not a heavy drinker by any stretch, but that night I had a couple of cocktails, in the spirit of the evening, you know. By the time I made it up to the stage, I was just as woozy. Not noticeably so (I don't think), but enough for me to know that my equilibrium was a little off. I had a time up there trying to perform. When the actual album came out, I had forgotten about the big party and all that, until I heard myself singing "All or Nothing at All." Well, some of the lyrics were just as thick and slurred, because of the liquor. I'm not sure if many people even noticed it, but I did. And I knew the reason why. It's funny to me now, but back then, I swore I'd never drink again before a show.

One of my most successful releases under Mercury (Fontana) was *A Very Gentle Sound*, which Jerry Butler helped produce. He came out from Chicago and we worked on it together. The album had "I Got Your Love," "The Summer Knows (Theme from 'Summer of '42')," "Never My Love," "The Reason Why," "Just Let Me Be Me," "A Sadness for Things," "More Love," and the title track, "A Very Gentle Sound," which my son, Richard Alleyne, cowrote.

A Very Gentle Sound did well. However, because I wasn't one of their top moneymakers, I really didn't get the push I needed in order to sell. And if I've learned nothing else in this business, I've learned this: When a company doesn't lay the money on the table at the onset, they've made a risk-free investment. They have nothing to lose. They are getting more than giving. If your records flop, they have very little to lose. If they sell well, that's more than they expected to gain. They have to get behind you, financially, in order for you to get the payoff in the end.

Still, somehow, it sold.

Over the seven years I was at Mercury, I recorded some great albums—*Intimate Moments; Here, There and Everywhere; Where It's At;* and *Soul*

Serenade. But my work wasn't pushed. In order to survive and stay on top of the charts, a push and a plug is always needed.

Financially, I was straining. Between trying to maintain my house and keep up with my travel expenses on the road and Richard's school tuition, my money started to dwindle. Money had gotten so tight that I came to the conclusion that I desperately needed to supplement my salary. Although Mercury was paying me my salary, and they're the only record company I can give that credit to, what I was making was simply not enough. In the fifties and sixties, artists typically received a 5 percent royalty (if they were lucky) on their record sales. In today's market, artists are getting anywhere from 12 to 15 percent, which is still so much less than what the record companies earn. If you've made a million, you better believe they've made ten million. When you think of the small percentage you receive as an artist, compared to the millions racked in by the record companies, it is criminal when royalties aren't paid. It's all by their design. Artists rarely get what they're worth. Hell, artists rarely *know* what they are worth.

So, I decided that I would go out and find a job. I didn't care what people had to say about it. I had that house to take care of, my mother, my son, I needed to make a living. I asked around and someone suggested I find something part-time, right in Jersey, where I was living. I was tight with some of the local politicians and found out there was a job available in the Bergen County Office. I applied and was offered a position as a license clerk.

This turned out to be a much bigger deal than I ever planned. I went down there, quietly, and really believed I could work in the office, mind my business, and make a little extra cash. But I had to be sworn in and the whole county was made aware of my appointment to the position. Then, the newspapers got hold of it, and of course they blew the story up. The New Jersey papers ran a headline that said:

"SINGER TURNS CLERK."

They wrote a downtrodden tale about me hittin' the skids and needing to go back to a nine-to-five gig. And what they didn't know, they made up. They blew it all out of proportion. Now, if they had just written that Gloria Lynne needed some money to pay her bills, so she had to get a day job, that would have been the truth. I needed a job and some money. It wasn't complicated. It was the simple truth.

The things I saw go on in that office made me lose all respect for city government. I was a license clerk, so if you needed a license for your business, you had to come to me. Well, it was nothing more than a title, because I had absolutely no authority.

I remember once, a black man had come to me for a license. He had a fleet of cabs and needed the license in order to run his business. He told me he had been coming down there for five years trying to get the license, so he was happy to see my black face sitting there.

Keep in mind, my single "I Wish You Love" was playing all over the radio, and thanks to the newspapers, everybody knew Gloria Lynne was working there. What they didn't know was that I wasn't making a dime on the record, even though it turned out to be one of my biggest hits.

Anyway, this man came to me and explained his position. He told me they had come up with all kinds of excuses to keep him from getting his license. So, I took over his case and brought it up with the department heads. Now, they held meetings every week in the place, which was a real pain in the ass. I told them that this man had been trying to get his license for five years and I didn't see any reason why he shouldn't be given the license to start his company. He had good references and fulfilled all of the necessary requirements. Well, the white man in charge knew exactly who I was talking about. They all did. So he took the file I had put together on the case and told me:

"Well, don't worry about him. If it gets to be too much, just send him to my desk."

License clerk, my ass. Those people were running a racket out there and it did not include black folks. They were determined to keep this man from operating his business in New Jersey and for no apparent reason, other than the obvious.

From day one, I got grief from the women in the workplace. They were upset that a "recording star" was working there and they gave me hell. They claimed that I had taken a job some other girl needed, and they didn't think that was fair, and I had no business being there.

"She's got records out. She don't need this job," they would say.

It got to the point where I had to hire two gold star detectives to carry me to work in the morning and pick me up at the end of the day. I was getting all kinds of threats. The women gave me so much trouble, I could hardly do the job.

No one had considered that I was qualified for the position.

Where I come from you work for a living, no matter what the job is. You earn your living the best way you can. And I wasn't making enough off my music to keep up with my expenses. But I guess people see you in a certain light and that's where they want you to stay. I had invaded their territory and they didn't like it. Well, this was really something because I was only making $5,200 a year there, but that little bit of money made a big difference.

Finally, my mother said, "If you need detectives to take you to the place and pick you up, you don't need that job."

So I resigned. They forced me out after three months on the job.

It was back to the road. I began touring again, doing sixteen and twenty cities, back to back. I was breaking my neck trying to make money. The road was brutal. We traveled by car or bus a lot of times, if the dates were close together. But it was really physically taxing doing so many cities in a short amount of time. And flying always took something out of you, physically, even if it was a lot faster. Jet lag is no joke. Going in and out of hotels, sometimes I'd wake up and I didn't know where I was.

There were good times and not so good times on the road. I remember the time I was booked for an engagement at Pep's Show Bar in Philadelphia, which is one of my favorite cities to play. You'd think I was born and raised there, I get such a great reception in that town. Every time I play Philly, the lines are wrapped around the block. I remember in the early days, Bill Cosby used to hang out at the clubs where we performed. He would come over and ask if he could go on at intermission, in between our sets, and do his bit, because we drew such huge crowds.

Anyway, my manager, Duke, had come with me on this club date, and of course my trio. The agent who had booked me on the date happened to be there that night, too. On the first night of my run, the club had just shellacked the floors earlier that day, so when I went on to perform, the floors weren't dry yet and my feet were sticking to the floor throughout the whole concert. In spite of that, it was a good show and the crowd was great. After the performance was over, we all came back to the hotel. Duke and my band members decided to go out to eat. I was too tired, so I asked them to bring me something back.

I was in my hotel room, getting undressed, when I heard a knock at my door. I thought maybe it was Duke or one of the guys. It was the agent.

I put on my robe and let him in. I didn't understand why he was coming by so late. It was about two in the morning, but I let him in anyway. I thought maybe he had come to finalize the payroll for the evening, or maybe he was looking for Duke or something. I knew him fairly well and we had worked quite a few jobs together.

Well, this man didn't want to leave. He sat around talking and talking and I was bone tired. But he just wouldn't leave. Right at the moment when I thought he was going to finally go back to his room, he turned on me.

As I walked him to the door, he grabbed me, tore open my robe, yanked my undergarments off. He pressed me down on the floor in such a way that I couldn't move. He pressed his weight on me, which kept me pinned down. I could not believe what was happening.

He raped me.

And of course, it all happened in a matter of minutes. He did it with a certain ease and familiarity, like he knew exactly how to catch me off guard and take advantage. I remember having on a full, one-piece garment, the whole bodysuit that fully covers you. He had it off of me in a matter of seconds. He had done this before. So, he did what he came to do, got up, left me there on the floor, and walked out.

When Duke came back, I called his room and told him what had happened. He came down there and was ready to pitch a bitch. His first reaction was to go get the man and beat his ass.

But I stopped him.

We had to think it through. Do we call the police? Have the man arrested? Risk a publicity scandal?

We didn't know what to do. As a woman, I knew that if a scandal got started, I would end up on the short end of that stick. I had my reputation and career to think about. Duke thought if I didn't want to go to the police, then we should keep the whole thing very quiet.

Violated was not the word for it. It was a brutal, low-down, unforgivable attack.

Because it's such a personal and violent thing to have happen, as a woman, your first instinct is to be quiet about it, to retreat and find your way through it alone. I understand why so many occurrences of rape go unreported. It's a horrific thing to admit to. You can't believe it yourself, let alone try to convince other people that it's happened to you. And I just kept thinking that no one was going to take my story seriously, since I knew the man, I worked with him, and I was the one to let him in the room.

The only thing I can say is, I hope this man realizes that what he did was the very lowest, most vile act he could ever do to a woman. Actually, I'm being kind, not mentioning his name, but he knows exactly who he is and what he did.

After this incident, however, I was really down on men. I didn't know what to think, what to feel anymore—I was numb. Considering my past, all the hurt and pain I had experienced at the hands of men in my life, you would have thought that I'd be bitter and angry, but instead, I think I was more hurt and confused than anything else. I didn't curse men, but I didn't embrace them either. I was no different than any other young woman out there looking for love, the right partner, a sense of security that you can achieve with a mate. But it wasn't happening for me. My refuge was my music. I never stopped working.

While out on the road, I checked in with Mom regularly to see about the house and to make sure she was doing all right. She kept track of all of the household affairs, took care of my mail and all of that.

One morning I woke up with a bad feeling and called Mom before even getting out of bed. I have always been a person that could sense things. I've always had vivid, telling dreams and other clairvoyant experiences. Well, on this morning, I asked Mom how things were, knowing something wasn't right, and she said:

"Have you heard about Dinah?"

I told her I'd had a disturbing dream about her the night before. In the dream, Dinah kept saying to me:

"I'm going to find a way. I'm going to find a way," over and over again.

When I told Mom this, she said:

"Gloria, Dinah's dead."

I was so sad about Dinah's death, and even sadder when I heard how she died. Now they can say what they want, but I knew Dinah and I know that woman did not commit suicide. Her death was accidental.

I know it just as sure as I'm breathing.

The Dinah I knew and loved like a sister would never, ever have killed herself. She was, in fact, preparing for the Christmas holidays with her two boys. She was newly married to Dick "Night Train" Lane, the ex–football player, who she was all excited about. I had spoken to her around that time and I recall her saying how much she was looking forward to some time off to be with her boys. And she would always get excited about Christmas. That was her holiday. She would go all out, buying presents and decorating like crazy. She had arranged her tour schedule so that she could have three weeks off before having to go out on the road again on New Year's Eve.

The way the media portrayed her death was just awful. They sensationalized it in all the newspapers, and there were contrasting stories about the cause of death. They said she had mixed prescription drugs or diet pills with alcohol, which, combined, had a fatal effect. She was only thirty-nine years old.

Though Dinah had always been obsessive about her weight and was known to pop diet pills, this was no reason to believe that she was abusing drugs, which the papers implied. They made her death sound very mysterious. And they guessed about personal matters that they had no way of knowing anything about. And with all of this mystery, a dark cloud was cast over Dinah's life, I felt, and the huge contribution she had made to the music world. Only people in the business, other artists and friends who knew her, were able to make sincere statements about her. If the truth be told, Dinah Washington's passing marked a great loss in the music industry. She was a dynamic woman and a phenomenally talented artist. When we lost her, we truly lost somebody.

Artists like Dinah only come around once in a lifetime.

I was working on the West Coast, and for the most part, had taken up residence in Los Angeles, at the time of Dinah's death. Her funeral was being planned in her hometown, Chicago, at her family's church, St. Luke's Baptist Church. Unfortunately, I couldn't afford to fly back for her funeral. I had no money to speak of. I told people I was working because I didn't want anyone to know how badly I was doing. It almost killed me. Dinah was so good to me. It broke my heart not to be there. She died in the winter of 1963.

And just like Billie, she was in her prime.

There were times like this that made being on the road and far from home very hard. No matter how professional you were, how reliable, losing a friend is losing a friend, no matter how you push it or pull it. It was hard to put on a happy face and go out there onstage and give a great show.

Smiling on the outside and crying on the inside, that's all it was.

Beautiful people in the business were just dying out. Every time you turned around somebody was gone. It was a very shaky time, the sixties. A lot of musicians and performers who had been popular in the forties and fifties were now in the poorhouse—living on welfare, barely scraping by, or dead from disease, overdoses, poverty, or just plain pain. It was a very deep period. Who could have predicted that these giants in the business would be gone before making it to middle age? But what could we do about any of it? We knew the deal, knew we were being used by a lot of the record companies, but that didn't stop us from needing to get up and go to work. But people were literally dying from the pressure.

In 1969, Joe Glaser passed away. I decided to leave ABC after his death because I didn't feel that I was getting the same treatment as I had when Joe was running things. Oscar Cohen, who had worked under Glaser for years as one of his booking agents, took over, and it wasn't the same. A lot of changes took place within the agency and they ended up losing quite a few artists. Joe Glaser was a gem. Agents like him are rare, few and far between. Joe was extremely wealthy. He was worth $80 million buck naked, but he was extremely generous. I remember him paying for students' full, four-year college tuition. He was known to finance the entire education of a lot of young people. College, law school, medical school, whatever they needed, Joe Glaser was a doer and a giver.

When I began looking for a new booking agent, Richard Carpenter's name kept popping up. He was a black agent who was supposed to be on the money. I met him in Englewood through a girl I knew, named Barbara, who I later found out was a stone nut. She told me that Carpenter had a great reputation, but I was still uncertain. After the Everest experience, I was very cautious about who I did business with. I remember Barbara saying to me, again and again:

"Gloria, you gotta trust somebody!"

Anyway, I was told that Carpenter was very well connected. He was also representing Dizzy Gillespie at the time. And my mother liked him. But then, she liked any abusive man. She liked these big, sturdy, manly men and Carpenter was huge. He had Mom in the palm of his hand. He could do no wrong in her book. Well, it turned out that *wrong* was all he knew how to do.

It was a fiasco. Carpenter made fifty million promises:

"I'm going to book you here, Gloria. I'm going to get you that gig over there, Gloria."

Please. He was so full of shit. All he wanted to do was sit up and eat. He and his wife used to come over to my house and have dinner all the time. We would barbecue on Sundays and their behinds would be sitting up in there, eating like dogs and drinking like fish.

Now, the strangest thing about working with Carpenter was, he was territorial with me, really possessive, but he didn't book me on any jobs. He was a power freak. I think he enjoyed knowing he had control over my career. He just wasn't doing a damn thing to further it. It was terrible. Instead of doing what he was hired to do, he sabotaged me. He had me under contract and, deliberately and willfully, did not book me on jobs. I asked him constantly to book me at different clubs because I needed the money, and he knew I needed the money, but he wouldn't do it. I would find out later, from club owners and other people that had requested me, that Carpenter was lying and telling them I wasn't available. Why he did what he did, I don't know.

Listen, that man turned down offers made on my behalf that could have skyrocketed my career. And he was very underhanded about the whole thing. He had me believing that he was working hard but that things were slow on the club scene, or he'd say certain dates had fallen through for one reason or another. Then, months later, I would get the real deal.

One of the most damaging things Carpenter did to me involved a job in television. While out at a function—I believe it was a concert at one of the big hotels—I met the actress Marla Gibbs. We were great fans of each other's work. I found out years after I had left Carpenter that I was wanted for the role of Florence on the popular television show *The Jeffersons*. Now, I found this out from Marla Gibbs herself. I was lucky enough to meet her further down the road. Now, this was years after Carpenter and I had parted company, but his lies were still lingering. She told me:

"Gloria Lynne, I always wanted to meet you. I have always loved your music. I wouldn't have gotten the job on *The Jeffersons* if it hadn't been for you. They wanted you, you know. When they created the role, they were interested in you playing the part. The only way I got it was because you weren't available. Your manager told the producers that you were too busy on tour to do the role."

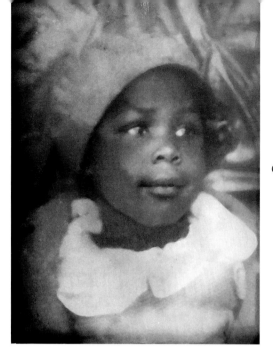

Gloria Mai Wilson, age five.

That's me at fourteen years old. This is pretty much how I looked when I entered the Apollo Amateur.

One of the all-girl groups I sang with in the 1950s, The Dell-Tones.
(Photo by James J. Kriegsmann)

229 West 134th Street.

Harry and me in love,
back in the day.

Me and Willa Mae, back in 1964, at her house in Philly. *(Courtesy of Duke McDougal)*

Me with my brother, John.

Me, stepping out in my new fur, at my apartment in the Lenox Terrace, up in Harlem.

On tour with my manager, Duke Wade, at the Kentucky Arts Center.

A friend, Allie White, my mother, myself, and Willa Mae.

Earl May and me.

That's "Curly"—
clean as a chitlin!

Ella Fitzgerald. Ella was "The First Lady of Song." Anything nice you can name, that was Ella. She set the standard for a lot of us coming behind her. She was sweet and sophisticated and completely dedicated to her music.
(CORBIS/Bettmann-UPI)

Billie Holiday. Billie was an incredibly talented woman. We all wanted to be as glamorous, as sexy, as bad as Billie.
(CORBIS/Reuters)

Dinah Washington. Dinah was a real glamour girl, all class and serious business. When I stood in for her at the Village Vanguard, for the first time in my life I felt like a real celebrity. (*CORBIS/Bettmann*)

Redd Foxx. Here's my buddy Redd on the set of his most successful TV sitcom, *Sanford and Son*. We cut the fool together all those years touring on the road. (*CORBIS/Bettmann-UPI*)

Ray Charles. Here's Ray, back in the day. I loved touring with him. He's a real sweetheart. (CORBIS/Bettmann-UPI)

Sarah Vaughan. My friend "Sassy" was very sweet, quiet, and reserved. Without a doubt, her voice was truly one of the most beautiful ever. (CORBIS/Bettmann-UPI)

Della Reese. Della was always such a striking performer. She has been a real force in the industry. Here she is during a taping of her 1969 TV show, *The Della Reese Show*. (*CORBIS/Bettmann-UPI*)

Mahalia Jackson. Mahalia was my mother's favorite gospel singer. Her voice had such soul and depth. She was so full of spirit that her voice transcended everything. (*CORBIS/Bettmann-UPI*)

B. B. King. B.B.'s got to be the hardest-working man in show business. He works 360 days on the job and the other five days he's traveling to a job. He is a living legend and one of the most wonderful human beings I've ever known.
(CORBIS/Bettmann-UPI)

Harry Belafonte. Harry has been a great inspiration to me. He is a tremendously talented artist, very focused, and extremely dedicated. He used to say, "You must love the art."
(CORBIS/Reuters)

The genius himself, pianist
Herman Foster, with saxophonist
Lou Donaldson.
(Courtesy of Tejas Records)

Me and my best friend, Helen Singleton.

Me and Helen's husband, Kenny, under the Christmas tree.

My son, Richard, at the piano.

Me and my friend Ruth Brown.

Drummer Billy Kaye.

My friend Ellen Mousari at a reunion party for Casablanca Records.

My "second son," Charles Champion.
(Photo by Melinda Kelly)

My good friend Frankie Hill.
(Photo by Buddy Rosenberg)

My dear friend Ricci Day.
(Photo by Richmond Lowe)

And I was sitting right out there at 495 Woodland catching hell with my house. I couldn't believe this.

Carpenter had lied again.

Well, fate is a wonderful thing and I'm not begrudging. Sometimes rejection can be your protection. It was obviously meant for Marla to have that job. If it had been meant for me, I would have gotten it. I do believe that. She is a very nice woman and I really appreciated her passing this information on to me. The thing that really got to me was Carpenter withholding the information from me. The fact that I was not even allowed to audition or meet the producers is what had me so outraged. I had no idea those people wrote that part with me in mind. It was almost unbearable. Here I was again, tied up in a rotten contract agreement with someone who didn't give a damn whether I lived, died, starved, worked.

Nothing.

Now, as far as my recording contracts were concerned, Carpenter could go to the record company and get money for what *he* needed, but I couldn't. They'd tell me that I didn't have anything coming. Carpenter could get all kinds of money from my supposed account with record companies, but he never shared any of it with me. Imagine that. He could get money off of my record sales, but I couldn't. He was a lousy thief. He stole me blind.

The only money I ever remember Carpenter going out to get for me was from Herbie Hancock. Herbie and I had collaborated on the Mongo Santamaria tune "Watermelon Man." I wrote the lyrics and Herbie arranged the music. Well, Herbie hadn't paid me an advance for writing the lyrics. So, Carpenter took me down to Herbie's office, which was in midtown Manhattan at the time, and asked him about my money. Herbie just played it off:

"Oh, yeah, yeah, Gloria, I've got something for you," he said. "No problem."

And he wrote me out a check for two thousand–some–odd dollars. Then as Carpenter and I were walking out the door, I asked:

"What about the sheet music? They have my picture all over the sheet music and my lyricist credit, but I haven't received any residuals from the sheet music sales."

So, Herbie wrote me another check. This one was for seven hundred–some dollars. Naturally I was glad to be paid, but I still wasn't sure if these were the correct figures. It all seemed very arbitrary to me.

Carpenter was in with a lot of the heavy hitters in the business and he used to bullshit his way and make all kinds of side money. Once, he tried to get Morris Levy, who owned Birdland, to approve one of his deals. Morris Levy was a very rich and influential man. He had his own record label, Roulette, and artists like Dinah Washington joined him. Now, Morris Levy had a reputation. He was loved by some and hated by others. I never had any run-ins with him until this affair. The Carpenter/Levy fiasco went down like this: Carpenter asked me to come with him to Morris Levy's office, and he was very mysterious about the reason why. So, I go down to Levy's office and sit and chat with him for a minute. He was living in New Jersey at the time and he asked me about my house and how I liked living in Englewood. He was a very nice man, a real professional. He asked about Richard and how he liked military school. And we rapped a while.

So after our chat, I walked back out into the lounge area, then Carpenter went in. The door to Levy's office was ajar, so I could hear what was going on. I heard Levy in there saying:

"I am not going to take that woman's house for collateral on your debt! I will not do it!"

Well, of course, my ears perked up and I had to fight the urge to charge through that door. As it turns out, Carpenter had owed Levy some money and tried to use *my* house to get out of it. Well, I will always appreciate Morris Levy for standing up for me. The way deals went down in that day, anything might have happened. I could have looked up and had my house turned over to someone else and would have had to get another lawyer on top of all the lawyers I already had, to get my damn house back.

Morris Levy refused to participate in his scam and kicked Carpenter out of his office. I still don't know the specifics of their arrangement, but I do know Carpenter was a lowdown bastard. He ruined my career. He is the reason I fell into hot water with my house and every other imaginable debt. I mean, this man was a real low-lifer.

After being on the road for long periods of time, I looked forward to coming home and spending time with my good friends and family. I remember once, I hooked up with my two brothers after coming off the road. We went out to the Elks Lounge in Englewood one evening. One of my girlfriends, Barbara, was with us that night, too. We were all sitting together having a drink, when this man came over to our table. He looked like he had already thrown a few back, but he stumbled over to our table. Then he looked at me and said:

"You're Gloria Lynne, aren't you?"

When I answered him he got all bent out of shape and started cursing me out. He said something about:

"All you black women marry white men when you get famous. Why do you put black men down like that?"

Well, none of us knew what the hell he was talking about. There wasn't a white man anywhere near us, nor had I ever been married to a white man. He kept on with this crazy talk, drawing all kinds of attention to our table. Then he became obscene, using all kinds of profanity. Finally, he wound himself up so tight, he had the nerve to push me. Well, that was it. I could take all his jive talk, but when he put his hands on me, I reacted. I used to carry a tear gas gun with me. It was one of those self-defense things that looked like a real pistol, but released tear gas when you pulled the trigger. So, I pulled the thing out of my purse and pointed it in this joker's face. Everybody in the place hit the floor and somebody called the police. I'd never had cause to use my gun before, so, when I went to pull the trigger, it jammed on me. There I was trying to fool with the thing to get it to work, when my two brothers decided to beat the man's ass. The cops showed up and took all of us to the Englewood police precinct. We made bail and were scheduled to return the following week.

I was still a fairly new resident in the community, so all of this was embarrassing. Of course, the press got a whiff of this, and the story came out that the gun I had was a real weapon, and that I had threatened this man's life. The day we went to court, it was jam-packed with people. Some were waiting to get the lowdown on my case, some had their own cases on the docket. Judge Leibowitz was the judge on duty. Well, there was such an uproar when my case was called, the New Jersey press was there. It was a mess. So, Judge Leibowitz cleared the court. After all of the facts were brought out, all of the charges against me were dropped.

As I was leaving, the judge called me back and spoke to me in confidence. He told me I had to be very careful about the places I frequented, that I needed to be very selective because I was too recognizable to go just anywhere. Well, he told me right. Hey, all that glitters ain't gold, it's true. Life in the public eye is very often a dangerous place to be.

I had to watch my back, money or no money, fame or no fame.

I remember crazy, crazy times being out on the road. I had a driver named Curly. His real name is Leroy McNeal, but we all call him Curly. He and my manager, Duke, have been best friends since they were teenagers. He used to drive me and my musicians around from city to city. Now, Curly is fine. He's jet-black with a head full of white hair. He is a stunning man, pretty as a picture. And Curly dressed to the nines. He always looked like he stepped right off the cover of a magazine. He was clean as a chitlin. And as nice as he could be. He was married to the singer Millie Jackson at one time. Well, at one point Curly was deemed legally blind. We used his van on short runs. One night, there was a bad storm brewing. It was a dark, dark night. I don't remember where we were coming from, or on our way to, but, Curly started driving crazy and the drummer Billy Kaye was in the car with him. Me and some of the others were caravanning behind them. Well, Billy got nervous and told Curly:

"Man, you're not driving right. You're swerving and carrying on."

"You don't like it," Curly said, "then get your ass out of my car!"

We were driving in the car right behind them and we looked out and saw this dark spot coming down the road. It was Billy. We pulled over and asked Billy what had happened and he said:

"He put me out the car! Curly put me out the car!"

I could sense that something was getting ready to go down, so I suggested that we speed up to catch Curly, then wave him off to the next rest-stop exit so we could all talk this thing through. Everybody needed to calm down. When we got to the stop, I asked Curly:

"What's wrong? Why did you throw Billy out?"

"He was trying to tell me how to drive!" he said.

"Well, Curly, you *are* legally blind!" I told him.

It got quiet for a minute, then we all just fell out laughing. You know, fatigue will do that to you, make you turn on your best friend.

Those guys were so crazy. I remember, many a day, we'd be traveling from city to city, and all five of them, my manager, Duke, my trio, and Curly, would have to go to the bathroom, at the same time. Well, they'd all get out the car and line up on the side of the road to piss. They were a sight! All five of them, lined up in suits and ties, good-looking men, standing there, side by side, pissing in a row.

Now why they had to do it together, I don't know, but that's how it was done. Usually Helen was with me, thank God, because I couldn't handle all of their foolishness by myself. These were fun, fun times.

At one point, my regular drummer, Grassella Oliphant, decided that he was going to carry a gun. The trouble was, a lot of times, we would do these gigs out on the road and somebody would always end up running off with the money. So, Gras just got tired of it and he said:

"I'm putting the word out that I'm carrying a gun."

Now Grassella had a real head for business. He acted, more or less, like our business manager. And he was dead set on this gun business. He even told my mother that if somebody even thought about not giving us our money, they were going to pay. I tell you, my mother may as well have had a confessional set up in the house, because everybody, at one time or another, would end up confessing something or other to her.

"Gras, you know you can't be out there on that road carrying a gun!" Mom told him.

"Mazie, I got to do what I got to do."

We had been touring with everybody—Ray Charles, Johnny Mathis, all of these big headliners—and somehow by the end of the night the club manager would forget about us.

"Enough of this shit," Gras said. "I'm going to carry a gun."

Well, he got the job done. Once word got out about Gras's gun, I swear, we always got paid. Getting paid on road gigs became a problem of the past.

I still speak to Grassella, every now and then. I tell him every time I talk to him:

"You know I love you for your brain."

He was one of the smartest guys I'd ever met. A real smart dude. He owns his own business now out in Orange, New Jersey. He's real tight with the mayor out there and he dabbles in politics. Grassella's a real go-getter and an all-around nice guy.

Most of the tours we did with big headliners, like Arthur Prysock and Johnny Mathis, cross-country and throughout the Caribbean, were arranged by Joe Glaser. The Ray Charles tours were organized by my manager, Duke, who is still good friends with Ray. These were always such great times for me, sharing the bill with not only big-name artists but with artists who I truly respected and liked as people.

Johnny Mathis is a sweetheart. He was always a joy to work with. And the women were something else. They were trying to rip his clothes off! Every time we toured together, Johnny would give us specific instructions on how to exit the venue. It was always some back-alley route. Well, it was absolutely necessary because I'd sneak a peek outside and there would be a mob scene, just full of women. Johnny is a stunning man, and he'd stand there singing all those ballads, "Chances Are" and all that, and those women would get so wound up that by the end of the show, they'd be about ready to pop.

Once, I was appearing at Leo's Casino in Cleveland and I had a run-in with the law. I was preparing to go out and do the second set. My band was already onstage—for this particular show, I was working with Grady Tate, Ike Isaac, and Hugh Lawson. The way the club was set up you had to go through the kitchen to get to the stage. I was walking through the kitchen when I heard all of this ruckus. I never thought it was the sound of bullets making all of that noise, until I felt something warm running down my leg. I was bleeding and Helen was there with me, screaming:

"Sissy! You've been shot!"

The next thing I knew, I was waking up in a hospital bed with all of these Cleveland cops standing over me. I asked Helen what happened. She said, bluntly:

"They shot you."

Evidently the police had been shooting at someone in the bar next door to Leo's and the bullets went flying everywhere, including into my left leg. While they apologized for the inconvenience, I had to cancel the run, which meant I missed out on my money. I was hospitalized for several days. When I came back to New York, I went to see my attorney, Maxwell Cohen, immediately.

"You cannot sue the City of Cleveland, Gloria," he explained.

End of story. Except for the pains I still have in that leg, that was the end of that episode. There would be no retribution.

My girlfriend Willa Mae Barnes used to travel with me a lot back in those days. Now, Willa Mae was insane. She was one of the funniest ladies I have ever met. One of the most hilarious things in the world was to watch Willa Mae handle her bill collectors. Willa Mae would go around shopping. She loved good shit. She would make all these bills, then, when the bills came due, she would tell her creditors:

"Willa Mae Barnes is dead. That woman's been dead. She's been dead five or six years now. I don't know how you expect to get any money from her."

And this was during the time when bill collectors would come to your front door. They would ring that bell, she would answer, and with a straight face Willa Mae would say:

"Willa Mae Barnes is dead. You need to go on and leave us alone. We're in deep sorrow and grief."

Once, Willa Mae wanted a new kitchen, so she got it fixed in her head that she would set her kitchen on fire and get the insurance company to pay for it. Before I could talk her out of it, Willa Mae set a match to her kitchen and only half of it burned down. When the claim adjuster came by to investigate, he said:

"It is amazing to me, Mrs. Barnes, that only half this kitchen is burned down and the other half is fine."

"What the hell do you want from me? My kitchen is half burned down!" she shouted at the man.

Well, Willa Mae got the money and the new kitchen.

I loved traveling with Willa Mae. She'd always keep you laughing. If there was a man in the audience that she thought was fine, worth looking at, she would come backstage and say to me:

"Girl, I think you need to take a peek at this."

And if he wasn't worth it, you might see his ass flying out the door. Willa Mae was a bold woman. She had incredible tenacity. She wasn't afraid of anything. And anything she put her mind to, she got. She was a hat designer, by profession, but when that wasn't working, she'd go on to something else. Willa Mae delved into a lot of things and she was good at just about everything.

The women I had traveling with me had to have a rough side. I needed them to be that way because I was that way, and I needed backup. Willa Mae, Helen, even Bertha Coultier, my secretary, were all rough around the edges when you got down to it. Bertha was very pretty and very petite, but she would let the people have it, if they got in her way.

It didn't matter who it was, Bertha could stop anybody dead in their tracks. Big, tall Negroes would be trying to get backstage and Bertha would say:

"You can't come through here." They'd look at her and try to move past her. She'd say, "Look, I done told you once, don't let me have to tell you again. Don't come back here!"

"Damn," those men would walk away saying, "that's a bad little wench there."

Bertha didn't play. All the women I had around me were full of fire. Gwen Nelson was another one who could do wonders with some hair but then pick up that brush and throw it at you if she needed to. She was really helpful to me. Gwen used to work with Joe Papp at the Public Theater in New York and she still works a lot of shows on Broadway. My makeup artist, Rosemary, who travels with me, is the same way. She pays attention to everything, never misses a beat.

These are good women with backbone. And I love them for it.

You had to cut the fool on tour. The money was always funny, but you learned to maintain your sense of humor. Even if things weren't all right, you had to make them all right.

I remember something Sarah Vaughan used to say, "We have a way of being happy through our trials and tribulations. The fun just keeps coming."

I remember doing jobs, ten days, back to back. In Detroit, they used to book you and split your time. They'd book so you were off on Monday, Tuesday, Wednesday, then go back to work on Thursday, Friday, Saturday, and Sunday. I would tell those people:

"Look, just clump me ten days, I'll do the job and get on out of here."

I didn't like all that waiting around to work, mostly because you had to spend money when you didn't work for four days. So by the time the people paid you for the job, that money just made up for what you spent hanging around town. This was discouraging, too. Because some performers would come through there and do one-nighters and make more money in one night than I made all year.

So, you had to cut the fool to stay sane.

You couldn't let all that shit get you down. But I thought to myself: *You mean to tell me I'm working five and six and ten days and people are coming in here working one-nighters, making more money than I ever thought I was going to see in my life!* It was absurd.

We did several tours with Ray Charles in the sixties. He was just great. I loved touring with him. We did the Astrodome together out in Houston and Ray split the bill with me. He didn't have to, but every single time I toured with Ray he made sure my name appeared on the marquee as big as his. I always appreciated his generosity. That kind of thing is rare in our business. Well, one time something happened and our plane schedules conflicted and we were having trouble getting back to the East Coast, so Ray asked my manager, Duke:

"How does Gloria and her band travel most of the time?"

He told him we either drove or took commercial flights, depending on where we were and where we had to go.

"They don't have to take no commercial airline," Ray said. "Y'all come on and get on my plane."

That's when I found out Ray was up there in the cockpit trying to fly the plane. You know, these blind folks are something else.

LeRoy Holmes, my old friend and producer from the Everest days, used to fly planes as a hobby. After I found out he had his own plane, I asked him if he'd teach me to fly.

"You want to fly," he said. "Come on."

We would take quick trips, from New York to Atlantic City, and when I got the hang of it I copiloted a trip to the islands. We went to St. Thomas Virgin Islands and Puerto Rico. I loved flying, but I knew my friends, Helen and Duke and all of them, were back there dying, just pissing in their pants. I did three or four landings and gained quite a few flying hours. I wish I had stuck with it. It's great for your coordination. And there's nothing more relaxing than flying.

On another occasion coming from the Dome in Houston—I believe this happened back in '62—we had trouble getting a connecting flight back to New York. We needed to be back for an engagement at Randall's Island. The concert was being produced by one of the industry's few black concert promoters, Teddy Powell.

Teddy was terrific. He was a top-notch businessman, and if you worked with him, you knew everything was going to be top-drawer, so we really didn't want to mess up the gig. We were getting nervous and thought we might miss it entirely. So, Duke did some finagling and got us on the private plane of John Glenn and some other NASA astronauts. They had just come from circling the Earth, and there we were with all this gear, instruments, bags and costumes, boarding their private jet. I don't know what Duke said to the airport personnel, because they kept the NASA jet. Well, we sure did. And they didn't mind. We had a ball talking to the astronauts. It was very cool.

There are a million and one road stories, and the fans I've come across along the way have been truly wonderful. I had men that wanted to kiss my gowns and women that would come up in tears, crying over the sentimental songs I'd sung. I remember once, after a performance in Philly, a man came up to me.

"Gloria Lynne," he said, "I made seven children on you."

"What do you mean?" I said.

I didn't know what he was talking about. And his wife was just standing there grinning.

"Well, you know, me and my wife—we made seven babies listening to your records."

I fell out.

They had brought all their Gloria Lynne albums with them for me to autograph, which I did, gladly.

When I started traveling on the road, in the sixties, I traveled with the Earl May Trio. Earl was my bass player and musical director. He had worked with a lot of New York musicians like Gene Ammons, Sonny Stitt, Miles Davis, and Mercer Ellington before he joined with me. The trio also included Herman Foster on piano and Grassella Oliphant on drums. The Earl May Trio is the band I'm associated with most. Herman Foster, who passed away recently, was a dear, dear friend. Herman was blind but he was one of the baddest piano players that ever lived. I learned more songs and more music from him than anyone I've ever worked with. He was really like our leader because his musical ability was so advanced. He was a brilliant musician.

Earl May and I were lovers. We were together for over eight years. The trio stayed together for ten. He actually protected me from a lot of madness that took place on the road, because everybody knew he was my man. Earl had two daughters from a previous marriage, Carol and Robin. Together with my son, Richard, we made a perfect family. The only thing missing out of our relationship was marriage. We did everything together. We even spent our off time together. We would have picnics in Central Park and go skating in Rockefeller Center, shop, wine and dine, go to the theater. We enjoyed each other's company.

"Earl, we have to get married," I said to him after about eight years of togetherness. "We've been together a long time. The kids love us and I think we really should be married."

He agreed with me, but the problem was he had never gotten a divorce from his kids' mother. They had been separated all this time but hadn't legally divorced. Well, his former wife knew Earl and I were together all those years and she never interfered with us. Besides, we were taking care of the children, financially and otherwise. I used to take those girls to Saks Fifth Avenue and all that. I always wanted girls, so they became my girls.

But somehow, after I posed the question of marriage, things fell apart.

I don't know the particulars of what went down between Earl and his former wife—why they never divorced or why they couldn't get a divorce at this late date, but there was a lot of confusion, and eventually it caused problems between us.

Earl and I were never able to get married. And though we were still traveling and trying to hang together, tension hung over our heads. Eventually, it broke us up. And our breakup caused the whole band to disband.

The breakup hurt my heart. It felt like something had died. I was feeling sort of lost and lonely. I mean, these guys had been with me since the beginning of my professional career. We had been together so many years. And I knew it would take me years to get that kind of chemistry and camaraderie with new musicians.

Both breakups were hard—the band and the man—but I had to keep going. I couldn't afford to wallow in sorrow, even though I was broke down, half the time, over it. The most complicated part for me was we broke up after my "I Wish You Love" hit. Now, when you have a hot hit record, every time you perform, people expect you to sing it. But the song reminded me of Earl and me together.

I sang "I Wish You Love" time after time, and each time I performed it live, people would say, "She's got tears in her eyes."

The Copacabana was a hot club in New York in the sixties. It was known as one of the top moneymaking nightclubs in the city. I was performing there one night, when Harry Belafonte walked in. He was there to see Billy Daniels, who was headlining, and I was singing in the lounge. After my show, Belafonte came over to discuss an upcoming television special that he was producing. Although he thought I was a little heavy, he thought I'd be great for the show.

"I want you to be a part of the project I'm working on for TV," he said, "but I'd like you to be a size ten by the time we begin shooting."

Believe me, I was far from a ten. He sent me to his doctor and I began a new diet, which got me down from a size sixteen to ten in time for the taping.

The show was called *The Strollin' 20s*. It aired on CBS in 1966. Sidney Poitier was the narrator. It starred Diahann Carroll, Sammy Davis Jr., Joe Williams, Brownie McGhee, Nipsey Russell, George Kirby, Duke Ellington, and myself. It was a theatrical piece that characterized Harlem during the 1920s. Langston Hughes wrote the script for the show. It was very poetic and captured the spirit of the community. The whole show was full of music and dance. It opened with a big dance number with all the dancers in period dresses and costumes. Duke Ellington performed "Sophisticated Lady" with his sextet. They built the set so it resembled the Savoy Ballroom, which, when I was growing up, is where all the black people went to hear good music, dance, and socialize.

We all had different characters to play that represented different Harlem lifestyles. My character was married to Joe Williams and we had three children, so Joe and I did a scene singing with the children around the kitchen table. I also sang "You've Been a Good Ol' Wagon" and the setting was a rent party where everybody there persuaded me to sing with the piano player.

"Come on, Gloria," they were saying, "you gotta sing."

Well, then, I walked over to the piano and start singing, *"You a good ol' wagon, daddy, but you done broke down . . ."* The dress I'm wearing in the scene is one of the dresses Harry promised me. I believe it was a pastel-colored chiffon dress. I remember Harry holding it up in front of me, saying:

"If you can get into this dress, you can have all of your costumes when the show is over."

That was all the motivation I needed. I got into that dress and never stopped wearing it. I wore that same little dress for I don't know how long, just because Harry Belafonte had given it to me.

Now, television was a fairly new experience for me. I hadn't done much TV at that point, other than my appearance on *The Ed Sullivan Show*, so working on a set with cameras and all that equipment was new to me. I remember one scene I did where I was supposed to be singing, looking out of a window. They had a four-pane window hanging there, and while the director was talking and getting things together, I decided to get a little rest and lean on the window. Well, I leaned too hard and the whole damn thing came tumbling down. I mean, I tore up the people's set. I didn't know that those set pieces were purely aesthetic and not made for able-bodied women to be leaning up against. That window came banging down, making all kinds of noise, the tech guys came running out there to save it, so they wouldn't have to build another one. It was a mess.

I finally got the hang of things, and I must say that the exposure I received was really great for my career. Television was the ultimate medium. Black people aired on the TV screen very rarely, so this was a chance in a lifetime.

Later, we did another similar special for CBS called *New York Nineteen*. Belafonte was a great inspiration to me and my career. He is a tremendously talented artist, very focused and extremely dedicated. He is really beautiful. Harry was all about the art. He used to say:

"You must love the art."

He doesn't play around. You have to show up on time to rehearsals, be prepared, get serious, and work hard. Harry gave me some of the most important advice I've ever received:

"Don't worry about fame. Concern yourself with longevity."

Television was a new experience for me. Although I knew a lot of the performers on both shows and had worked with them on the nightclub circuit, this was a brand new venue for many of us. Featuring black performers on television in the sixties was still a relatively new idea. So I was especially grateful that I was asked to be a part of this. It exposed me to a wider audience and it also raised my moneymaking potential. I owe a big part of my following today to those television specials.

Because Harry Belafonte was so special to me, I have always felt that I needed to let him know just how much he meant to me. It is a rare occasion when you are able to sincerely express your gratitude to someone, when the time is right and the place is convenient. Oftentimes, years pass without friends ever knowing how much you appreciate their friendship. With that said, this is for you, Harry:

> *I'm so glad our paths crossed. You made a huge difference in my life. You were always in my corner and spoke such wonderful words on my behalf that they reached the audience I've been so blessed with. I remember your words of wisdom, telling me to strive for longevity in my career. Sometimes, during the most difficult times in my life, I would hear your words, as if you had whispered them in my ear, when I needed them most. I have even had the opportunity to use those same words to encourage others, so I thank you for your love and support. I thank you for your example and the true hand of friendship you extended to me.*
>
>

Love,

Gloria
>

9

Loose Ends

*L*iving pillar to post was the reality of my existence for a while. I was in Los Angeles working on a deal with Canyon Records and making plans to move there, permanently. I tried to get Mom to move to California with me but she refused. It didn't set well with her. She really didn't think California was a good move for me. She stayed in Englewood. I was ready for a change, so I went ahead with my plans.

In 1970, the black-owned newspaper *The Amsterdam News* published my obituary. They wrote a blurb that said: "The tragic life of Gloria Lynne has come to an end." They had absolutely no information on which to base my supposed death, so they made it up. The whole piece was vague and misleading. If you read it, you might have thought I died of an overdose or perhaps was murdered. This just added more fuel to the fire that had me hightailing it out of town.

When I first went out to California, I had planned to get a house in Los Angeles, so I moved a lot of my furniture from the Englewood house to California. This was the worst thing I could have done, since I had to put everything in storage until I found a house. I made all kinds of mistakes in my haste to get out of there. I was also in love. I met a producer, Frank, who was working with Canyon at the time. We met in Englewood at a party, through my friend Barbara—the same woman who introduced me to Richard Carpenter. He was good-looking, smart, and a genius at sound engineering. Frank and I really dug each other, which convinced me, even more, that the West Coast was where I needed to be.

Meanwhile, Richard Carpenter did something to anger the management at Mercury Records around the time my contract was up for renewal. I was given very little information about what went down. All I knew was that I was suddenly out of a job and without a record company. So, Canyon was not only a good opportunity, it was a necessary one.

I remember bumping into the NBA star Wilt Chamberlain one day, on Seventh Avenue in New York, and he was opening nightclubs back then. He had been dating one of my white girlfriends, Fran Mansfield, so we knew each other fairly well. We talked for a minute, then he said:

"You've got to come on out to California and sing at my nightclub, Gloria."

I believe he was one of the owners of Basin Street West back then. So, everything seemed to be pointing in a West Coast direction. I was California-bound.

I didn't do much socializing when I first got to LA, because I was so busy working, but I was invited to parties all over the place. The night Frank and I met, he offered to give me a ride home from the party. I accepted. From that night on, we saw each other almost every day. We went to the movies, to dinner, to nightclubs, to parties, everywhere together. We used to talk a lot about the business. He'd tell me his horror stories and I'd tell him mine. Frank was actually a genius at sound engineering, a child prodigy. He worked for Ray Charles when he was only a teenager, about sixteen or seventeen years old. He told me about all the hell he had to pay for being young and gifted. No one really trusted that someone so young actually knew what he was doing. And even after he proved himself to be outstanding in the field, some people in the business were still uncomfortable having a kid around working for them and getting paid top dollar. Between the young and old, I don't know who gets treated worse.

Frank was very cool to be around. I loved his company. With him, for the first time in a long time, I felt like a whole person. I thought I had finally found someone who cared as much about me as I did for him.

There was just something about Frank.

I was in Los Angeles when Mom had to be hospitalized. My girlfriend, Stormy Redcross, called me with the news. It wasn't anything in particular wrong with Mom, but everything in general. I believe she had gotten depressed living in the house alone. I was gone all the time. She didn't suffer long with sickness, thank God. She was hospitalized for a week or so, then died shortly after that at home. Mom was sixty-three years old. It was 1971.

Stormy was so good to my mother. She watched out for her while I was out in California working. She would always go by to see her and check on her for me. She was the one to put her in the hospital when she became very ill. Stormy was the only one. All of those other people—who used to come around and eat their dinner and drink up all the liquor while I was out on the road, sitting around talking with my mother—were nowhere to be found. People were saying that I had deserted my mother. Well, we didn't have any money, so somebody had to go and see about getting some. I was working to keep that house note up and maintain our style of living.

I didn't have much money to pay for all of the expenses, which depressed me to no end. Mom didn't have much insurance. I had been taking care of her down through the years. There were hospital bills and funeral expenses that needed to be paid. I made a desperate attempt to get money from Bernie Solomon. Surely, I thought, he won't refuse me now. I went to see him at his office in Century City and told him about my mother's passing.

I said to him: "You've never paid me what I was worth. Now my mother is dead in New York and I have to get there and bury her."

Did he give it to me? I want the world to know this man's name. And if he's dead, I want him dug up. The man sat there, expressionless, and said:

"Your records haven't been selling and there are no royalties due."

My faith in God got me out of my seat, out the door, and into my car. I could not believe this man would not budge to try to help me. The man who had made millions off of my records since 1961 could not, in 1971, find it in his heart to give me the money I so badly needed. Money that I felt was due to me.

Faith and only faith kept me from killing that man that day.

Thank God I had a friend, Ricci, who I could always depend on. Ricci Day traveled with me on the road, as my hairstylist and dresser. He and I were very close. He always called me "Gertie." Whenever we traveled on the road, Ricci would always find a church for us to attend. He always looked out for me. Well, he was living in the Los Angeles area, working as a cosmetologist. He did hair, makeup, and wardrobe. Ricci used to help me pick out my gowns and things when I was on the road. He was always a big help to me. I can't recall all of the times through the years that Ricci saved the day. He was also very close to Mom. She regarded him as a son. The news broke his heart, but he took one look at me and knew I was in a real state.

So, he started making calls and taking care of all the funeral arrangements for me. I struggled to provide a decent burial for Mom. I had very little support. And my money was short. God took her, but you've got Earth to deal with. All of her affairs had to be taken care of, but Ricci was there for me. He flew back to New York with me and took care of every last one of the details. He helped get the funds together to pay for a lot of the expenses, by borrowing, pleading, collecting on old debts.

I have always prided myself on my ironclad memory. During the time of my mother's passing, I remember very little. It was like I died with her. With the exception of getting myself back to New York, I was in a complete daze. All of the pain I ever felt or could recall came down on me, and I was numb.

I don't remember crying at my mother's funeral.

I had a premonition about her death. A week before she passed, I found myself always in tears, crying all the time, day and night. I had dreams and visions about her. And strangest of all, memories, things that happened between the two of us kept entering my mind. I would find myself lost in recollection about our lives together. All the good and all the bad. My mother used to say:

"I'm going to stay here as long as I can and leave when I just can't help it."

One night, these words kept playing over and over in my head. I knew my mother was leaving. I could feel it.

I cried so much because the thought of Mom's life and all the hardships she endured just broke me down. Her life was never easy, and even when she should have been happy she wasn't. There was something brewing at the bottom, as if something was always deeply disturbing her. Happiness escaped her. So I cherish the few moments in time that we shared joy. I pray to God that she felt a semblance of happiness in her life. I hope that I was able to give that to her.

My mind spun with memories.

I thought about the second grade. The teacher told my mother that I had been acting up in the classroom. She told her that she should come to school and beat me in front of my class. That would set me straight, she said. My mother agreed. She went to school with me the next morning and when the class was seated, the teacher announced what was about to take place. My mother was going to beat me in front of everyone.

At the very thought of that day, my eyes fill up with tears.

There are no words to describe how I felt. I lived with this scar all throughout elementary school and junior high, because most of the kids at my school ended up at the same junior high school. Most of them were from the neighborhood, too. So there was no escape from the humiliation.

That night, at home, I heard my mother telling Mr. Johnson what she had done and his response surprised me:

"That was wrong," he told her. "You shouldn't have embarrassed her in front of her classmates."

He thought that kind of embarrassment would be difficult to overcome.

This was the beginning of a period when I thought my mother did not love me. I never spoke about it, but I harbored this feeling deep, deep inside. I could not believe my mother had beat me, in front of my schoolmates, knowing how badly Mr. Johnson beat me at home.

His beatings made scars. Mom's beating broke my heart.

I cried over an audition. One day after auditioning for an off-Broadway musical, I ran home to tell Mom about it. She asked me how things went and I told her that I would find out in a few days if I got the part. Then, I told her that the auditioners told me I was very pretty.

"They lied to you," she said.

Up until that audition, I don't ever recall anyone ever referring to me as pretty. Her reaction stole away any joy I may have been feeling at the compliment. It hurt. Her words, "Pretty is as pretty does," are still glued in my brain. I never felt pretty. I had no reason to believe I was pretty. To feel pretty, you have to feel loved, and I rarely felt loved, growing up. When you're a child, it is difficult to comprehend loving yourself. Usually, children emulate those around them. If you feel love around you, it is only natural to feel good about yourself. You feel worthy of being loved. It took me years to learn self-love. Years.

There was another memory of a little girl, Geneva Moore, who my mother spoke of often. Geneva was a little kid who lived in the same building as my mom when she and my father first arrived in New York. They rented a room from Geneva's mother at 124 West 135th Street. When my father was out working, my mother relied on Geneva to show her around or pick up things for her from the store. Since my mom was pregnant when she came to New York, she was sick a lot. Geneva would run to the pharmacy and get medicine for her. Mom said she never would forget how good Geneva was to her. She didn't know a soul in New York and Geneva really helped her through the hard times. Although my father had some money, it didn't do my mother much good, since she didn't know the lay of the land. She often said my father was a hoarder. He was known to have hidden away in the house jewelry, cash, coins—all kinds of monies. But what good was money, she used to say, if you don't know your way around, where to go, who to trust? Geneva was a blessing to Mom. She was grateful to her. She stayed in touch with Geneva all her life, until she was a grown woman. She never forgot her.

Wyandanch, Long Island. I remember Mrs. Susie Anderson, who lived in Wyandanch. She was one of my mother's friends. She was a very heavyset, real black lady who always had pretty, pretty things. She owned a building on Ashland Place in Brooklyn, before she married her husband and moved to Wyandanch. She was the first black woman I knew who was married to a white man. They had a son named Donald. When he acted up, Mrs. Susie Anderson would place him on the hot stove top and burn him. Wyandanch, Long Island. It was a very pretty town.

Honestly, during this time, I felt like I didn't have a friend in the world. As many people as my mother had helped when their rents were due, or when they needed money to feed or buy clothes for their babies, even money for hospital bills, none of these people were around.

And bill collectors were calling around the clock.

My house notes were all backed up, the money was slow. It wasn't coming in. I couldn't keep up. Trying to get money working the nightclub circuit and steadily fighting with my manager and record company about money took its toll. I had nowhere to turn. My brothers couldn't help me. They were working nine-to-five jobs and their incomes were limited. I thought, it's no sense in me trying to struggle with this alone, so I found a real estate man and put the whole thing in his hands. He told me he could find a way around foreclosure, where I could still recoup some of the money I had sunk into the place.

Well, whatever he had up his sleeve didn't work. I lost my house. I still don't know what kind of shady dealings the real estate broker put into play. I do know he walked away with money on the deal. And I never heard from him again. He handled things and never contacted me to finalize matters or to even let me know what transactions had taken place. If I called his office, he was unavailable to speak to me. If I wrote letters, they went unanswered. I was too exhausted at this point to fight another man. But I do know that the joker is still in the real estate business over there in Jersey somewhere, probably ripping off somebody else as we speak.

Then there was Richard Carpenter to deal with. After being shiftless and trifling, and after I had broken my neck to book my own gigs and get work for myself, the man tried to sue me. He filed a lawsuit against me for $40,000, stating that I owed him in back contracts. He claimed that since he had me under contract, I owed him a cut of whatever I was making, even though he hadn't booked me on the jobs. He was a real piece of work.

Judge Leibowitz, my old ally, helped me on the case. He did some finagling to get the case heard in New Jersey, instead of New York, and was able to use his influence on my behalf. Carpenter had to prove that he had booked me on jobs and show every last one of the contracts, pay stubs, commission checks, etc.

Well, he hadn't done a damn thing, so he didn't have a damn thing to show. I won the case. The suit was only part of his wanting to control me. When he saw that I had gone out on my own and gotten jobs, he felt that he had lost control. I'll never forget something Billy Eckstine used to say—he called, managers "damagers," and he ain't never lied about that.

I wanted out of this contract with Carpenter. I had no intention of starting over in California with him on my trail. Now, he also had my son, Richard, under contract. Richard was interested in producing, writing, and singing. Initially, Carpenter thought he could spark his career in the industry.

Well, after the shabby job he had done for me, I just couldn't have that. He had messed over me, I wasn't about to let him do that to my son. So, I contacted Richard's father. I called Harry and told him:

"This man's got not only me under contract, but he's got your son."

Now, Harry was a wild, wild, wild beast. He was not to be fucked with. Three days later, I got a call from Carpenter saying he had released us both from our contracts. The resolution was simple, as far as Harry was concerned. He took care of it. He told Carpenter:

"Turn my people loose."

Harry and I stayed separated for years without getting a divorce. During the years of our separation, he was out there doing his thing, messing around with different women, and, once, word got back to me that one of them was pregnant. She ended up having twins. Well, that affected me.

I knew we had problems, but damn, I thought, he never gave me no twins. It's kind of comical when I think back on it now, but my feelings were hurt.

Then, a few years later, he had another baby by another woman. Well, after that, I said that's it. And I went and got a quickie divorce in Mexico. I wanted to feel freed up and so did he. I didn't have anything to do with who he was with and vice versa, and it was evident that we both had strayed away from each other. There was no possibility of us getting back together, so I went to Mexico.

Richard was thirteen years old when we finally divorced. I wanted the divorce to be a quiet thing for Richard's sake, but it leaked out. He was in school when some of his friends came running over to him with a *Jet* magazine:

"Say, you hear your mom and pop got a divorce?"

Harry and I probably should have never gotten married because we were such great friends. I don't think either one of us really knew what we were getting into when we got married. Most people don't, but that's the way it goes. We tried. The divorce never ruined the friendship, thank God. I could always count on Harry when I really needed him.

I took a moment to breathe and consider my next move. Then, a rumor started flying around that I was hooked on dope. This really stung my ears when I heard it. Of all the dope addicts out here in the business that continue to work and make tons of money, I thought, *they want to start this shit with me and I don't have a dime.*

I believe I was blackballed.

It hurt me a lot.

And being blackballed, baby, has an effect like no other.

Of course, I was compelled to clear my name, so I was put on the defensive, going around trying to convince people in the business that the rumors weren't true. I mean, this thing could really damage your career, if club owners didn't want to book you because they thought you would be a problem or record companies didn't want to deal with you because they thought you were "trouble." This was cause for you not to be hired by anyone at any time.

The drug scene was a real trip, especially for someone like me. I was always scared of my own shadow, damn near. You would hear all kinds of stories about people enticing you to do dope, and my mother would tell me:

"Watch what you eat, watch what you drink, don't take this from that one and don't drink that with this one. And always watch your back."

I was leery about being anywhere close to dope, so for this rumor to be spread about me was a real blow. Anyone who knew me, knew better, but public perception is something you are forced to deal with when you're in the public eye. It became very important for me to prove the rumors wrong, to show the world that I was healthy. I may not have been wealthy, but God knows I was wise.

The most important decision for me at this time was determining if I felt like starting all over, which is what moving to the West Coast would mean. I had to determine for myself how I would be positioned in the new music market. I took a long look at my recordings. I thought about how hard I had worked and where that work had gotten me. Then I prayed that all of the work would pay off for me in Hollywood.

Hollywood

Funk. Soul. Rhythm & Blues. And plenty of Rock. Any way you want it. Soft. Hard. Punk. Glam. Heavy/Metal—all in stereo. Standard issue: synthesizers, drum machines, Moog and Mellotron. Berry Gordy has moved Motown to Los Angeles and spread the sound all over the country. They are the biggest black-owned corporation to date. Stevie Wonder, Marvin Gaye, Diana Ross, the Spinners, Smokey Robinson & The Miracles, the Jackson Five, and the Commodores are on the tip of everybody's tongue. Then there's tantalizing Teddy Pendergrass to turn on all the ladies. And Aretha Franklin is the "Queen of Soul." The Isley Brothers, Earth, Wind & Fire and the Commodores, Rufus & Chaka Khan have added something new to the formula. Funk is: Parliament Funkadelic, courtesy of George Clinton. The soundtrack form Shaft wins an Oscar for Isaac Hayes, the first black composer to ever clasp hands around that trophy. When Melvin Van Peebles makes Sweet Sweetback's Baadasssss Song, studios take note. He makes a mint on an independent film, and word of mouth is his main method of distribution. Next thing you know here comes another load of copycat movies, lumped together in one tripped-out moneymaking period that's called blaxploitation. Superfly, The Mack, Foxy Brown, and Cleopatra Jones were all hits at the box office, putting some quick cash in the pockets of black actors like never before. Then again, Sly and the Family Stone says, "Everybody is a star." Television introduced the situation comedy featuring the black family— Good Times and The Jeffersons, with sprinkles of black faces spread across the screen in police dramas and soap operas. And it's all about style—El Dorado, Riviera, Lincoln Continental, Cadillac cars. Donna Summer and Gloria Gaynor are the divas of disco. Jazz clubs are closing to make room for dance floors and deejays. It's a wild, wild time. And so it goes in the seventies. Flamboyance dances her dance . . .

10

Hollywood Haze

I had big expectations of life in California. The scene was so different from New York and I felt like I was off to a fresh start. The black music scene had its old standbys, jazz and rhythm & blues, but now there was funk, soul, rock and roll. It was a time of big bands, but not like Duke's or Basie's, instead it was Parliament/Funkadelic, the Ohio Players, Earth, Wind & Fire.

Disco was the big deal.

Freda Payne, Gloria Gaynor, and Donna Summer were the big names in the industry. Backup singers became a fixture. Every solo artist and singing group had girls in the background singing the harmonies.

There was such a thing as black Hollywood because black actors were starring in films and appearing on television in greater numbers than ever before. I remember a time when you saw a black person on TV, you ran and told the whole neighborhood. It was news. Now, we actually had black superheroes, Shaft and Superfly. Black women were appearing in films, kicking ass in thigh boots and halter tops with shotguns strapped across their shoulders.

It was wild.

On television, we had black families shown for the first time. It was a new day in show business. And everybody felt the change. Black performers were free to be flamboyant and outrageous. The very pulled-together look of women from my era was clearly over. We had Rufus & Chaka Khan, LaBelle featuring Patti LaBelle, the Pointer Sisters. The new sound was electric guitars and synthesizers. I could see then that electronics were taking over. They were piping that music in through all kinds of new technology. I used to tell a lot of the fellas I worked with:

"Don't you see what's happening? In a minute, they're not going to need live musicians. You are not going to have jobs, if you don't pay attention. You all better wake up."

Over time, you heard less and less of the acoustic sound that had been popular in the jazz era. It was a very loud time.

Loud, in every sense of the word.

However, on the jazz side things were becoming very "lite." The jazz instrumentalists who were hot during the seventies were people like Chuck Mangione, Bob James, Earl Klugh, and Grover Washington Jr. The pure jazz sound was fading. Even pioneers like Dizzy and Miles were trying new things, new ways to reinvent themselves and stay on top of what was happening in music. The jazz vocalists who were on top were the same people who were on top way back in the day, like Sarah Vaughan, who was a superstar by this time, and Ella Fitzgerald, who had become a living legend. Lena Horne, Roberta Flack, and Nancy Wilson were also hot at the time. I was excited at the new possibilities LA offered, although my place in it all . . . honestly, I didn't know.

Canyon Records promised me the world. The president of the company, Wally Roker, was anxious to get me on board. They set me up in grand fashion. They moved me into a beautiful apartment right on Sunset Strip. The building was absolutely gorgeous. It's known as the Jockey Club today. It was a magnificent place, still is. They made arrangements to pay my rent and all of my personal expenses while I was under contract.

I released *Happy and in Love* on Canyon Records in 1972.

There I was in my new California-style getup on the album cover. I was sporting a pair of bell-bottom pants with a big paisley print and a matching cape. I was in full regalia with my gold satin puff-sleeved blouse, frosted lipstick, and matching eye shadow and fabulous gold shoes. It was really a sight.

It was a good, solid album. It could even be considered my crossover album. Because things in the record business were changing so much, we added some uptempo tunes with heavy rhythm in there so people could dance to it. We recorded "Whatever It Was You Just Did," "How Did You Make Me Love You," "Can You Take What I'm Gonna Do," "If You Don't Get It Yourself," "Love's Finally Found Me," "What Else Can I Do," "Seems Like I Gotta Do Wrong," "Don't Tell Me How to Love You," "I'm So in Love," and "I'll Take You All the Way There." I even used background singers on this album—Lady Helena, Elaine Hill, and Genie Brown. My boyfriend, Frank, did the engineering, the editing, and the remixing for the album.

When *Happy and in Love* was released, I was still waiting on payment from the company. Come to find out, Canyon had given my payment to Richard Carpenter. They claimed to have given him a check on my behalf long before. Well, if this was true, Carpenter would make sure I didn't see a dime of that money.

I knew I would never see that check. Meanwhile, I began to get suspicious about things at Canyon. They continued to make promises, but as time went on, they hadn't backed up any of them. Things at Canyon began to crumble.

The specifics of the Canyon contract, I don't recall, but it was the last contract Richard Carpenter negotiated on my behalf, before Harry got on his ass and ran him out of my life. Anyway, I had to hound the record company for information on the album, bug them to do publicity, harass them about my money. The same old story.

Then, one afternoon, I found an eviction notice posted on the door of my fabulous Sunset Strip apartment. It turned out that Canyon had not been paying the rent on the place like they promised. I was left hanging in California, with all of my furniture in storage and no place to go.

I was stranded.

I really needed Frank. But he had other ideas. He waited until I had permanently moved to Los Angeles to act a fool. This is the time he chose to get funky with me. When I fell on hard times—I mean, I had lost my mother, lost my house, my career was on shaky ground—he was nowhere to be found. I tried calling and calling but he wouldn't return my phone calls.

Frank had vanished.

At the time, my manager, Duke, had about thirty or forty rooms in

California he could book me in, which was my saving grace. If I could get a trio together, I would. Otherwise, I would perform with only piano accompaniment.

Vocalists need at least four or five musicians at their disposal at any given time, but the pianist is the most important. You can always get sidemen, but you really need an outstanding pianist that knows your book.

Duke always made sure I had what I needed. There was Concerts-by-the-Sea, where I worked pretty regularly; Safari; and the Lighthouse in Hermosa Beach, which is one of the oldest jazz clubs in the country. We even did cruise ships, like the Queen Mary Jazz Festival in Long Beach. Luckily, Las Vegas was nearby, and we could usually book dates in one of the hotels there.

But I also worked a lot of small rooms to supplement my income. I call them side-of-the-road rooms. I think I've worked every corner bar where they threw up a stage and said, "This is Jazz." The only problem was, one by one, a lot of these clubs were petering out. The jazz rooms were turning into discos. Eventually, Duke went back to New York, where he could do steady business.

I found a one-bedroom apartment on the first floor of a building on Horne Street in Hollywood. With the money I made from nightclubs, I was able to get my things out of storage and set up house. The Canyon experience threw me, but only for a minute. I had become so accustomed to being jerked around by record companies, that after a while I almost expected it. But being in California took on a different meaning for me. I was away from New York and its problems. I had a chance to establish myself among new audiences and experience a different side of the business. I still felt good about the move. I loved the atmosphere in California. Being there was very therapeutic for me. I think if I had stayed in New York, or at my house in Jersey, it would have been too difficult. Too many memories, you know. So, California dreaming was working for me. I unpacked and didn't look back.

No sooner did I move into my new apartment, when Richard and a whole carload of his friends showed up at my door. He hadn't called and told me they were coming or anything. They just jumped in a car and drove all the way from New York to California. Here they were with no money, no place to stay, and no explanation as to why they came. I didn't

Bass player Mickey Bass.
(Photo by Bob Vogel)

My accompanist, the
incomparable Roy
Meriwether.
*(Photo by Paula Norton,
Norton Photography)*

Michael Fleming, bassist.
(Photo by J. Kramer)

My drummer, Vince Estor, and friends Etta Jones and Elaine Patterson.

Backstage at the Apollo Theater, with Neil Cole, Janette Zuckerman, Greg Bandy, Mary Ann Niehaus, Bernice Easter, and Ann Rubino.

In the Bahamas at the Annual Jazz & Blues Festival, with Nancy Wilson, Bill Lockett, and Hal Jackson.

Hal Glickman, who owned Sherry's on the Strip, my friend Cardella Di Milo, and me.

Coming offstage after performing "I Wish You Love" with Joe Williams (left). That's actor Robert Wagner (right) helping us offstage.

During a performance in Washington, D.C., at Tacoma Station. (*Courtesy of Carol Tyson*)

Having dinner with my friends Bernice Lundy and songwriter Juggy Murray. Juggy wrote a lot of music with Ike Turner during the Ike-and-Turner days.

Entrepreneur Percy Sutton and me.

Me with my friend Gwen Nelson, who traveled with me.

Roy Meriwether, myself, and Phyllis White, leaving on a cruise to Bermuda.

Me and jazz saxophonist Stanley Turrentine.

Backstage at Fat Tuesday's with my friend Rosemary Sterrett.

Me and Lionel Hampton.

Dionne Warwick and me during the benefit concert
at the Beverly Hills Hilton.

Performing here with the Japanese All Star Band.

Meeting with Michael Bourne at WBGO in New Jersey.

Smokey Robinson and me at the Rhythm & Blues
Foundation's Pioneer Awards ceremony.

My two "daughters," Carol, Earl May's daughter, and Barbara Jackson,
at the Rhythm & Blues Foundation's Pioneer Awards ceremony.

Dell Long, Mark Green, me, and Jeff Eaton.

During a recording session with Rodney Jones, who produced "This One's on Me" (MLISE) Records.

Me with the O'Jays backstage at the Apollo Theater.

My "daughters," Earl May's girls, Carol and Robin and her little girl.

Duke and me at Priority Church out in New Jersey.

Me and Dr. John.

Me and my good girlfriend Etta Jones.

have room for myself, let alone for five grown kids. I had to go to the landlord just to find space for them. Mr. Liederman, the landlord, was kind enough to let them use one of the vacant apartments in the building. I didn't have any of their parents' names or addresses to notify their families. The only one I knew was Richard's best friend, George, but I had never met his family. I didn't know how I was going to explain this to his people. And all of them were intent on staying in California. I had very little to offer them in the way of assistance because my own situation was shaky. But here was my son, with four white kids showing up at my front door. Things worked themselves out. We all just kept going. What else could we do? The kids eventually made their own way and settled in. Richard stayed with me for a while.

I tried to date a little to lift my spirits. I met a guy named Robert, who was a few years younger than me. I was very vulnerable, but Robert made me feel good. We saw a lot of each other. We hung out at different clubs together, ate out a lot, went to the movies, all those good dating things that you do. I hadn't been to his place, but he used to talk about it a lot. He lived in a penthouse apartment in a gorgeous high-rise.

Well, finally he took me there to see it. It was fabulous! I never knew exactly how Robert made his money, but he always had plenty. He was very concerned about me and what I wanted and needed. He used to say:

"Don't take jobs singing in low-class clubs. You don't have to do that. You've got me to depend on."

I couldn't believe what I was hearing. It was strange to me. In fact, I had a hard time accepting his generosity. I was so accustomed to taking care of the whole world. It had been a long time since someone had offered to take care of me. His hobby was photography and he was really good at it, so we used to go out and take pictures of different landscapes, on the coast, at the beach. Now, Robert was a sweet guy, so girls were attracted to him. He was part of the "in" crowd in Hollywood. Everybody who knew him liked him. After dating for a few months, he asked me to move in with him in his penthouse apartment.

We had our little honeymoon period of living together, like everyone does, then after about three months, an old girlfriend popped into the picture. She came by to see him on more than one occasion. Robert had never mentioned her before, so I didn't find out, until after the fact, that they had dated for years before I met him.

I finally confronted him about her showing up so much, unannounced. I told him, in a very nice way, that it made me feel uncomfortable.

Well, baby, he spun around on me like a viper. "You're just jealous of her because she's younger than you," he said, raising his voice. "You're intimidated by her!"

This tirade went on for a while and then the real truth came out: She was pregnant with his baby.

We tried to go on with our relationship, acting as if the pregnancy wasn't going to affect us. We both knew better, but we really enjoyed each other's company and weren't ready to give that up yet. Robert said he intended to take care of the baby, but he had no plans on getting back with the woman.

We even moved out of the penthouse, thinking that would help our relationship. We rented a beautiful house in the Hollywood Hills. The house was owned by Marvin Mitchelson, the famous attorney. It was completely furnished with Asian furniture and fixtures. Marvin told us he and his wife had visited the Orient, then decided to build this house. But they had outgrown it and had built an even larger house.

Anyway, Robert and I tried to do what we could to patch things up, but nothing seemed to work. We had all kinds of fights and arguments until, finally, I asked him to leave.

And he did.

So, there I was in this fabulous house in the Hills, by myself. I knew I had to hurry up and move to a less expensive place before my money ran out. I found an apartment, shortly after our breakup, on Doheny Drive in Beverly Hills.

A funny thing happened just months after I moved into the new place. The apartment complex was run by a white woman whose name I've forgotten. And I had met someone new, Joe Saucier, who was so fair, he looked damn near white. He used to take me out on dates and we hung out for a while. Well, one day he came by the apartment looking for me and ran into my landlady. When I came home from a gig later that night, she made it a point to tell me:

"Oh, you had a visitor." She paused, then said, "I didn't know you dated a white man."

"What white man?" I asked.

I didn't know what she was talking about and was much too tired to try to figure it out.

"There was a white man here to see you," she said. "He was tall with mingling gray hair, very handsome."

I tried to keep a straight face:

"He's not white," I said.

Well, this really got under her skin.

Next thing I knew, the woman went up on my rent five dollars!

I told Joe about it and he fell out laughing. We both got a giggle out of it, but I jumped on his case for showing up like that. And I made him pay the extra five dollars every month. Well, he probably only ended up paying about twenty bucks altogether, because we didn't date very long.

By now, I had found some nice clubs to work in and I stayed pretty busy. Even though Robert and I broke up, I was beginning to feel whole again.

I attribute this to work. There's nothing like a steady flow of work for an artist. We spend half of our time looking for work and the other half trying to keep the work we've got.

Once I got on my feet, I bought a little yellow Toyota. Now, talking about putting things in perspective, after owning a Mercedes, a Lincoln, and other luxury cars, this little car meant more to me than any of them. It represented my triumph over hard times. I had scratched and saved for my little yellow Toyota, and it was just what I needed at the time. And there's no feeling in the world like having what you need, when you need it.

On my fortieth birthday, I threw myself a little party. I cooked all of this food—fried chicken, collard greens, black-eyed peas, potato salad, baked macaroni.

Well, there was a minister who had befriended me in the neighborhood, and called himself being sweet on me, so for a birthday present he brought me two dogs, a poodle and a shepherd. I didn't have the heart to tell the man that I couldn't afford to maintain two dogs. So, I accepted them.

I named them Othello and Iago. When it came time for them to eat, they ate what I ate.

There was never any dog food in the house.

One of my neighbors, Angela Dunn, had two Great Danes, Daphne and Chloe. Angela was a journalist. She worked for one of the local papers. And she would take care of the dogs whenever I had to hit the road. I'm not sure at what point Chloe decided she was in love with Iago, the shepherd, but I came back off the road and they were all over each other. I mean, they were really honeymooning! And poor little Othello was kicked to the curb. They didn't pay an ounce of attention to him.

Then, Angela told me the news: Iago had knocked up Chloe.

Well, they were a motley pair, completely different breeds, God only knows what kind of creature they would bring into the world. So, I told Angela:

"We've got to do something about this."

We didn't know what to do because we both loved our dogs and didn't want to hurt them. The vet recommended an abortion. This was the first time I had ever heard of a doggie abortion. I didn't know such a thing was possible. Well, Angela paid for half and I paid for half.

I had to give the dogs away eventually because they were eating up too many of my dollars.

Speaking of birthdays, they've taken on a whole new meaning for me as I've gotten older. Every last one of them is important. My good friend Etta Jones and I throw parties together every year to celebrate our birthdays, which are close together. Oh, it's an extravaganza, baby. We go all out. We spare no expense and make sure we have an absolute ball. Etta Jones is another great singer. She's the closest thing to Billie Holiday that we have. Etta is a pure jazz singer. I never considered myself strictly jazz because I'm known to sway. I'll throw some pop or soul in the mix. But Etta is a purist, with a gorgeous voice.

My friend Ellen Mousari moved to the LA area just months after I did, for job-related reasons. I tell you, that Ellen could always find a good job. She worked mainly within the music industry, but when she couldn't find work at a record label or an agency, she would just try something else. I always admired her sense of direction. She never let grass grow under her feet. And if I had a problem, I could always talk to her. Her brother, Ernie Benson, had a popular facial spa in Hollywood called The Face Place, a hot spot for celebrities. I believe he recently closed it, but it was very, very popular in its day.

Ellen and I had been friends since the sixties. New York was home for both of us. So, when we got together, we had years to reflect on and talk about. I was happy to have a friend in the area. She pulled me out of a blue funk many a day. We used to go out to eat constantly. She would call: "You feel like going to lunch today?" And that was all it took. We hit our favorite spots and ate like pigs. I mean it. We ate until we had to walk around after we pulled away from the table. Now, everybody in LA drives, but we had to walk off all the gas from eating so damn much. This is the God's honest truth. We ate like there was truly no tomorrow.

On one of our regular gorge-fests, we were out walking on Santa Monica Boulevard, and we ran into a little shop called Good Scents. Ellen had mentioned it to me many times before. They sold all kinds of oils, incense, candles, botanicals, all kinds of holistic healing aids. It was a lovely little shop.

Well, we went crazy in there. It was decorated so beautifully, it made you feel good just being there. We were walking around the shop when we heard someone holler out:

"No, she's not in my store! Not Miss Gloria Lynne! It can't be!"

Ellen and I froze. The owner, Charles Champion, had come over to us, all excited, smiling and nearly jumping up and down. It turned out that he was a huge fan of mine, and he told me he owned all of my records. This was surprising to me because he was so young. He said he had grown up on my music because I was one of his parents' favorite singers. I was completely overwhelmed. This was the last thing I expected walking in there. Now, Charles has this fantastic personality and he is as handsome as he can be. I remember being so impressed with him. He was so young and talented, and his store was beautiful. We stood there talking for a long time. He told me that he was also an actor. At the time, he was doing a lot of television commercials and soap operas. Well, from that day forward, Charles and I became very close friends. He is such a beautiful person. I regard him as my second son.

Now, Charles is extremely spiritual. He was into holistic health and metaphysics long before it was popular. He introduced me to the Science of Mind Church in California. I began attending one of their churches, in my area, and I thoroughly enjoyed it. They had a wonderful bookstore, full of all kinds of spiritual and inspirational books. I read everything. This information was like a breath of fresh air to me. They taught practical living principles—how to achieve a spiritual relationship with God and how to live a happy and whole life while you're here on Earth. Their teaching never made you feel guilty or full of fault, nor did they burden you with man-made customs and beliefs. It was liberating and spiritual, as opposed to dogmatic. I had seen the likes of the so-called religious in my childhood and I wanted no part of that kind of "religion." I had experienced so much abuse at the hands of people who called themselves devoted Christians, which definitely had its effect on how I viewed the church.

I saw people march into church every Sunday and come home and beat their kids damn near to death.

And I thought, What the hell are they teaching them in church? My experience at Science of Mind really helped me get back on track.

I have always believed in God and my faith is strong and intact. However, when you grow up in an environment where "religion" is used as an excuse for physically abusing a child, trust becomes an issue. I wouldn't just walk into anybody's church.

It took me some time to put things together and realize that God had nothing to do with the evil that I experienced as a child.

Before this time, I had been going around the block from my apartment to the Christian Science Reading Room to pick up their pamphlets, which they gave away free. They were extremely generous and encouraging people. In fact, when I first moved to California, the people there made me feel very much at home, which I never will forget.

Science of Mind, however, was more in line with my own thinking. I took classes in metaphysics, meditation, and Bible study. It almost felt like being in college. They told me if I completed a certain level of study, I could become a practitioner and be able to practice healing, which was always one of my interests.

The time I spent at the Science of Mind Church really helped me to come to terms with my past, especially my childhood and my relationships with my mother and father. It gave me a better understanding of what had happened and how I had been affected by all those years of abuse. It also helped me to put it all in its proper perspective, so I could get on with my life. Gradually, I opened up myself to healing, and most important, I learned forgiveness.

Funny thing is, when I was about seven or eight years old, I had heard something about Science of Mind from someone somewhere. I don't remember where I got my information, but I liked what I heard and I re-member telling my mother:

"When I get grown, I'm going to follow those people."

Well, she just laughed and told me I didn't know what I was talking about. I don't know how I knew at that young age that I'd end up right there in the Science of Mind Church. But God knew. Science of Mind tuned me in to my own spirituality, which is what I had been lacking for so long. Many times, in the past, I went to church feeling low in spirit and came out feeling the same way. With Science of Mind, I found another dimension for my life.

On the music scene all kinds of things were going on. Most of the big name artists out there were new, at least new to me. The jazz artists that I came up with had really taken a backseat to the new music forms—disco, funk, soul, R&B. Disco was spreading like wildfire. Donna Summer's "Love to Love You, Baby" and Gloria Gaynor's "I Will Survive" were disco an-thems. When disco came through, a lot of critics complained that the music lacked substance, but the fans loved it, lived for it. It was a carefree period. The seventies were much more relaxed, in a sense, than the sixties. The civil rights movement had accomplished many of its goals, though a lot of lives were lost, but generally, in the seventies, everybody chilled out. The drummer Milford Graves once said, with regard to what was happening in music at the time:

"The 1970s was like everybody went to sleep."

Although on the jazz side there were women who were holding their own. Nancy Wilson, who I love and regard as a baby sister, was doing well. I know she's had her share of hard knocks in the business, but she has a good manager, John Levy, who is one of the most respected black managers in the industry. He's kept a keen eye on her career. And there were a few others who were doing well, but only a few.

I was in a whole different state of mind. I was working on myself. Of course, if work came up, I jumped at it. But overall, I was working on *me*.

I was performing at the Parisian Room one night and I met Cardella Di Milo. She approached me after my set, we talked and exchanged num-bers. We stayed in touch from that night on. We clicked right away. She used to host shows at the Parisian Room every Monday night. She was so popular that every Monday night she would pack the room. In addition to her hosting job, she was also an actress. She did a lot of films, wrote songs, appeared at nightclubs in the States as well as overseas. Cardella was also a columnist for one of the local newspapers. She is a really dynamic woman.

When we met, things hadn't been going so well for me. I was moving around from apartment to apartment. I couldn't get situated because my money was so up and down.

I think Cardella sensed this. She always tried to help me. One day, she took me to meet Hal Glickman, the owner of a nightclub, Sherry's on the Strip. Hal had a trio playing at the club all week, and on this particular night I sat in with the band. After hearing me sing, he offered me a regular job singing on weekends for as long as I wanted.

Neither of them knew that I was down to my last dime and I was about to be evicted from my apartment. This was the break I needed to get my finances together. I mentioned to Cardella, very casually, that I needed to find a new place to live, without telling her that I was about to be evicted. Cardella went to Hal again and asked him to help.

There was a house, just up the hill over Sunset Strip and not far from the club. Hal knew the owner, Keith O'Connell, and asked him to rent it to me. A lovely house with three bedrooms, a living room, dining room and a den, it had a magnificent view of the city. And it was fully furnished, complete with a baby grand piano in the living room, directly in front of the windows, which went from the ceiling to the floor. The house rented for four hundred dollars a month and Hal arranged it so that my weekly pay at Sherry's on the Strip went toward the rent. Talk about singing for your supper.

The piano was my peace. I played on it every day and wrote song after song. I sang at Sherry's every weekend, unless a job out of town came up. At this time, however, out-of-town jobs were few and far between.

Cardella watched my back.

She used to call every day to see if I had food, or if my lights were on, or if my telephone bill was paid. She had done so much to help me that sometimes I wouldn't tell her the real story. I'd say I was doing fine. Only God knew I was struggling.

In spite of my financial troubles, it was a time of introspection. I had been too busy working to realize that I needed some time alone to think. Cardella is a very spiritual person. We used to go down to the ocean and pray together. She would always take time out to commune with God.

Cardella is the kind of person you can call on to pray with you, or pray for you. She'll do it right there on the spot. This was very comforting for me. I've been to a lot of churches but I've yet to come away with the same feeling of balance and serenity that I get by simply praying with a friend by the water. I was very alone during this time, still mourning the death of my mother and trying to reconcile myself with everything that had happened back home in New York. Cardella really saved me.

Cardella and I were a mess together, though. She had this little piece of a car. It was just as raggedy as it could possibly be, but we would get in it and try to get down there to the beach to pray. Well, each and every time, it was a struggle with that car. We always had to take a bottle of water with us, to pour into it, because the car would spurt and spout, and the water would just jump up out of there. So, you had to have water to put into the radiator or whatever it was.

We always had to have water.

I remember one day, after we filled the buggy with water, Cardella was showing me all around Los Angeles and pointing out the different landmarks. Oh, she was really doing her thing, letting me in on things, you know, showing me the sights. Well, all of a sudden, there was a pause, and I looked over at her. Cardella had fallen asleep at the wheel. And we were just rolling down the road.

"Cardella!" I shouted.

She jumped, then said in a calm voice:

"Oh, I was sleep."

God looks out for babies and fools, it's true. Because together, we were two bona fide fools.

I ran into Michael one night at Sherry's. Now, Michael was a man I had met when I first got to California. We met during the time I was with Robert, but he didn't say much to me then, but I knew he liked me. I mean, you always know when a man likes you, no matter who you're with. Anyway, we hadn't seen each other for a long time, so I was glad to see him that night. He stayed for all three shows, and at the end of the night, he asked if he could come by and see me sometime. I agreed and gave him my phone number. The next afternoon, Michael called. He wanted to come by my place, which he did, and we spent a very pleasant evening together.

Michael was a dream. He was fine, sweet and sophisticated. He was so cool to be around and he could do anything—he cooked, he gardened, he could fix things. He had a way of cheering me up like no one else. I enjoyed every last minute I had with him. There were days when we didn't do anything more than go for a drive up the coast. With Michael, it was glorious.

I wrote a song about him, about us, called "More Love."

Michael was a musician but not a crazy musician. He had no problem working jobs that were outside the business, as long as they were legit. We would sit and talk for hours. Michael told me all about his years in the service and I told him about growing up in Harlem. We shared a lot with each other, which was very comforting for me. Michael knew I was wounded and trying to heal, so he found ways to soothe me. He restored my faith in relationships. Because I had come to the conclusion that if there was a room full of men I could walk in and, invariably, choose the wrong guy or the wrong guy would pick me and I'd like him. But Michael was different. He was very laid back.

He made it easy for me to love him.

Keeping busy helped a great deal because during this time my son, Richard, and I had lost contact. He had gone back to New York, but I couldn't find him. After my mother's death, he began to wander. He took it really hard, and to this day I know he still grieves. My mother gave him anything she thought he might want and everything he asked for. I used to try to tell her not to spoil him so much, but she insisted.

"Hey, he's my only grandchild. Just leave me alone about it," she would say.

When Mom died, I couldn't pick up where she left off. I could no longer afford it. Well, I was a nervous wreck not knowing Richard's whereabouts. I didn't know anything. I didn't know where he was living, who he was with, or how he was getting along.

When he first came to California, he was on his own, for the most part, because I was always working. And he really didn't know how treacherous people could be, and even though he had been raised in New York, he lived a very sheltered life. We protected him from everything. Soon after he arrived in LA, the car his grandmother bought for him was stolen. After that happened, Richard said he wanted to leave California and go back to New York. I didn't feel good about him leaving, but I let him go back. Now, here he was, nowhere to be found.

His father, Harry, was still in New York, so I just prayed that he would get in touch with him. Harry and I always stayed in touch with one another. He always had my address and phone number, no matter how much I moved, and I always had his information. I called Harry several times to let him know that Richard was in the area, but each time he said he hadn't heard from him.

I wanted Harry and Richard to be close. Even though we weren't together, that was no reason for the two of them to be distant. I remember when Richard was about seven years old, he went out to spend the summer with his father. Harry was living in Brooklyn at the time with his girlfriend, Joyce. I used to call him every day to see how they were doing and he would tell me about all the fun he was having. Though he was just a subway ride away—Harlem to Brooklyn only took about forty-five minutes on the train—he was thrilled to death to be hanging out with his dad.

Richard had been at his father's maybe a month, then one day, we couldn't reach them. During this period, my mother was still living, and she called several times. Then, I called. Still, no answer. We took turns calling all day, trying to track them down. After several hours passed, we got worried. Because Richard knew I called him every day and wanted to hear from me. We called at least twenty times that day and still got no answer at the house.

The next morning, we started all over again with call after call. They weren't at home but I knew Harry wouldn't have taken Richard out of town without my permission, so I didn't know what was going on. Then Mom got to worrying. We continued like this, then after making a thousand and one calls, Mom and I were sitting in the kitchen trying to figure out our next move when our apartment buzzer rang. My mother answered the buzzer.

"Who is it?"

"It's Joyce," a woman said. "Is Richard there?"

She was asking for Richard, so Mom buzzed her up, which we almost never did. Usually if someone came to visit, we knew about it, but we'd never buzzed someone up who we weren't expecting. Well, we waited and waited and Joyce never came up.

Now, we were curious.

I knew Joyce was Harry's girlfriend's name, but I had never met her. I didn't even think she knew where we lived. So, I went down to the lobby to see if I could catch her and no one was there. Not a soul. I went back upstairs and called over to Harry's again. No answer. Well, we were fit to be tied at this point.

We decided to head to Brooklyn and see what the hell was going on. A neighbor drove us. When we reached Harry's block, we asked the people out on the street if they had seen Richard.

"Yeah, I just saw him go by on his skates," one guy said.

As he was telling us this, here comes Richard flying up on his roller skates. Well, my child was filthy dirty, from top to bottom, his clothes, his face and hands. I couldn't believe he was standing there looking like that. He told us he had been out in the street all day, since early that morning, and his father had gone somewhere, but he didn't know where, because the lady that he was living with was dead.

Of course, Mom and I thought Richard had gotten the story wrong, that maybe something had happened, but maybe he was too young to understand. We both knew that Joyce had just come to our house, rung our bell, asking for Richard. So, we asked one of the neighbors who was sitting out on the stoop and he told us that Joyce had died that morning.

Well, this just stopped us cold.

Then we really got to thinking, maybe Joyce really did come to the house to warn us about Richard and let us know that he was outside, alone in the street. My mother was a firm believer in spirits and otherworldly things, so we took a look at each other and we knew it was true.

It was Joyce.

Her spirit had visited us.

Harry, we figured, must have gone out to take care of things and probably forgot to give Richard the house keys. So, Richard wasn't able to call us.

I told Harry about the "visitation" after things had calmed down.

"I can believe that," he said, "because Joyce was crazy about Richard."

When we got home, I asked my son about what had gone on in Harry's house. He told me that Joyce had been sick in bed with an abscessed tooth. She and Harry had been arguing about something all night. They used to fight a lot, he said. Then, early that morning, she died. Richard was just a kid, so his description was very plain and simple, but I think he saw something that caused him to become very distant to his father. After Joyce died, Richard grew further and further away from his father. They just couldn't get close. I prayed this would change but it never did.

So, here was Richard, twenty-something years old, back in New York with no family ties there. He was there all alone and he didn't get in touch with me to let me know his whereabouts. It drove me nearly out of my mind. Just when I couldn't stand it anymore, I got an offer to do an engagement in New York. It wasn't a lot of money, but transportation was paid for. I accepted the job, hoping I could find Richard while I was there.

I went down to Sherry's on the Strip and told Hal that I needed time off to take the job in New York. He had no problem with it, but he didn't understand why I was going for so little money. I told him how worried I was about my son and that I was really going to try to find him. To my amazement, he said, "I'll go with you and try to help." He thought he might enjoy New York, anyway, since he had never been there before. In the meantime, I had some old numbers of a few friends of Richard's. I made call after call and was able to get bits and pieces of information as I went along. Some gave me addresses where I might try to find him, and once I hit New York, I started searching. I went door to door searching for my son.

I finally found him at a friend's apartment in midtown Manhattan, in the forties on the West Side somewhere. I was relieved to see that he was intact, but I sensed that something was not right with him. I just didn't know what it was, exactly. I asked Richard to come back to Los Angeles with me.

"I'm just not ready to go back there," he said.

Hal was standing there in that little tight apartment with me and he offered Richard a job, right there on the spot. We did everything we could to convince him, but he said he wasn't ready, and I guess he just wasn't ready. He refused. So, I had to go on without him, but I was never happy about leaving my son in New York alone.

I didn't know the people he was living with, or who his friends were. It was an uncomfortable time between us. He was a grown man, but he was still my son, and like any mother, I worried about him and only wanted the best for him. In this particular space in time, I felt like a stranger with my own son. Something told me that Richard was suffering, that he was having some deep problems that he could not tell me about. And I had to make peace with the fact they he didn't want to share it with me. I headed back to California.

I was performing at the 9000 Room in Los Angeles one night and I was approached by two men from Liberia. They waited around for me after the show. They told me how much they enjoyed my performance and asked me if I'd be interested in coming to their country to perform. I was flattered but didn't give what they were saying any real consideration. I could barely afford to stay my behind right there in California, much less to try and get to Africa.

They gave me their business cards, took down my contact information, and told me to expect a call from them within three weeks. Before they left, they began this very deep conversation about the problems they were having in Liberia.

"Is there someone in your country that could possibly help us?" they asked.

The only person I could think of was the Reverend Jesse Jackson. Jesse and I had met some years before in Chicago while I was performing there. I felt comfortable enough to call him. He was still very active in the political scene in the seventies, and I thought he'd be interested. I set up a meeting between the three of them.

After the Liberians met with Jesse, they made a point of calling me to say how impressed they were with him and to thank me for the referral. The rest of the details of their meeting I read in the paper, like everybody else. I never heard from Jesse after the meeting was set.

He went to Liberia to meet with their government officials and the trip got plenty of press. They showered him with gifts and thought he was the best thing since running water.

In the meantime, the two Liberians were still trying to get me to perform there. We discussed it further and they offered to send me $3,500 as a deposit fee. Another $3,500 was to be paid after our arrival. They told me they would pay to fly my band there and pay for all of our expenses, which is the only way we could have afforded to go.

After about three months, they told me they couldn't pay the balance of the fee. And they demanded that I come for only the $3,500 amount.

This money would have to cover transportation, salaries, and expenses for five people.

It was impossible.

So, they went over my head and convinced my band into coming without me. At that time, I was working with Karen Hernandez, pianist; Stan Gilbert, bass player; and drummer Frank Wilson.

Then, I got a call from Jesse asking me to come, telling me that the Liberian government was expecting me. I explained to him exactly what had happened, what they had promised, and what they had delivered.

"I cannot afford to come," I told him. "They promised me a certain amount, then they reneged."

I never heard from him again. Next thing I know, the Liberian government got so angry with me that they passed a law against me, stating that no girls in the country could ever be named Gloria. This was pure craziness. It all boiled down to money.

What could I do?

I was not in the position to travel to Africa. I could not imagine leaving one country, broke, to arrive in another one, broke down. And the fact remains they did not fulfill their promise, so they gave me no other choice. I couldn't stop my band from going, but I pleaded with them not to go, to back me up on my decision.

They went anyway.

Then, they came back here, traumatized. It turned out to be an awful trip and they claim to have escaped within an inch of their lives. God only knows what was happening in Liberia at that time, but I followed my intuition and stayed home. I apologized to the Liberian government and concluded that it was all a big misunderstanding.

———∞∞∞———

11

Sweat & Tears

$\mathcal{A}$BC Impulse Records approached me around 1974 about a two-album deal. They offered me the contract with the understanding that I would have very little artistic control. Esmond Edwards, a black producer, selected all of the songs, all of the musicians, everything. I just had to show up and sing.

We recorded *I Don't Know How to Love Him.*

The album included "The Shelter of Your Love," "We Are the Dreamers," "Thank You Early Bird," "I'm Thru with Love," "I'll Be Passing By This Way Again," "Visions," which had a beautiful saxophone solo by John Klemmer, and "How Will I Know." The only songs on the album Esmond didn't choose were "Out of This World" and "I Don't Know How to Love Him," but he did the arrangements on both songs. The other arrangements were done by Johnny Pate and Wade Marcus. He didn't even allow me to use my regular pianist. There were some talented musicians on the album— Sonny Burke, Clarence McDonald, Jerry Peters, Lee Ritenour, Ray Parker Jr., John Horrell. But more than anything, a vocalist really needs her accompanist, particularly if you've been working together for a lot of years. You develop a certain chemistry that you just can't always get in one session with musicians who aren't familiar with your style.

Now, Esmond didn't hire me, the owner of the label, Mr. Rubinstein, hired me. I remember Esmond coming to me, saying:

"Well, we heard you had problems, so . . ."

"What kind of problems?" I said. "If you thought I had a problem, what the hell do you want with me over here?"

The drug rumors were still circulating. And no matter what I said or what I did, people believed what they wanted to believe. But it continued to hurt my feelings. As hard as I had worked *not* to make mistakes in the business, my reputation was ruined anyway.

Around this time, Duke Ellington had passed and there were many, many tributes being organized in his name. I was approached by his son, Mercer Ellington, to perform a tribute tour with his orchestra. Up until this time, I hadn't worked with the Ellington family, so I was pleased to be a part of the tour. Mercer was very kind and generous with his time and energy. It was a very good experience. I don't recall all of the singers and musicians that participated, but I do remember there were many jazz greats on the tour. We traveled throughout the Midwest and Canada. It made a great impact on audiences. They were able to witness what a giant Duke was, and how much music he contributed in his lifetime.

I Don't Know How to Love Him hit the charts three weeks after its release. When they told me the news, I went to the jazz charts to look for it but couldn't find it. I called the record company back and told them I couldn't find it.

"It's on the soul charts," they said.

And sure enough, there it was on the soul charts with a bullet.

Next thing I knew, I was fired.

The record execs at Impulse felt they had signed me as a jazz artist, but my sound wasn't being recognized as jazz by the record-buying public, so they let me go. I went to the big man, the boss, Rubinstein. "Mr. Rubinstein," I said, "if this record is showing up on the soul charts, I don't mind following suit. Music is music. Can't we do something to pump up the record and keep it going?"

My contract was still revoked.

Since I was signed to do two albums and only completed one, I filed for unemployment. I went down to the office and explained that I had been fired from my job for reasons that I felt were unfair. They told me to bring my contract in and they would call ABC Impulse on my behalf.

I lucked out because when they called them, the Impulse people slammed the phone down on them, which made them curious enough to look even deeper into my case. Turns out that my application opened up a whole can of worms. I don't know if many people know this, but there is an IRS office within every unemployment office. They are informed on each case that passes through unemployment.

Anyway, I filed the necessary paperwork and went home. The very next morning I got a call from the IRS office.

"Miss Lynne, would you bring your contract in?" they said. "We feel that we're going to pursue this issue because we have a lot of artists coming in here with the same story."

Record companies were famous for giving young, aspiring artists "hand-outs," which was enough money to satisfy you, but it wasn't money you could necessarily claim as earnings. Some companies were known to hand over cold cash, so they wouldn't have any legal obligations or complicated payroll issues. I, on the other hand, had a legitimate contract with ABC Impulse. I had gotten an advance from them and everything.

They tried my case right there in the unemployment office. Impulse insisted that the advance they gave me was not considered "earnings." "It is most definitely earnings," the IRS said, "and you're going to pay her unemployment."

"But she's not an employee," the attorney for the record company said.

"Well, what is she then?" the IRS asked. "You have a contract on her. What do you call her?"

"She's just an artist," he replied.

The IRS was really angry about this, so they wrapped things up by saying:

"You're going to pay this woman."

Within the next week, I received eleven checks in the mail at once.

This case blew their cover. It made the IRS aware that many record companies were not paying into unemployment for their artists. Categorizing people as artists and not as employees was just another ploy in their bag of tricks.

I was simply going to get what I thought was mine.

When I was with Mercury they always paid into unemployment and took out all of the appropriate deductions. With Impulse I thought:

They fired me, so I'll get unemployment.

"You realize you may never work in the business again after this," I was occasionally told.

And they had a point.

Winning this case had repercussions.

This is a business where people "put the word out on you" and your career is ruined. From then on, the word on the street was that I was "trouble." So I went from "having problems" to being "trouble."

In 1975, I had a sudden urge to get stronger, physically, get in better condition, so I joined a health club.

One year after this epiphany, I learned that I had fibroid tumors and the doctor said they needed to be removed immediately.

Well, I procrastinated, even though I realized the urgency. I was so sick and weak from constant bleeding, I stayed in bed all the time. I had trouble getting out of bed. When I did get up, there was a trail of blood on the floor.

My son was living with me at the time and there was no way I wanted him to have to deal with all of this. A good girlfriend of mine, Frankie Hill, used to call the house every day to check on me, and each time Richard would tell her I was asleep.

After a while, she got suspicious and just came on over. When she arrived, she found me lying in a pool of blood. She wrapped me in blankets and took me to her physician, Dr. LeRoy Weekes. Now, Frankie was a funny girl. I remember arriving at the hospital and I guess the people weren't moving fast enough for her, so Frankie told one of the nurses: "If you don't hurry up, you're going to be completely un-assed in here." That was her word, *un-assed*. She'd talk about, not a kicking of the ass, but a "total un-assment." Oh, Frankie was funny. Well, when Dr. Weekes got a look at me, he immediately admitted me into the hospital. I couldn't have the surgery to remove the tumors right away because of the huge blood loss, so after several transfusions, they proceeded with the surgery.

After I had been hospitalized for nearly three weeks, the doctor informed me that I had to have a hysterectomy.

Dr. Weekes was a great doctor, very well known and well loved in Los Angeles. I felt blessed to have him as my surgeon. I wasn't upset about the hysterectomy. My main concern was my health and to be well and strong again. The surgery was successful. However, I was placed on estrogen therapy, which blew me up like a balloon.

Once I began to bloat and gain a lot of weight, I called Dr. Weekes and told him I would heal on my own. I refused the estrogen and began to use prayer and meditation as my medication. I was very serious about it and dedicated myself to living healthy. I reached levels of spirituality that I had never imagined. I dedicated myself to a daily regimen of morning prayer and afternoon meditation. I clutched my Bible and allowed my body to heal.

I also felt blessed to have Frankie. She was one of the people I met through Cardella. She was an aspiring actress, dancer, singer, and she also modeled. Frankie had a lot of ups and downs in her life, but she would always find a way to overcome her problems.

She told me when she was in college, she was very inspired by my music. She entered a contest and won, singing one of my hit singles on Everest, "I'm Glad There's You." She graduated with a degree in music from one of the schools out in California. It may have been UCLA.

Frankie found an apartment in Brentwood and we shared it. This was a real learning experience. Until Frankie pointed it out, I hadn't noticed that when I wasn't singing and performing, all I would do all day long was write songs, write lyrics, and concentrate on music. Michael and I were still hanging out, but we weren't quite as close as we had been. I was too distracted. I was sitting around waiting for the phone to ring with a job offer on the other end. I moped around feeling sorry for myself.

I missed recording and I missed performing. I'd had so much success in previous years that I sat at home, wondering: Where did it all go? It is difficult making the transition into working sporadically. I often thought back to the fun times on the road, with Duke and the guys, Earl, Herman, and Grassela, even though, at the time, we were all complaining about the rigorous touring schedule. I had reached some tremendous heights in my career—Top 20 hits, the Playboy Jazz Award, top-selling albums, cross-country tours, headlining with Ray Charles and Johnny Mathis, sold-out concerts, but nothing ever prepares you for the day when it begins to slip away. I remember Ella Fitzgerald told me, all those years ago when I was just a teenager:

"When you make it, you must remember that you have to be just as enthusiastic when you're successful as you were on the way up. The greater you are, the harder it is to stay on top."

One day, Frankie said to me, "You know, you have a great voice. But it is not going to see you through all you need right now."

I told her that I was very bored, waiting by the phone for job offers. I had no management, no agent, no record company. So I had to depend on myself to get work.

Frankie suggested that I do what she did, secretarial temp work. She said it paid well and at least I'd be making money to cover my expenses. So I made the appointment with her temp agency, reluctantly.

The appointment was set for one week later. Frankie gave me the whole lowdown. She said I'd be given a typing test, which just wore me out, because I learned to type in high school, but I was never good at it. I could only type thirty to forty words a minute, and that's if I was typing from my head, not from a piece of paper. It had been decades since I worked in an office situation.

As a teenager I had odd jobs around Manhattan but nothing long term or really lasting. I had worked as a receptionist at an ad agency, once, and also had trained as a physical therapist, but, really, I spent most of my life singing and performing. So I had mixed feelings about the whole thing.

I got to the office about fifteen minutes early, so I could relax before the interview. I filled out the application, then came the typing test. After that, there was a two-page written test, then they began the interview. My interviewer said, right off the bat:

"You've been out of the workplace for a very long time, haven't you?" She proceeded with the interview and at the end of it, she said, "You've passed all of the tests. You just need to brush up on your typing."

Then she gave me my first temp assignment.

It started the very next day.

I was actually surprised by how good I felt after following up on the temp work idea. I felt better about myself, because not working was miserable. This was a new adventure—a chance to meet new people, make new friends. I worked for advertising agencies, real estate offices, banks, purchasing companies, accounting firms, and each job prepared me for the next one. If I went to one job and didn't know how to do something, I'd say, "Oh, we did it another way at my other job."

So they would be forced to train me.

I learned something of value every step of the way. It was a different world for me, but it afforded me both worlds. If I had a singing job, I could do it, but at least this way if I wasn't performing I could maintain.

I went to the union to see if I could get some assistance paying for my hospital bills. I explained the entire situation to them and showed my pay stubs from various nightclubs as well as my recording contracts. If you are a member in good standing, have earned money in the industry during the past year, the insurance benefits kick in. In my case, I qualified for all of the above. As it turned out, my fight for unemployment insurance worked in my favor, because AFTRA submitted to paying the entire hospital bill. They didn't require that I pay one dollar of the insurance copayment or any of that.

I also received a lot of help from the governor's office. Jerry Brown was governor of California then and his office had my back the entire time. I wrote letters to them explaining all that had taken place between me and ABC Impulse and they stayed on top of things, from beginning to end. I owe them a debt of gratitude. They made sure my financial assistance from the union and unemployment was on time and in time.

In the summer of 1979, my father died. Miss Pearl, his longtime girlfriend, called to tell me, so I got on a plane that same day to New York. I remember it was the hottest August on record. My father was living in the same apartment that he had given Harry and me when we got married. Everybody who knew my father knew that he was a pack rat. He supposedly had lots of cash and jewelry stashed away in that apartment, but no one ever found it. If they did, they never told me.

The day of the funeral, John, Harry, and I showed up together. Miss Pearl had made all of the funeral arrangements. Well, that woman had my father laying up there all day long, in an open casket, in that incredible heat.

"Why do you have my father up there like that? What time are things going to start?" I asked her.

She said she wanted to wait for the rest of the family to arrive.

"We're here. His children are standing right here. I'm here. John is here. And Harry is here."

We were the only people I considered family, but of course, Miss Pearl had children by other men. They all called my father "Daddy" or "Granddaddy." Her children were given educations and all that, while my father chose not to do a damn thing for the children he brought into the world.

Anyway, we took a seat in the church, away from the other family folk. The whole thing was a fiasco, as far as I was concerned. I was ready to go the minute I got there. I didn't feel like it was my father who had died. It seemed like somebody else's daddy had died. I was at a funeral for a stranger. It really made me sick. So much so that I didn't even go to the burial. I got on a plane later that afternoon and went back to California.

Miss Pearl really worked her show. She stuck up under my father all those years and kept her hands buried deep in his pockets. They were together over fifty years. Growing up, I remember thinking that she was such a nice lady. Of course, I grew up and got hip to her game. After my father's death, I saw the real side of Miss Pearl. There was a lot of confusion about who was to get what. I hadn't expected my father to make any provisions for me and my brothers in death, because he hadn't done it in life.

In fact, I was surprised to receive a check for $101, weeks after he was buried. Evidently, he had taken out a small insurance policy and named me as the beneficiary. This inspired me to do some further investigation. I did some research with regard to his pension and the longshoreman's insurance, but I found that all of that money had been claimed and collected. Then I found out that Ms. Pearl had skipped town and moved to North Carolina. She bought a five-bedroom house and moved in with another man.

Miss Pearl got all of my father's money.

I was living at 1131 Alta Loma in a really nice apartment. Bob and Vicky Walter managed the building and we became good friends. They knew my situation and always looked out for me. Around this time, Richard had returned to California, and he was living with me.

When I went on the road, they watched out for Richard, who was suffering from a severe back ailment after having three really bad car accidents, one of which was in my little yellow Toyota.

Vicky was a pianist and we spent a lot of afternoons writing songs and singing together. They were such great people. Bob and Vicky were the kind of people who make you feel so comfortable that it takes the edge off of living. This was one of the most memorable times I had in California because they were such nice people. It was a time of meeting nice people along the way.

There was still not much happening on the singing circuit for me in

LA, so I continued working temp jobs. Sometimes I'd be at a company for a day, sometimes a week. It was tiring, but it paid my bills.

Around 1981, I went to work for Bank of America. I never used my real name. I used my middle name and married name, Mai Alleyne. I felt more comfortable with them not knowing who I was, since I was still performing on the side when I could. It began as a temp job, but after about three months they found out that the girl who I had been replacing was not coming back. My manager, Florence, who was a very nice woman, came to me and said:

"Mai, do you want this job?"

Well really, I didn't. It wasn't a matter of wanting the job but of needing the job. It was paying seven hundred dollars a month. I had gotten tired of running around chasing after jobs, so I agreed to take the position with the hope that I'd be offered more money and the opportunity to be promoted, which eventually happened. Every so often they'd give me a raise.

Then, in the blink of an eye, three months turned into three years.

My friend Charles Champion had a fit when he found out I was working at Bank of America. He could not understand it. He said:

"What are you doing working nine to five? You're a great singer. You shouldn't be wasting your time at a bank!"

Charles wanted me to think seriously about going to Europe or Japan. Now, he is a world traveler. Charles really lives. He does it all. And everything he does, he does well. He's one of those people who enjoys life to the fullest. He would pick up in a minute and go to Paris or Milan for a few weeks, then come back to California and pick up his acting career where he left off. Well, he was just furious that I had gone and taken a day job. He insisted that the European market would eat me up. He said they had bins and bins of my music over there, and my audience would be ready-made if I'd just go. He mentioned Paris, London, Milan, even Tokyo as places to consider living. But at the time, I just couldn't think that far ahead. I was concentrating on my immediate needs—rent, gas, lights.

Music was still my love but it was not my bread-and-butter. I joke about it now, but honest to God, I wrote more songs on Bank of America's time than I can count. I used to save up my sick days and vacation time in order to do gigs out of town. My coworkers thought I was chilling out on my off days, but I'd be hightailing it to Chicago or Detroit or even New York, singing somewhere in a club.

Very few people in the music industry knew that I had taken a day job, so from time to time, they contacted me about different engagements. During my time at the bank, an old friend, Neil Cole, called me. He worked as a promoter and event planner. He told me that he wanted me to do a nostalgia concert with the Earl May Trio.

Neil used to work with the hospital union, Local #1199, and he organized concert events for them. So, he knew a lot of singers and musicians. He worked with Nancy Wilson and Billy Eckstine and a lot of the other top black entertainers. He worked with large corporations to get backing for the events. Around this time, he had become associated with some of the large concert venues in New York, like Lincoln Center and the Brooklyn Academy of Music.

So I told him I was interested in doing a reunion concert, if he could get everybody back together. Trying to put your hand on musicians is a trip because they spend so much time traveling. Anyway, Neil said he really wanted to do the concert, so he'd get the ball rolling and get back to me.

I did my best to stay busy. Once, I was asked by the comedian Slappy White to appear with him on a monthlong engagement at the Las Vegas Hilton. Of course, I said yes, since my money was tight (and Bank of America's little checks couldn't hold a candle to live performance pay). His manager arranged everything, including the hotel arrangements. I was given a suite at the Hilton, and apparently Slappy had made other plans for his housing.

However, he still wanted to use my suite as a pit stop. He left some of his clothes in my suite, which was fine, but he also told his friends that they were free to use the room whenever they wanted. So I'd come in from performing each night and there'd be a room full of people in my suite. They were in there doing everything illegal under the sun. There were bowls of cocaine all over the place, liquor bottles, drug paraphernalia. I was scared to death the entire time I was there because this nonsense went on daily. I had heard that Slappy was a low-lifer, but I needed the gig. I never imagined all of this would be going down.

Slappy asked me to come back to Vegas on another engagement some months later, and I told his manager:

"Yes, I'll do it, but I have to have my own private room. I can't have Slappy and his friends coming in and out of there with all that dope and shit. I cannot have that around me. Because if the police come, they're taking us all to jail."

And I was very, very fortunate because I found out later, several of those people who had been running through that suite had gone to jail.

I was living at 1131 Alta Loma at the time and Slappy lived around the block. One day he called me saying he wanted to discuss the upcoming engagement.

"Why don't you come on over and let's talk about it," he said. My girlfriend Frankie was with me when he called. So, I told her:

"Frankie, come on and go with me over here to Slappy's place."

And I was right to take her with me because when that man opened up his front door, he was standing there buck naked! Frankie was standing behind me, so Slappy didn't realize she was there. Frankie stepped forward and looked at him:

"You know, you ought to be ashamed of yourself!"

Slappy didn't say anything, but he could see neither one of us were studying him. But that didn't make him go put on any clothes. And we left his naked ass standing right there in the doorway.

Slappy was a wild, wild dude.

I did a second Vegas engagement with Slappy, for the money, of course, but I went back to my bank job as soon as it was over. I had to work to build up some more sick days. But I accepted a booking at the Parisian Room and without my knowing it they advertised the show heavily. It was all in the papers and on the radio that Gloria Lynne was performing in concert there. They had my picture on the advertisement and everything. The very first night of the run, there was a great crowd. The vibes were real good that night.

Well, at the end of the set, the houselights came up. I looked out into the audience, and the club was completely packed, full of damn near every last one of the Bank of America's employees. Someone had seen one of the advertisements with my picture on it and spread the word throughout the bank. I was shocked. They found me out. They were all there, the president of the bank, some of the VPs, everybody.

And I had to show up to work in the morning.

It was really unbelievable. I think they thought they were being supportive by coming to my show, but it was humiliating for me. The next morning at work the vibe was very different. People were coming up to me asking me to autograph albums. Then others became resentful of my being there, which was a little reminiscent of my New Jersey Bergen County days. So, after that, it just didn't feel the same, after I knew *they* knew. I wasn't comfortable there any longer, so I resigned.

I didn't stop temping, though, because the money was still absolutely necessary to my well-being. I went on doing one-day, two-day and one-week assignments. The whole time I worked as a temp, I caught the bus. I rode buses all over Los Angeles because they didn't have a subway system at the time. And even if they did, I wouldn't have been on it. I had long since left the subway system alone. I stopped taking subways when I was nineteen, living in Harlem. I have always preferred staying aboveground, on the bus. Anyway, one evening I was coming home from a job and the driver was a black dude. Well, this man stared me down. He looked at me hard.

"You're Gloria Lynne, aren't you?" he finally said.

Before I could say anything, the man went off.

"Oh, my God, Gloria Lynne's riding my bus!"

He asked me where I lived, then commenced to drive me all the way home, off the regular bus route, to my front doorstep.

"You're going to get in a world of trouble if your supervisor finds out," I said. "You know you're not supposed to be driving this city bus down residential streets." The other passengers on the bus didn't know what the hell had happened.

"I don't care what my job has to say about it," the man said. "I'm an old fan of yours and I'm dropping you at your doorstep tonight. And that's all there is to it. Hell, you're Gloria Lynne!"

12

Years Go By

*I*never wanted to become "local," because then you get local money. Whatever level you've climbed to diminishes when you work in small dives or clubs that don't book comparable acts to your own. God knows, I wanted to sing more than anything, and temping was starting to bring me down.

But I did what I had to do.

I ran across a girl I knew, Amelia Patterson. She was the nanny for the Jackson Five. She traveled with them and took care of them when they were young. She asked me what I had been doing and I told her I had been working mostly as a temp.

"Gloria, would you do me a favor?" she said. "I need you for about a week." This was right after Michael Jackson had gotten burned shooting the Pepsi commercial. They were getting fan mail by the truckload. "We need someone to separate the mail. Michael's been getting fan mail from all over the world and the post office won't separate that mail from his business mail."

She thought I was the perfect person for the job because I could recognize the difference between the regular mail and an ASCAP or BMI check or other theatrical mail.

So, I went over to his father's office. Amelia had told the truth, because you couldn't get in the door for the mail. I sat there all day long, sorting and opening huge bags of mail. Every once in a while, I'd answer the phones. I'll say this, that boy is well loved. I experienced it firsthand. People were calling from all over the world. Little children, four and five years old, were calling the office "to speak to Michael Jackson." And they were speaking every language known to the world. I can sincerely say that I have attempted communication with every country on this planet.

I stayed there two weeks. They paid me well. I had never met Michael's father, Joe Jackson, before, but he recognized me. One day, he came in and brought me lunch and thanked me for helping them out. Curiously enough, he never once asked me what I was doing there. It was a little odd. Somehow I expected him to ask:

"Gloria Lynne, what are you doing here? What's happening with your career?"

But he didn't say anything.

I guess he thought it was none of his business. I did the job for him and he paid me well. But in all honesty, I couldn't be in the same position and have a Dakota Staton, or an Etta Jones, walk in knowing they were performers in the business, without asking them:

"What's up?"

I went to work for an answering service, Crestview Answering Service. The owner's name was Mary Jane Kniser. She was a great boss. She had a lot of aspiring actresses and showbiz types working there. The great thing about that job was you could come and go and still come back to a job. I stayed there a while, making ends meet, but continued to look for singing engagements.

Around this time, I started searching for a new record deal. All I got were rejections. It was hard for me to understand. I even got a little paranoid. I started thinking my name was on a list or something, because I'd walk in the door, and they'd look at me like I was crazy for even asking. You would have thought I was an amateur or an outsider, that I had no years in the business at all.

A record deal really could have eased my money situation and given me some sense of security.

I had also been spending a lot of money on attorney's fees, because my battles with Bernie Solomon and Everest were ongoing. So these fees, on top of my monthly expenses, were hard to maintain. But working at Crestview was very cool. The clientele was strictly celebrities. We answered phones for Kirk Douglas, Bette Davis, Tina Turner. All of the girls that worked for Crestview had other ambitions, so we had that in common. We had a ball in the office. It never felt like work.

A new club opened in the area, called the New York Club. I knew the two women who owned the club, so they asked me to perform there, from time to time. They wanted to set a jazz tone in the club, in hopes that they could get a regular following of jazz lovers. One night, I was up on the stage, singing "Watermelon Man," and I saw this young girl, down front, dancing and singing along with me. She looked familiar, but at first I couldn't place her face.

Then I realized it was Chaka Khan.

Once I recognized her, I pulled her up onstage and we sang the ending of the song together. After the show was over, Chaka asked me to do a favor for her. She wanted me to ride out to the Hollywood Hills with her, to Natalie Cole's house. I asked her why, and she said:

"Natalie's in kind of a bad way."

"I don't know Natalie," I told her. "I knew her father, but I've never met her. I don't think I should drop by her place unannounced."

Chaka insisted that I go.

Natalie had this beautiful home in the Hills. It was really incredible, and when she answered the door she said:

"Oh, Gloria Lynne's come to my house."

She was very sweet, very gracious. Well, we walked in there and she had other guests. There were several men there, hanging out. And they all looked at me like I was the Wicked Witch of the North. I said to myself: *I can't get into this woman's business.* I didn't know what they were smoking or drinking, but it was apparent that something had gone down. Natalie and the rest of them looked completely out of it. I sat down and immediately began to pray silently: *Whatever this is, Lord, take care of it. If Chaka feels that there is something I can lend to this situation, let me know what it is I can do to change this thing around.*

After I prayed, I turned to Chaka and said, "I have to go now."

The next night, Chaka came back to my show at the New York Club and she brought her whole family. I met her mother and aunts and cousins.

"Could you give Chaka a few words of encouragement?" her mother asked me. "We all look up to you, Miss Lynne, because you have sustained yourself in the business."

"I love Chaka," I told her. "You've got a very sweet baby. She's going to be all right. Chaka is going to do well."

And she has.

About six months later, I heard that Natalie Cole was back on her feet. She had cut all of that stuff loose. To see Natalie today, it's as if none of it ever happened. She's as beautiful as ever.

I had been trying to get a new band together and get back out there, in full swing. I started searching for a new trio. I scoped out clubs on my own that I could work in and make good money. Some jobs I booked before I had musicians. Now, some people didn't know that I had broken up with the Earl May Trio, though we had been apart for years. So, I called my friend Della Reese to see if she could help.

"Della," I told her, "I have a job to do and I need a musician."

"I'll send you Marvin," she said without hesitation.

Marvin Jenkins is a remarkable pianist. From that moment forward, he became my saving grace. He bailed me out of more tight spots. He was Della's pianist but he helped me out whenever I needed him. He was a wonderful musician and a really great person to be around. Marvin is very positive and encouraging. He was responsible for helping me get my mind back on my music.

Della's friendship is one I'll always treasure. I could call her for anything and I'd be sure to get a positive response. Della's a big kid at heart. I remember she had a beautiful doll collection and she would ask you:

"Are you going to come over and play?" And she was dead serious. She wanted you to come to her house and "play." I always loved being around her. She taught me, "never forget the little girl inside." She told me to cherish that little girl spirit within and never let it go. This is advice I live by. It was especially poignant for me because of all my childhood experiences.

I remember when Della got married. She had a wedding at Robert Schuller's Crystal Cathedral. Well, baby, a wedding it was indeed. It looked like something out of *The Arabian Nights*. She looked like a queen and her husband, Franklin Lett, looked like a king. They were so beautiful together. There aren't many events that leave a lasting impression, but this was certainly one. I was so pleased to be a guest, so happy I could be there to witness such a fine affair. It was absolutely beautiful. And I was truly happy for Della.

Around this time, I started working with Mickey Bass, who was fresh out of Howard University. He was my bass player. He had played with Carmen McRae and was always like a little brother to me. Greg Bandy was with me, too, as my drummer. We hit the road together in the eighties.

We had some good times out on the road. My girlfriend Bernice Lundy was traveling with me then. I had put together another good trio with a great sound. The only problem was that one of the musicians I had hired had a bit of a drinking problem. (I'll keep his name to myself.) Anyway, every gig we got, there would be some episode with this dude, either on-stage or off. He'd be so tore down some nights, we wouldn't know what to do with him. We'd be hanging out in the hotel suite and he'd come busting through the door:

"I'm going to kick everybody's ass in here!"

He didn't mean no harm. It was the liquor.

I'd have an engagement and we'd all be sitting there waiting on him. Well, he would be sitting in a bar somewhere talking about:

"I'm supposed to be with Gloria Lynne. But, hey, what the hell can I tell you?"

He stayed drunk. There was one time, I believe it was in Baltimore, where he didn't show up for the date. I was distraught because the place was packed! And I knew these people didn't feel like hearing any shit out of me, talking about, "I'm minus one musician."

So, we started the show without him. I sat down at the piano and I told Mickey:

"Just keep playing and I'll keep singing, and where I can tinkle, I will."

Mickey was another godsend. Now, I'm not a pianist by any means. I can do a little something, but that's about it. This was during the time when the union reps used to come around and sit in on shows to make sure the artists were being properly taken care of by the club management. They could also bust you for booking a gig as a vocalist and trio, then performing with something other than that. Wouldn't you know, a union rep showed up and saw me sitting there on that piano? But I couldn't concern myself with him at that moment, we had to get through the show.

Suddenly, clear out of the blue, I heard a keyboard accompanying me on a song. I didn't know where it was coming from. I said, Lord, something's not right here. I looked around, behind me, and I saw this black man with his electronic keyboard set up, and before I could say anything, he said:

"Keep singing. Sing anything you want, Miss Lynne, I know it all! I know everything you thought you were going to sing."

And he played it. It was pretty incredible. It was very touching to me, knowing that someone loved my voice and my music enough to show up and play and give something to my performance. But that night, it was absolutely necessary, because this other dude never did show up.

I remember once, we were performing in Washington, D.C., at the Hilton. Late one night, after our show, this musician was in his hotel room. Well, I guess he got up to go to the bathroom and forgot where he was. So he walked out in the hotel hallway buck naked. He didn't know where he was. When he realized what he had done, he came down the hallway, knocking on people's doors:

"Let me in!"

He came to our door.

"Don't open that door," Bernice said. "He's out there drunk."

Well, earlier that evening, he had lost all of my music, which I didn't find out until later. So he decided to check with the concierge and see if they had found the music. He marched down to the hotel lobby, over to the concierge, showing his natural born ass. It turns out, they had found it and were holding it there for me. He told the man:

"If you tell my boss that I lost her music, I'll kill you."

Now, the man was nervous. He called my room to try to get me to come down there and get him. And Bernice insisted:

"Leave him down there."

But they had to get him back in his room, because his black behind was down there strolling through the lobby, ass out. The next day, the concierge came over to me, whispering and shaking:

"Miss Lynne, did you get your music back? The gentleman here left it in the hallway and we held it for you. I would have told you before, but he threatened to kill me."

He was a funny drunk. Thank God, he's cleaned up his act now.

I'm glad to say he's totally clean and doing well.

I worked with so many different musicians in those years. I met the pianist David Benoit when he was just a kid. He was new on the scene and I was double-booked on New Year's, which was common for most singers. I had an engagement at Concerts-by-the-Sea and another job after that one, at one of the big hotels in the area.

Now, I had a piano player for the first job but not the second one, so I called around and my friend Cardella introduced me to David. He was just a freckle-faced kid from Hermosa Beach. His mom's a schoolteacher, I believe, and his father's a psychiatrist. Well, he played for me that night, and we hung together for a while after that. I knew he was a major talent, way back then. One night, I told him that I'd had a dream about him. In the dream, he was sitting at the piano in a huge, huge auditorium, onstage by himself. And now that dream was manifested because David Benoit is the biggest thing going on the contemporary jazz scene.

I got to know his parents well. They invited me to their home on several occasions. I went there on the Fourth of July one year, and I have never seen such a celebration. It was the biggest Independence Day celebration I have ever witnessed. You would have thought there was a war going on. They had guns fired and all the pomp and circumstance. It was a real patriotic affair.

David was the only white guy in my band, which was tricky at times, especially when we did shows in all-black areas. I remember once, we were in Detroit at a club called Dummy George, and David disappeared on me. The bass player and the drummer I used on that gig were local guys, so I didn't worry about them. But after traveling on the road for as many years as I had, I knew the dangers and my guard was always up.

Now, David was this little white boy from California, so I knew I had to watch out for him. I used to tell him when we were in certain areas to stay nearby, because things happened and I didn't want him to get wrapped up in any mess. He was tickled, I think, by my overprotectiveness, but I used to tell him:

"David, stay where I can see you."

So, after the show one night, I didn't know where he had gone. I went back to my hotel room, worried sick. Hours later, David shows up grinning, talking about how the guys took him out on the town to see the sights. I was so upset. I didn't know what happened to him. David got a kick out of me. I guess he never expected to have a second mother traveling with him out on the road. He was young at the time, but he was also grown.

After I came off the road, I went right back to Crestview Answering Service. I worked very hard to make things happen in the music business, but slowly it all started to slip away. I never chose to leave the business, but without management and without a record company behind me, it became almost impossible to get work. I was continuously rejected by record companies. I couldn't get a deal to save my life. It's like I looked up one day and no one knew my name. Throughout my life, I devoted nearly all of my time and energy to my career. There was rarely any downtime. So, I never thought I'd be in a place where I couldn't work as a singer, where people in the business would be unfamiliar with my work. It was very frightening.

The artist's life can be all-consuming. It takes over everything, your mind, your thoughts, your conversation, your interests. Then, next thing you know, what you do for a living becomes who you are. You can't discuss anything else, you don't involve yourself in anything other than the art, and your interests become very limited. In retrospect, I can appreciate the time I had away from the business. All of the temp jobs and other odd jobs helped me to realize that I had another side to my brain.

Now, living through the experience of being on the outside of things was frustrating as hell, because, of course, I'd rather be singing than typing correspondence but evidently these were necessary lessons for me. Through this experience, I became a whole person.

It's funny when you look back at what your initial intentions were and how things actually turned out. I know now that my move to California had very little to do with my career in the music business but everything to do with my personal growth and healing. Time away from New York and everything that was familiar to me gave me time to work on myself.

Those years made a woman out of me.

Even with all of the ups and downs, I hadn't really contemplated leaving California, until Neil Cole came out again to see me in Los Angeles.

"Are you still interested in doing the nostalgia concert?" he asked me. "I've got Earl and everybody together, if you want to do it."

Years had gone by since Neil first approached me about getting back together with the Earl May Trio. And I knew that he hadn't forgotten the project, because Neil is a real go-getter, he follows through on everything. Very little was happening for me in LA, so when he made the offer, I said:

"That sounds like a plan."

I packed up and went home. It was 1986.

Home

God, let this be the right move for me. Go before me and make the way smooth and easy. I'm stepping out on faith, Lord, and I pray that each decision I make is the fulfillment of your will. There are days when I have trouble keeping my head up, and some days, I feel very lonely. But I have found peace in your Word. For I know you are with me always. That is your promise. It's been a long, winding road and I am truly grateful for my many blessings.

God, you know my heart. All I've ever wanted to do was to sing your praises, to allow your light to shine through me. And if someone can feel joy in my music and life in my songs, then I know I have done my part. Father God, help me to stay focused. I sometimes miss the mark, and I let the obvious obstruct my view. But in quiet times, I know that your Grace has lifted me. You are the strength of my life. I don't know what lies ahead, but I thank you, Father, for showing me the way. I thank you for healing my mind, my heart, and my spirit. I will go forward with a holy boldness, knowing that you are my defense and my deliverance.

Amen.

13

Home Revisited

The first nostalgia concert was held at the Brooklyn Academy of Music. It is a gorgeous music hall with beautiful architecture. It's right in downtown Brooklyn. For the third time in my career, I felt like I was starting all over again. The Brooklyn Academy of Music might as well have been the Apollo Amateur, some forty years ago. I had been out of the public eye in New York for so many years. A lot of my fans on the East Coast didn't know what had happened to me. Some thought I was out of the business altogether, some thought I was living in Europe somewhere, and some thought I was dead. The Earl May Trio and I hadn't performed together in over twenty years. So, I didn't know what to expect from the audience. I was in my dressing room, and of course, I was nervous, then here comes Neil. He came backstage to tell me:

"There's standing room only, Gloria. The show is sold out, and there's a line out the door of people trying to get in."

That evening, when I hit the stage, memories from the sixties flooded my mind. Earl struck up the band, and to coin an old phrase, it was just like old times. The crowd let us know we had been missed. They loved us. I sang my songs from the Everest years, and with each song the audience became more ecstatic. By the end of the concert, the auditorium reached a fever pitch. The crowd was on its feet. We got a standing ovation.

Honestly, the reaction of the audience that night convinced me that

I had made the right move. I decided, right then, to get back in the business, full force, because to make a comeback and get that kind of reception was very reassuring. It was a sign that I was doing the right thing, in the right place. It was much more than I expected, because times change and so do people. After the Brooklyn Academy of Music, we did another reunion concert at Lincoln Center and the reaction was just as strong.

In all of the years I worked in New York, I had never performed at Lincoln Center. It is the home of opera, jazz, classical music, symphony orchestras. It has quite a legacy. Lincoln Center is considered one of the greatest halls of music in this country. So it was very cool to be headlining there, especially with my old buddies Earl May, Herman Foster, and Grassella Oliphant. Neil had really done it. He promised me a sold-out house and he delivered. The concert was backed by the Phillip Morris Company. They made sure everything was laid out for us. It was one of the most glamorous and exciting evenings in memory.

I will always love Neil Cole for taking me by the hand and bringing me back to New York. Coming back, and performing the reunion concerts, gave me a fresh outlook on my talent and my career. I was able to put things in their proper perspective. And seeing Earl and Herman and Grassella felt so good, I didn't want it to end. It was extraordinary. I have Neil to thank for that. He's still doing his thing. He manages the Lenox Lounge up in Harlem, which came back to life once he laid hands on it. It's appeared in a lot of films and music videos. It is now one of Harlem's landmarks.

Soon after my Lincoln Center debut, my friend Bernice Lundy called to say that she wanted to include me in a spread for *Essence* magazine, to be called "Jazz's Grand Divas." Bernice was well connected in the fashion and beauty industry. She once owned a modeling agency. Bernice is another go-getter. She has always kept herself very much on the move and in the know. I was happy to appear in the magazine. Susan Taylor, the editor in chief, tells me, to this day, how my music brought her together with her new husband. They are both big fans and they grooved to my music while they were dating. The spread was great publicity for me, but more than that, it was a testament to the years I had put in the business and motivated me to keep on going. I remember during my photo shoot the photographer asked me:

"Who would you like to listen to?"

Well, I couldn't decide, so I started rattling off my favorite male singers: Jeffrey Osborne, Peabo Bryson, Joe Williams, Billy Eckstine, Jon Lucien, Arthur Prysock. Then, I said:

"Put on Luther."

I've always loved Luther Vandross. Baby, they put on Luther's album and my pictures turned out just divine. The whole layout was beautiful. It also featured Dakota Staton, Abbey Lincoln, Betty Carter, Nancy Wilson, and Carmen McRae. There were mentions, of course, of the pioneers, Billie Holiday, Sarah Vaughan, Dinah Washington, and Ella Fitzgerald. It was very special to me, since I had just got back in town. It was another warm welcome.

When I first arrived back in New York, I stayed at the Ramada Inn in midtown Manhattan. I really hadn't had the time to take it all in yet, because once I got to the city, it was all about preparing for the concert engagements. There was so much buzz and excitement surrounding my concerts, I barely had enough time to unpack. Then one day it hit me: Mom wasn't there. Nothing attached to the life we had together was there. My father was gone. Aunt Elsie had passed on. Helen had her life with her family. Harry was living with his girlfriend of many years. And my son, Richard, was still back in Los Angeles.

I looked up one day and I was alone.

Naturally, there were many acquaintances and people that I knew who were still living in the city, but no one who was really close to me was there. The transition was odd because New York is my hometown, so I never expected to go "home" and be so out of sync with what was happening.

It had been over thirteen years since I left New York. And, of course, things had changed. Everything cost a fortune. Manhattan looked even more crowded than before. The atmosphere felt different to me. The city was crowded and dirty and loud. After living near the ocean and among palm trees, it took me a minute to snap back. Some of the old clubs and restaurants that I used to go to were gone. Although I had popped in and out of town to do different jobs over the years, I hadn't stuck around long enough to notice all of the changes. I would do a show, then turn right back around and head to LA. I tried to settle in the best I could, but I couldn't shake this lonely feeling.

Harry was happy when I came back. I remember him saying, "Well, you're home. At least nobody has to worry about you now."

He was living with a woman at the time. He had a son by her, Steven. He also had a set of twin daughters by another woman. Harry and I stayed in touch over the years, for Richard's sake, and also because we considered ourselves friends. A lot of time had passed, though, and he had his life and I had mine. I knew I could call on him if I needed him, but we rarely engaged in casual conversation. My old boyfriend Michael and I kept in touch. We talked every once in a while after I left LA. After all the fanfare at Lincoln Center, Earl May and the guys had other gigs to do, so they weren't really around after our reunion concerts. With all the hoopla over, it all fizzled down to me, sitting alone in a hotel room.

A visitor in my own hometown.

I don't think there's a lonelier place on the planet than New York City. Although there are 10 million people in the streets, there is a feeling in New York of "you're on your own" that can really get to you. It's a very strange paradox of being surrounded by people, but all alone in the crowd. No familiar faces, no one to bump into on the street who knows your name, who you can hang out with. It's everybody and nobody all at the same time.

I remember getting very sick around this time. I had a very bad cold, so I used to go across the street, from the Ramada Inn to the corner deli, and get soup every day and bring it back to my hotel room. My room was dull and drab. It had very little sunlight. There really is no sunlight in midtown Manhattan because of all the tall buildings. There was nonstop noise outside my window, cabs and buses and people. And the hotel hallways were full of tourists, running in and out of their rooms. The cleaning people would come and they didn't speak English half the time, so it wasn't like you could stir up a conversation with them. And when you're lonely, you'll talk to anyone who'll listen.

But nighttime was the worst time.

Melancholy crept in like an evil spirit who had come to do me in. When night fell, the vibe in that room changed to something sad and lonely. Sleep was my only escape. I forced myself to sleep every night, and some nights the feelings of desolation were so bad, I wished someone would come and just knock me in the head, so I could pass out.

I knew I was going to have to get right back out there and drum up some work. After the rough time I'd had in California trying to land a deal and get steady work, I believed New York would be more receptive. I was anxious to get my career back on a roll. But New York had something else in mind. I was in a haze and could not see my way through.

The only person I felt close to was Helen. When she found out I was sick, she asked Harry's son, Steven, to come and get me.

"You can't live up there in that hotel, eating deli food every day," she said. "You have to come to my house." So Steven came and got me, and when I got to Helen's she said, "Sissy, you got to stay here until you get on your feet. You don't need to be staying in no hotel."

So I moved in with Helen and that's how I found out she was gravely ill.

Helen never told me how sick she was. The only thing she told me was that she was "not feeling good." I had to move in there to see for myself. Helen was a diabetic but she was having all kinds of complications. The doctors had her on forty different pills. And her eyesight was beginning to go. It was really frightening for her because none of the doctors could tell her exactly what was wrong. I went through the muck and mire trying to get help for Helen.

After a few short weeks, I had booked some club dates, so I asked Helen to come along with me, the way we used to do. She started feeling like her old self again. She and I were hanging out in nightclubs and partying and carrying on. She was feeling good and looking better. Her grandchildren were around the house then and they couldn't believe the change in her. And as far as I was concerned, they weren't treating her the way I felt she deserved to be treated. Helen would ask them to do things and they'd walk right past her. So I had to play the wicked witch. I'd snap at them:

"Don't you hear your grandmother talking to you?"

Hell, I knew these kids before they were born.

I lived at Helen's house for nearly two years. One night, after I had come home from performing at St. Ann's Church in Brooklyn, I got into a bad argument with one of Helen's kids. I don't even remember what it was all about, probably something small, but things turned ugly. There was a lot of tension in the house, mostly because of Helen's illness. Everybody was worried and stressed out. So emotions were flying everywhere and it turned into a big mess. People started saying things they didn't mean, and everybody's feelings got hurt. I didn't want to leave Helen but I knew that night it was time for me to go.

I called my girlfriend Bernice Lundy. She was living up on Riverside Drive in Manhattan. When I called her, I was crying so much, I could hardly speak. She said, "I'm coming to get you." And I left Helen's house that night.

Now the entire time I lived at Helen's, I worked and pulled in my share. I tried to make her as comfortable as possible. It was hard enough knowing that Helen was not well, but after all of the hardships I had been through in my life, this argument with one of her children was my breaking point. Everything swelled to the surface. It had cut too close to the bone.

Now, Bernice was staying with her son. They had a two-bedroom apartment. The one room she had, she shared with me. She had a boyfriend at the time and I remember I used to have to call before I came home at night: "Is it clear?" Here we were, good and grown, carrying on like a couple of teenagers. I was so grateful to Bernice and her son, because I really didn't have anyplace to go. I love her for it. She made me feel at home in a tight situation. And she didn't have to do it, but she did.

Four months after I left Helen's house, she passed away. Her daughter, Ernestine, called to tell me. She took it hard and so did I. She told me, the day Helen died, her baby granddaughter, Kimberly, crawled up on Helen's lap, latched on to her, and would not let her go. If somebody tried to pick her up off of Helen, the baby would have a tantrum. She knew death was on her.

I lost my dearest friend when Helen died. She was a godsend in my life. We were friends our entire lives. Helen was the closest thing I had to a sister. I used to be able to pick up the phone and tell her almost anything and be guaranteed a positive response. I've stayed in touch with her children over the years, especially Ernestine, who I saw come into the world. I think of Helen always. I miss her dearly.

Helen's death put me in a different frame of mind. I began to think that maybe New York was not the place for me. It was such a sad and confusing time. I had given it three years, but things weren't clicking the way I had hoped. I was performing in a lot of nightclubs, but I could not get a record deal. I continued to get rejection after rejection from every label I went to. Every day I'd tell my friend Bernice:

"I'm going back to California. I'm going to buy my plane ticket today."

She and I were still living together, so she knew firsthand how frustrated I was. I wanted to stop imposing on her, too. She was kind enough to let me stay with her, but I needed my own space and so did she.

One day, I was looking in the paper, the *Village Voice*, I believe it was, and I saw an ad for a sublease. It was the first time I had ever heard of sublets. So I set up an appointment with the owner. It was a last-ditch effort because I was truly ready to get the hell out of Dodge. The woman who owned the apartment interviewed a lot of people, but God was with me.

"I'm going to give *you* the apartment," she said.

It was on 106th Street between Broadway and Amsterdam Avenue. When I walked in, the place was fully furnished. It had everything—pillowcases, plates, pots. She and her husband were both professors. He was over in Italy teaching and she taught at Rutgers University. They were both getting ready to go on sabbatical. So I stayed there for one year. The rent was nine hundred dollars a month.

While I was living in that apartment, I experienced some really, truly broke days. I mean, I was living on the edge. I was trying to scrape together work but things were slow and money was even slower coming in. I never will forget the day I gathered up all the change I had lying around the apartment. I put it in a small can and walked down to a neighborhood bank that was on 96th and Broadway at the time. I don't even think that bank is still there. Anyway, I was really desperate. I had gotten down to my very last.

So, I went in, feeling embarrassed and ashamed, but needing the money. I spoke to a Hispanic man that worked there. And I told him very quietly, "I'm down to my last dime. I have these coins and I'd like to turn them in for cash." He understood and without saying a word that man took my coins, left me standing there, and came back with my cash. He just smiled an understanding smile and told me to take care of myself. I will never forget his kindness. Whoever he was, he has no idea how he saved my life.

I was under a lot of stress to make things happen, but I learned, you can't force it. I didn't socialize a lot because I didn't have the money to go out. So that left me at home doing a lot of thinking, which if you're not careful, can make you crazy. I thought about friends that I knew who had regular jobs and were looking forward to their pensions and all that. They had property and investments. It's a real trip when you think about most artists' lives. Too many are living on the edge of society, with no guarantees and very little security.

During this time, I heard from my old buddy Charles Champion back in California. Although I was moving every five minutes, Charles always kept in touch. He wrote me to tell me he had gotten married and sent me a picture of himself and his bride. I remember thinking that Charles was such a free spirit, that marriage may be more of a burden than a blessing for him. Anyway, when I saw his wedding picture, I called him and said:

"Charles, what was going on with you when you got married? You both are standing there looking scared to death."

I didn't find out all the details then, but the marriage lasted only two years or so.

And baby, when Charles's divorce came through, the whole wide world knew about it.

He sent me a sweet letter and a hysterical picture of himself. In the picture, there was Charles, standing in his living room, buck naked, with only a red, heart-shaped balloon covering up his privates. The balloon read, "I Love You," and the whole apartment was filled with multicolored balloons. In the letter, he said, "I was so happy to be free, I had to get naked." That's Charles.

Around this time, I hooked up with Bobby Timmons, who was an incredible pianist; Ike Isaac, a bass player who was married to Carmen McRae at one time; and the incomparable Grady Tate on drums. They were a bad-ass trio, baby! We did some wicked things together. We hit the road together.

The road was just as much a trip in the eighties as it was in the sixties. We did a lot of gigs up and down the eastern seaboard, from Boston to Baltimore. I was really pleased with the work we did together. Audiences used to go nuts when they heard us. But sadly, Bobby Timmons died in his thirties. He had a liver condition that could not be cured. It was tragic. Everybody in the music world knew how gifted Bobby was. It broke all of our hearts to see him pass away so young.

My friend Phyllis White was traveling with me. She was like a niece to me and I was very close to her mother, Dot. Now, Dot helped me through a lot of rough spots.

During the time I was staying out at Helen's house in Long Island, Richard was still living in an apartment that my girlfriend Frankie Hill and I shared in Brentwood, California. One morning, Richard called me in a state of flux. He was upset because the U.S. Marshals were there, trying to put him out of the apartment. Now, Frankie and I were living in that apartment when I left to come back to New York. I still paid her half the rent every month because I didn't want to let go of the apartment, just in case I decided to go back there. I was spending money to maintain that apartment as well as paying for my share of Helen's household expenses.

Anyway, Richard was angry because he knew I had a lot of nice things in that apartment, and he didn't want to leave my things in there. I didn't know what to do because, usually, by the time the Marshals show up to throw you out, you've been given a lot of warnings. If they come to kick you out, they don't leave until they do. So I told Richard to leave everything there.

What else could we do?

Frankie, evidently, had not been paying her share of the rent, but she never told me. We could have worked something out, if only I had known. Instead, I just kept sending my share of the rent out to her every month, unaware of any problems she was having. When I came to New York, I only brought the bare necessities with me. I left my nice jewelry, a lot of clothing, and all my furniture in that Brentwood apartment. There were a lot of things in there that had sentimental value, and all of it I had worked very hard to get. I lost it all.

Richard stayed with a friend in LA for a few days, then he flew to New York. When he finally hooked up with me at Helen's, we had to find a place for him to stay. Instead of cramping up Helen's space even more, Dot called and said Richard could stay at her house. She knew our situation and wanted to help. She and her husband, Nat, lived in Queens, and they had an extra room. Dot showed me what true sisterhood meant. They treated Richard like family. I will always love and appreciate what they did for me. At the time, Richard was not in good health. He was still suffering with his back injury, so I had to do what I could to get him back on his feet.

Phyllis helped me out a lot by traveling with me. We went on a lot of jobs together. She had a military background, so I didn't have to worry about a thing if she was with me. Phyllis ran a tight ship. There would be no shit going down if she was around. I remember once, we did a gig in Boston. I was performing at a very high-class nightclub there. I loved clubs like this one, where everything was laid out for you and you wanted for nothing. God knows we worked in a lot of dumps over the years, where you had to get dressed in the owner's office because they had no facilities and no dressing rooms for the artists. This nightclub was definitely on the money. It was gorgeous. It was a theater in the round. The stage circled as you sang. We had been there a few nights already and each night was jam-packed, but this particular night was unusually crowded.

During the show, Phyllis noticed that there were a lot of couples in the audience. Well, when I started singing "Love, I Found You," she noticed a couple who was sitting down front, paying a lot of attention to each other. Suddenly, she didn't see the woman anymore. Next thing you know, a waiter came along, pulled the tablecloth up, and here comes the woman out from under the table. She had slid up under the table and planted her face between the man's legs. They were having oral sex right there in that club. That woman had hiked up her skirt and got down on her knees to please this dude during the show. So while she was down there handling her business, I was onstage just singing my heart out.

We could not believe it.

And the crazy part about it is the owner somehow blamed me for this nonsense. He came over to their table and asked the couple to leave. Then, come to find out, they weren't the only ones carrying on. I saw people hugging and rubbing and kissing all through the show, but when I sang "Love, I Found You," it looked like the whole place had fallen in love. The owner told me later they found people all in the bathrooms cutting loose during the show.

"Miss Lynne, we were anticipating you coming and singing all these love songs," he said, "but we've never experienced *anything* like this."

I never went back to that club. And they never asked.

Phyllis and I had fun together. She is a very talented hairstylist, so my hair was always whipped. She also helped dress me. Phyllis would stay on the lookout for things she thought I might like. If she saw a dress or a pair of shoes or a piece of jewelry, she would buy it for me. She knew my taste better than anybody. Phyllis was a single mom raising her daughter, Regina, by herself. I always admired Phyllis's sense of discipline, especially on the road, because, from town to town, you could find yourself in the damnedest situations.

Once, we were in Washington, D.C., appearing at a nightclub on a four-day engagement. My boss told me, at the end of the night, to come back to his office to pick up my salary. Now, Phyllis usually took care of the payroll, but he insisted that I, personally, come pick it up. Phyllis and I decided we would both go get the money. We went back to his office but he wasn't there. *Oh, here we go again, the man ran off with the money,* I thought.

So, Phyllis went to find him. In the meantime, his brother shows up. He came into the office and said:

"Gloria, I have your payroll."

I really didn't think anything of it. After all, he was the boss's brother. But then he switched up on me. He started telling me how much and how long he had been in love with me. He was very descriptive. I began to feel a little uneasy. There I was, with this man who I had never set eyes on, in a very small, tight office, and he was talking all this love stuff. I just smiled at his flirtation. I didn't say a word. Then he reached down toward his pants and I thought he was reaching for my check, but what he reached for shocked the hell out of me. The man sat there and pulled out the biggest, longest, hardest penis I had ever seen in my life. It was so erect, he had to struggle to get it out of his pants.

"This is what *you* need!" he said.

He started flinging himself around in front of me, which I guess was my cue to go for it, you know, grab it. Well, I was so stunned by his advances that, all of a sudden, I started laughing. I just fell out laughing at the man and could not stop. I laughed so hard, I was in tears. This didn't stop him. He didn't care. And he was a very distinguished-looking businessman. By all appearances, he was the kind of man you take home to mama—handsome, intelligent, well dressed. Well, who knew he had a freaky side? I never would have guessed, by looking at him, that he was capable of such a thing. He was a damn exhibitionist. There's no two ways about it.

By the time Phyllis walked back into the office, he had got himself together. But when I told her what happened she hollered! I mean, we embarrassed the man so bad. He got up and left the room. We got our money from the boss and got on out of there. After that, we vowed to never leave each other alone with anyone, unless we made it perfectly clear that we wanted to be alone.

When my ex-husband, Harry, realized I was trying to make a comeback in the business, he called my old manager Duke Wade. He told him:

"Gloria's back and she needs your help."

Duke Wade, I tell you, ain't nobody else like him. He was semiretired from the business when I came back home to New York. I was scheduled to appear at Carlos I in the Village, so Harry asked him to come by and catch my show.

When Duke walked into the club that night, I was thrilled to death. I was so happy to see him, looking good and still the same ol' Duke. He told me he had taken on a nine-to-five job and had been on the job for a while. Duke was always very devoted to his family: his wife, Carol, and his four kids, Michael, Mark, Mona, and Reba. He told me:

"Gloria, I'm not doing too much in the business anymore, but I'll make some calls for you and see what happens."

Ironically, the first job he got for me was at the Apollo Theater, which is where we met all those years ago. From that moment to this one, Duke has worked very hard to keep me working.

As a black manager, Duke has never gotten the breaks he deserves. He never had access to the same clubs, money, or bookings, as other managers with half his experience. The kind of opportunities he tries to provide for the artists he represents are not available to him, for no other reason than the color of his skin. Duke has more experience in the industry than any agent out there, but he has frequently been given second-rate treatment by club owners, record companies, nightclubs, and radio stations.

He has endured being disrespected and disregarded throughout his career as a manager.

Nonetheless, he has a resilient spirit and a positive outlook. He has helped more careers than I can name. Duke will find a way out of no way. He knows what's out there and what he's up against, and he has found ways to outmaneuver the best of them.

As artists, we look to our managers for guidance and support, and Duke has given me that. There really aren't enough words to say about all that he's given me, because he's so close to me. I can't imagine doing what I do without him.

I was working at Carlos I, down in the Village, when I met Ann Rubino and Mary Ann Niehaus. They came to see me perform there regularly. They were longtime fans of mine and really wanted to meet me. So, one night, after the show, Ann came up to me. She said:

"Can I show you some of my poems?"

I didn't mind, so I took her book home and started reading it. Some of her poems were really quite beautiful, so I put them to music. In a very short time, Ann and I became friends. We wrote a lot of songs together.

I remember the time I worked in a club called McHale's. It was on the upper West Side, around Eightieth Street and Amsterdam Avenue. McHale's played people like Chaka Khan and Ashford & Simpson, all the big names would run through there. This particular night, Jon Voight, the actor, came to see my show. He came with Ann Rubino and Mary Niehaus.

After the show, we took him up to Sutton's, up in Harlem. Now, Sutton's was famous for their chicken and waffles, like Wells', which was the first up in Harlem to do the chicken and waffle combo. Well, we had a ball up there. We ate damn near everything on the menu and Jon kept us laughing the whole time. Jon was surrounded by women and I was surrounded by white folks, and there we were sitting up in Harlem in the middle of the night, whooping and hollering and having a good time. When it came time to pay the bill, Jon went into his wallet and pulled out his credit card. Yvonne Redcross, the owner, came over and said:

"Oh, we don't take credit cards here." And Jon didn't have a penny on him. Here he was the big movie star without a dime.

So I said, "Hey, Jon, don't worry about it, we'll take care of it."

But he never got over it. I never will forget how disgusted he was that he didn't treat us all to dinner. He was the nicest person and we loved his company. So who cared? He was Jon Voight. My evening ended on a high note because that's when I got my kiss. Jon and I said good night and we kissed right on the lips. It was short, but very sweet.

Meanwhile, the Apollo Theater job that Duke had booked me on was coming up. I was scheduled to perform with Skitch Henderson and the New York Pop Orchestra. Ann and Mary Ann showed up to the concert and they brought with them Herb and Janette Zuckerman. Herb Zuckerman was the former mayor of Palisades Park, New Jersey.

After the show, the Zuckermans came backstage to meet me. We talked for a while and they asked me what my plans were.

I told them, "This is probably it for me. I'm going back to California and settle down."

Well, they didn't hold their tongues. They didn't know me, but you would have thought these people were my long-lost relatives. Herb Zuckerman said:

"You're too talented to leave. Don't give up your career."

"You don't need to go back to California," his wife, Janette, said.

It was very uncharacteristic of me to tell all my personal business to strangers, but I told them all about the frustrations I was experiencing with record companies, with my finances, and with my housing situation, because after my sublet was up, I didn't know where I was going to live. So, without missing a beat, they said:

"Oh, we'll take care of that."

I told them I was paying nine hundred for my sublet, which I thought was steep, but I hadn't realized that New York rents had gotten so outrageous. The Zuckermans kept track of my apartment hunt. They asked constantly:

"Did you find a place?"

I told them I was trying to find something in the nine-hundred-dollar range.

"You're not going to find it," they said.

Janette suggested the Princeton Building, up on Ninety-fifth Street between Broadway and Amsterdam. I made the application and called Janette to let her know.

"Well, which apartment is it?" she asked.

I told her the one-bedrooms were going for $1,450 and the two-bedrooms were $2,500 a month, so I had chosen a one-bedroom. I never will forget Janette telling me:

"The one-bedroom is not big enough for you and Richard. Get the two-bedroom. Go ahead, take it." I couldn't bring myself to ask them to pay so much rent for me. I didn't know them well and I thought it was great of them to offer to pay at all. So I took a one-bedroom apartment.

It was a beautiful apartment. The Zuckermans bought my furniture, paid all my monthly bills, and gave me $2,500 a month to sustain myself, so I could write and devote all my time to my craft. Herb Zuckerman is

dead now, but I love him. I never will forget his generosity. Janette Zuckerman and I always stay in touch. But these two angels stuck by me when
I was in desperate need of friendship. They helped nurture my career back
to health and they are really the cause of my staying in New York.

Janette is a high roller in Atlantic City. She knows everybody there.
In fact, she produced a few concerts for me at the Bally Grand in Atlantic
City. She would put up the money for the show, what's called a four-waller,
and our shows did very well. Whenever I played there, she made sure that
my accommodations were always top of the line, that I had everything I
needed and then some. She and Herb were always looking out for me.
They had a deep respect for my talent and never wavered in their support
of my career.

One night, I was preparing for a show and Janette insisted that I go
to my room to relax.

"Take a bubble bath, Gloria. Relax."

I told her that I was hungry and I wanted to get some food first. Well,
she said:

"Go to your room and I'll take care of it."

I went to my room only to find a Jacuzzi full of bubbles, champagne,
and sandwiches, and to top it all off she sent a butler. See, Janette Zuckerman always gets butler service when she shows up in Atlantic City. I
heard a knock on the door, then in walks a man dressed in a tuxedo with
white gloves, a bow tie and cummerbund, the whole nine yards.

"I've come to feed you, Miss Lynne," he says. "The staff tells me you're
hungry."

I couldn't believe it, because I never really associated "high class" with
Atlantic City, but it's there, you just have to know the right people. So
there I sat in a tub full of bubbles, with a glass of champagne and a lovely
man in a tux hand-feeding me sandwich after sandwich. Now, I was hungry
but I didn't want to ruin the ambience, nor did I want to bite the man's
fingers off. So, I laid back and played the part.

Around this time, I had Billy Kaye with me on drums, and a Japanese
pianist, Kinichi Shamazu. Kinichi was new to America and had just recently begun working with me. He was a talented musician. He learned
my entire book in a matter of weeks. He had great respect for music and
great respect for me. Kinichi had degrees in math and science but chose
music as his career. My longtime friend and pianist Herman Foster inspired

him to pursue a career as a pianist. He really admired Herman's style of playing. And I hired him because he sounded like Herman.

Well, Kinichi could play, but he couldn't speak English worth a damn. Right in the middle of our show that night, I noticed a long pause. I didn't hear Billy Kaye playing. So I'm just standing there in front of the audience, smiling and grinning, waiting for Billy Kaye to hit the next number. I didn't want to turn all the way around, so I look over at Kinichi and I'm whispering:

"What happened?"

He whispered something back that I couldn't understand.

So I said, "What?"

"Heseep," he said.

"What?"

"Heseep."

I still didn't know what he was saying, but I was trying to play it off.

"Kinichi, I can't hear you. What happened?"

"He seep!" he said, big and loud and into the mike.

I turned around and there was Billy Kaye, knocked out to the world, asleep at the drums. Well, the audience went up. We all fell out laughing.

I've worked with some wonderful, talented musicians over the years, but I must say, I got back my old groove when I met Roy Meriwether. I believe it was around 1987. Kinichi had gone back to Japan, so I lost him. I was going crazy trying to find a pianist. And a lot of other talented guys around town were committed to other singers or they were out doing their own thing. I was going nuts, because I had jobs coming up but didn't have a band. I really needed a pianist and I wanted the best I could find.

My friend Bernice saved the day, again.

"Oh, I know a piano player," she said. "His name is Roy Meriwether."

Now, Roy is a genius. And sometimes the geniuses like to be left alone. He really doesn't have to play for anyone but himself. He's done me the great honor of acting as my musical director and accompanist for the last twelve years.

Roy comes from an extremely gifted family of ministers and musicians. There's a whole gang of those Meriwethers. His father was a big minister at a church in South Jersey. When Roy was five years old he was sitting in church one day when the pianist didn't show, so his father sat him down at the piano and had him play for the entire service. He's been playing every since. He still plays for his father's church and works with the choir. He's a self-made musician. Over the years, he has studied and trained, but really, Roy is a raw musician. His talent is completely organic. There's really nothing you can say but that he's God-gifted. If you've ever witnessed his playing, you know that it is out of this world. His gift has little to do with academic conventions. Roy is connected to his instrument in a way that very few can claim.

Behind the scenes, we cut the fool. Now, we fight like cats and dogs. And when Roy decides to trip out on us, we just get some water to sprinkle on him, because we know he's got to be crazy, because the boy is a genius. When you're that brilliant, you're entitled to a couple of moments of insanity per day. It's only fair. Roy's a lot of fun. I love being around him. He's always got a nice joke to tell you, something to tickle you. And he always makes me feel like I'm the biggest star in the world. Ain't no star bigger than me. He's been my right hand. And I love him dearly.

14

Pick Up the Pieces

In the latter part of '89, I landed a record deal with Joe Fields at Muse Records. After three years of searching, I was happy to finally sign a new recording contract. I found out there was yet another hurdle to jump in the business: age. I knew New York was going to be a whole different trip because times had changed, but I never thought my age would be a deterrent to getting a deal. If anything, I thought all my years of experience would be an added plus.

I was in for a rude awakening.

Before signing with Muse, I was getting turned away from record companies who didn't think my sound was young enough or hip enough. My intention was to bring to the table my years of experience and a finely crafted style. I still believed there was a place for my music, my voice, and my style. Honestly, I have never thought of music as something that dies or fades. I can sing jazz, pop, gospel, soul, R&B, all of it. And I don't need twenty-five musicians or dancers or special effects onstage with me to do it. In my day, we perfected our form with trios. There were no more than four of us on the stage at one time. In my day, we didn't even have backup singers. Either you could produce the sound or you couldn't. You had to stand and deliver.

I have a great deal of respect for women who have been able to maneuver around age barriers, like Tina Turner and Patti LaBelle. It's hard work trying to stay on top in a business that changes on a dime.

Nowadays, there is more of an interest in rap, hip-hop, and even R&B has taken on a slightly different sound than the sound of, say, the fifties and sixties. Traditional jazz is being replaced by instrumental "smooth" jazz. In fact, some of the old jazz labels have folded or been bought out by huge corporations. The corporate element in the industry is new as well. Large record labels are run by accountants and lawyers. It's nothing like back in the day, when creativity and imagination were appreciated. It's a whole different ball game.

Nonetheless, the young artists are getting paid for their music, which is definitely a switch.

I considered all of the great work I had done down through the years and how much things had changed. It was really astounding. By now, I had at least thirty-five or forty albums to my credit. I was still associated with hit tunes like "I Wish You Love" and "Love, I Found You." All those hit albums on Everest and Mercury I recorded, hit singles like "Lonely and Sentimental," "Soul Serenade," and "Impossible," had to count for something. I still believed in the superior quality of this music, and I knew there was more where that came from. Surely, I thought, there's a place for this kind of timeless music. But record companies wanted bankable talent. The market they use to measure what was hot or not was an under-thirty-five crowd. Kids.

What is so disturbing about what's happening in the business today is the way young people are being thrust into the limelight with little or no preparation. I do not understand how record execs can allow a kid to record and not know what he's doing. It's reprehensible. A lot of young people are coming in with no knowledge, no education, no musical training but given quickie deals, then sent flying out the damn door.

I've never seen more one-hit wonders.

I thought things were bad when I was coming up, but the music business today is ridiculous. The kind of money they're dangling in front of these kids' faces is more than a lot of artists of my generation have seen in an entire career.

And there is very little mentoring going on.

These kids have almost no one to turn to for assistance or guidance. Record companies are so hungry for that next hit, to make that next dollar, that the age of grooming a career and ensuring its longevity is long gone. It's more treacherous now than ever before. There is so much more money at stake. Today, black music is internationally marketed and promoted. And with all of the new technical innovations, things are happening at such a terrific speed that you can't keep up. There's a lot more at stake, money-wise, which creates a different kind of atmosphere in the industry. One that has less to do with quality and more to do with dollars.

Anyway, I was very optimistic about my new record company. Joe Fields had a long, successful track record in the industry. He'd worked with people like Gladys Knight & the Pips, Donna Summer, and a lot of big singers that were hot in the seventies. His career spanned decades in the business. On the Muse label, he had recorded James Moody, Sonny Stitt, Kenny Barron, Etta Jones, Morgana King, Dakota Staton, Kenny Burrell, Della Griffin, and Arnett Cobb. A lot of the jazz people from the old days recorded with Joe Fields. The only problem with Joe was he was not a creative person, although he appreciated quality. He was one of the few who would give a jazz artist a contract, but he had very little to offer, artistically. At Muse, there was very little marketing and promotion done for newly released material. The word was, if you worked with Muse, you had to be rich, so you could do your own publicity.

With Muse, I was looking to do some good work. I wasn't looking for any hype or fanfare. I've been in the business long enough to know how to work around such problems. Down through the years, I have worked with little or no promotion, no agency representation, poor representation, no promotion, no advertising, no hype. I knew ways around all of that. I know that good music is good music and it finds its way to the people. So these problems don't shake me anymore. I don't expect the hoopla, but I do expect respect.

My first album for Muse, *A Time for Love*, hit the charts three weeks after its release. It included "I'm in the Mood for Love," "Lend Me Yesterday," "But Beautiful," "He's Out of My Life," "Trust in Me," "Thought About You," "Love Is Blind," "You Keep Turnin Me On," and the title cut. Everybody's happy when their album hits the charts, and I was thrilled to death.

Now, I was beginning to feel like I had really made a comeback. Then one day I looked at the charts and my album was gone. I called Joe Fields and asked:

"What happened? It's supposed to be climbing."

"Don't feel bad," he said. "It was probably bumped."

It was bumped by Anita Baker's album. I decided to have a conversation with Joe about promoting my album.

"Well, maybe if you push the album a little more, we could get the momentum back."

"That's ego talking," he fired back.

His reaction was beyond me. I could not understand how he associated ego-tripping with matters of business. The implication was that I was supposed to be grateful to have an album out.

"You don't have an ego?" I said to him. "Ego is self. Everybody has an ego." *Here we go again,* I thought. I said to myself, *I've got to find the magnet that draws these kinds of white folks to me.*

I was with Muse from '89 to '98. Joe Fields kept renewing my contract each year. I did three albums on Muse, *A Time for Love, This One's on Me,* and *No Detour Ahead,* then I called it a day. I should have done more albums while I was there, but I chose not to. Joe wouldn't pay you, unless you asked. But having to ask for money from a record company, not receiving royalty statements, and being treated like you're ignorant of the business was more than I could take.

I thank God that I'm strong and I tried not to let this cut through any of my creative abilities while I was there. And it's not all Joe's fault. After so many years in the business, I didn't feel like spinning through that vicious cycle again. I was not going to open those forty-year-old wounds.

To tell the truth, I went to plenty of record companies and I was either turned down, or I had to turn *them* down because, again, the money they offered was what they were paying their secretaries. And Joe Fields knew this. He knew that a lot of older artists in the business couldn't get deals. Around that time, he was preparing to record with Joe Williams. The legendary Joe Williams didn't have a deal, which was hard for me to believe. I think a lot of artists, realizing age is an issue, take what they can get from Joe Fields, because, hey, at least he will record you.

Speaking of Joe Williams. I was lucky enough to perform with him one last time before his passing. He was a great, great artist. I loved him. I was asked to participate in a benefit concert out in LA, for the Whitney Houston Foundation for Children, Inc., and the Starkey Hearing Foundation. Now, Whitney I've known since she was a little thing running around, because her mother, Cissy, and I go way back to the early days. The benefit concert was produced by David Gest, and half of Hollywood was there. There were performances by Mariah Carey, Chaka Khan, Carole Bayer Sager, Michael McDonald, Smokey Robinson, Carol King, and a lot of other artists. Well, David Gest, who I've worked with on many functions in past years, asked Joe Williams to come onstage with me, so we could sing "I Wish You Love" together. Before we could reach the stage, we got a standing ovation. We had known each other for so many years. We watched each other grow over the years. It was a beautiful moment between us. And it was the last time we'd see each other.

That's one of the things that's wrong with the music industry today. They throw out their old people, especially if you're black. Too many black legends are casually discarded after contributing four and five decades' worth of music to the industry.

On the white side, they have their Tony Bennetts, Frank Sinatra still sells like he's alive, and even Elvis's ass isn't dead yet: He's on a U.S. stamp.

But on the black side, there are hardly any comparable black vocalists or musicians that are revered in the same way. We let our old people fall through the cracks. We're partly to blame. Jazz artists, especially the instrumentalists, play to more European and Japanese audiences than black American audiences. There was a time when black music was upheld in our community. It was the beat of the black neighborhood. Now, we're buying whatever we're told to buy and our loyalties are left to whim and the latest trend. It's sad.

The truth is, I've done better than most. Most black musicians after they reach a certain age cannot get a contract. They spend decades developing themselves as artists. They try to keep up their craft, keep themselves in good condition, they work at their art until they die, but it goes unappreciated. They're looked down upon by people who don't have their years of experience, level of expertise or training, and haven't paid their dues.

In opera, they don't do this. They don't even think you *can* sing until you're in your forties.

After a while you become numb to the mistreatment, even though you know it isn't fair. The harsh reality is the success of most black artists is marginal compared to their white counterparts. Especially if you're measuring success in dollars. Black artists must depend on their devoted following, the people who will buy their albums, come to their shows, and really support them, year after year. Without a faithful following, you're out there in the wilderness to fend for yourself.

Like I said, I've been luckier than most, and I thank God for my fans every single time I grace a stage because I know it could be another story entirely.

In the past few years, the black entertainment business has lost a lot of its pioneers. I, personally, went through a period where every year one of my friends in the business was gone. Sarah Vaughan left in '90, Redd Foxx in '91, Dizzy Gillespie in '93, then years later, there was Carmen McRae, Ella Fitzgerald, Mercer Ellington, Betty Carter, Joe Williams, and my dear sweet friend Herman Foster. It's been one after the other. And these were giants in the industry. Irreplaceable, unforgettable people! The work now is to ensure that they are not forgotten.

Today, so little attention is given to quality. You have all of these supposed hit-makers out there exploiting kids, waving gold and diamonds in front of them. It's really ironic that the older generations of artists were barely paid for their contributions, but what they contributed will never die. It was too good. Talent was the thing. Originality. Style. Quality. Now, it's a crapshoot. Every once in a while a true artist sneaks in there and gets to do their thing.

Videos have introduced a new element to music. While they are, in essence, a productive and often creative way of presenting music, I cannot understand the exploitative and obscene nature of many of them. I watch all of the video shows because I'm always interested in seeing the new kids coming up.

But I am disturbed when I see music videos that are denigrating to women. I sit there and say to myself:

Why does the little child's ass have to be out? Why is half her bust hanging out of her blouse?

Every video now has the shaking of the ass, and it's so distracting that you can't hear the lyrics. It makes you wonder, what are they really selling? Come on, get musical. Let the music make its mark. A beautiful lyric or a melodious line will always outlast a bust or a behind.

And now, live performances are live only in the sense that the person up there is living and breathing, but you see young people without a single musician onstage. Instead, they have dancers. And with all of that "show," the audience can't fully appreciate the music. You can't focus your eye on the artists long enough to even hear them. Whatever other gimmicks record companies are using to sell these records are only fleeting. Good music is good music.

And it will endure.

During the time I was recording with Muse, my living situation was still up and down. The seesaw continued. I was living at a place called Skyview on the Hudson. I was renting with the option to buy, and I had sunk a lot of money into the apartment. When I fell behind in the rent, the landlords took me to court. They wasted no time. It was back to the courthouse for the umpteenth time. I told the judge how much money I had put into the place and that I was renting with the option to buy. I even explained my financial situation to him. I told him I was waiting for royalties to come in. It didn't make any difference. I was behind and that was it. I was out on the street, in the dead of winter.

By this time, Herb Zuckerman had passed on, but Janette still had their house in Palisades Park. She travels a lot and she owns other property, so she said:

"Take my house. I'm never there."

I stayed in her house for a year, until I got on my feet. She threw me another lifeline. I know there are angels on this Earth. No one can tell me differently.

I was working the club scene, but jazz money is not a lot of money, unless you're high on the roster. It also helps if you're a man. Jazz is a male-dominated field, always has been.

Like I said, a good secretary can make as much as a jazz artist.

So when times were tough, Janette made it a lot easier for me. She understood my situation and never judged me or questioned my choices. She just offered help. And it was unconditional. She never asked for anything in return.

Her house was really beautiful and she gave me full reign, so I was very comfortable there. They had a maid, Catherine, who would come every Monday to clean. I started to look forward to her visits. She is a lovely woman. She raised both of the Zuckerman's kids. I remember Herb was crazy about her. Catherine made sure I had everything I needed, but more than that, she kept me company.

The phone rang one afternoon and I knew, even before I picked it up, there was bad news on the other end. I started not to answer it. But I did, and there was a voice telling me that Harry had died.

It hit me hard. I went through all of the emotions you go through when the love of your life dies. I was OK one minute, then distraught the next. One minute I'd be laughing at something we had done together, then in the next I'd be in a crying fit.

Harry was my only true love. He was my best friend and husband, the father of my only child. Harry gave me a sense of family in a time when I felt alone. When we were married, I felt like I was part of something.

His passing cut right through me. It didn't come as a shock. I mean, we're all getting older. Harry had been suffering with diabetes for quite some time. At one point, he had to have his left foot amputated.

I spoke to him the day before he died. He was in the house with his granddaughter, Simone, who was the sweetest and prettiest little girl. Both Steven, Harry's son, and his granddaughter were as sweet as they could be. Harry was in there eating McDonald's or something with his grandbaby.

"You better get some wholesome food in your system," I told him.

He had a really bad cough and seemed to be suffering from a bad cold. I'm not really sure what was ailing him, but he died at home the very next day. It seemed like once I got the news, I started missing him right at that moment. I would never see my friend again. It hit hard.

I reflected on our years together. We were such good buddies before we hooked up. We were neighbors, grew up right across the street from one another, and all the girls in the neighborhood loved Harry.

You couldn't tell me he wasn't the finest thing Harlem had ever seen.

But things were so hard back then. Black men weren't allowed to be men, but they damn sure tried. Harry always supported his family. He was a hard-working man. And we were so young. Nineteen is young, no matter how you cut it. But in those days, by nineteen you might have had a couple of babies to feed, a wife, a stack of bills, and three jobs. You may have fought in a war, by nineteen.

There were so many limitations on us. We were mice in a maze. Society told us what we could and could not do, what we were, and what we most certainly were not, what we could become and what we'd never be.

He wanted the world for us, but there were too many barriers and he couldn't knock down them all.

Harry had big dreams, but he never saw them manifested.

And in the end, Harry did me wrong. He knows he did.

Maybe Harry and I should have never been married. Marriage just confused things between us. Maybe we weren't ready. Maybe it wasn't us but everything surrounding us that got in the way. Maybe being apart was better for the both of us. Maybe.

Harry had been living with a woman for several years. They were never married, but she took over planning his funeral, as if she was the wife. When Richard and I showed up at the church, she had us seated up front, but on the opposite side of where Harry's family was sitting.

People were nudging me, asking me why I wasn't sitting with the family. But I didn't worry about it. I looked around, and I didn't notice Harry's twin girls there. And I wondered if she had even bothered to let them know their daddy was dead. The longer I sat there, the angrier I got. It was clear to me how she had decided to handle things, separating her family from the rest of us, as if they were the only people close to Harry. I looked at the program she'd had printed up and it read: "Harry Alleyne leaves to mourn a wife, a son, Steven, *and two friends* Gloria and Richard."

Now, I try to be a woman at all times, in my mind, soul, body, and spirit, what I think a woman is. I didn't mind that she had me listed as a friend, because Harry and I were good friends, but what she did to my son was vicious. She knew she was wrong.

Because I had gotten a Mexican divorce there was more red tape to muddle through. I had to show proof of my marriage, my divorce, and Harry's death in order to receive widow's benefits. Well, I only had to go to the undertaker to get Harry's death papers, but I had lost track of all that other stuff over the years, since I moved so much. When I couldn't find our marriage certificate, my thoughts ventured back to our wedding. I went into a state of inner panic. I thought back to that jack-legged preacher my mother had brought in there. And though it may sound crazy, I began to question whether Harry and I were ever truly married. Because my parents were so against it, I started wondering if my mother had gotten a preacher who wasn't legit, so the marriage wouldn't be legal. My mother was capable of doing that kind of thing.

I said to myself, *Lord, what if Harry and I were never really married?*

I searched all around and went through all of this muck and mire, trying to get my hands on our papers. I was able to get a copy of our marriage certificate through city hall, which eased my mind a bit. Then I had to get the divorce papers. So, I contacted the Mexican consulate. This was a fiasco. They were so busy trying to rip you off, by the time you got what you needed, you ended up paying more money for the *copies* of the divorce than you did for the divorce itself. They wanted a certain amount of money to research, a certain amount to make copies, a certain amount to send the copies.

It was a trip.

So Spirit told me to go another route. I went to the attorney who drew up the divorce papers, Maxwell T. Cohen. Now, Cohen was old when I got the divorce, so I didn't know if he was still around. I called his office and they told me he was no longer practicing, but gave me a number where he could be reached. Before getting off the phone, I asked:

"Pardon me, but does he still have it all together?"

The receptionist caught my meaning, so he said, right away, "Oh, he's cool. He just wrote a book."

I was able to reach Cohen and he made things very simple: "I'll write a letter so you can get your benefits immediately."

That's all it took. In a matter of days, I received a large retroactive check, then the benefit checks started coming regularly.

The whole ordeal was funny after the fact. It was some forty years later, Harry was dead and gone, and there I was, still wondering if I really had a husband.

When it came to knowing about my own social security benefits, I had to get all of that information from Herb Zuckerman. Before he passed away, I'd done a show at the Bally Grand in Atlantic City and he'd come to see me. Coming home in the limousine, Herb asked me if I had applied for my benefits. Herb and I were the same age, although he always treated me like a little girl.

"Baby, did you apply for social security?" he asked.

He told me to go down to the office the next day and see what I could get. I lived all my life as a performing artist, I rarely worked nine to five, except those years when I was temping. So here was another one of those common knowledge issues that a lot of artists pay little attention to.

Honestly, the life of an artist is different in so many ways. It's like we all live on another planet. We're living in a dreamworld until reality comes crashing down. I was sixty-two years old and hadn't given a thought about retirement planning or any of that.

Anyway, I applied for my benefits and when I saw what showed up on the computer, I couldn't believe it. I was eligible for benefits but only on the basis of the nine-to-five jobs I had done. Those little jobs turned out to be a real blessing, because very little of the money I made on my recordings was ever reported.

"This can't be all of my earnings. This can't be true," I told the administrator.

"Miss Lynne, I know it's not true, not with all the albums I have by you."

It was an interesting experience. It was too late to change the situation, so I accepted what little money they had to offer and went on. However, I do feel that some kind of legislation should be put into effect to assist artists. You shouldn't work in an industry all your life, then once you're a senior citizen have less to retire on than the rest of the working world. It's not fair. When you stop to think about all of the people who benefited from your artistry, from record execs to radio stations to record stores, it's sort of ridiculous that money is a constant issue in your life. Everyone enjoys your music, but very few realize the extremes you've gone through to put it out there. Show business is the only business in the world that has no real laws to govern it. It's a circus.

15

Looking Deep, Searching Near

*I*t's good to be appreciated. I was performing at Maxim's on Madison Avenue in Manhattan once. I did a weekend run there. My makeup artist, Rosemary, told me after the show:

"Tupac Shakur's mother was here. She said she came to see you to get her soul together."

This was just months after Tupac had been murdered. I sent word to her that I was so glad to be there for her in her darkest hour. It was really touching to know my music was healing for her. When people drop those kinds of compliments on you, it melts away the madness.

In 1997, I got the surprise of my life. I received a letter from the Rhythm & Blues Foundation. I was being honored with the foundation's Pioneer Award. Well, that just blew me away. It was like a breath of fresh air, music to my ears, and every other cliché you can name. It was incredible. I didn't know whether to cry or shout. I think I did both. The award came with a substantial monetary award. And honestly, I cannot describe how heartwarming it is to receive this kind of award. It has a way of washing away all of the bad stuff and highlighting the good stuff. To be considered a pioneer, an icon, a real tribute to your craft is what it's all about. No matter what's going on, when you're honored this way you realize why you got into the business in the first place, why you fought the good fight all those years.

The ceremony is held the day after the Grammy Awards, either in Los Angeles or New York. That year, it was a huge celebration at the New York Hilton. Aretha Franklin was mistress of ceremonies. It was full of stars. There were jazz people, folks from R&B, blues, rock, soul, everybody was there. I saw people I hadn't seen in years. It was such an overwhelming experience. It felt like a fantastic, fast-moving memory. It was so magical that each moment something incredible would happen and I'd think, *God, I don't want to forget this. I'll never forget this.* My head was in the clouds the whole night.

I was honored along with William Bell, Gary "U.S." Bonds, Clarence "Gatemouth" Brown, Gene Chandler, the Four Tops, Little Milton, Smokey Robinson & the Miracles, Ruby and the Romantics, the Spinners, Paul Upchurch, and Van "Piano Man" Walls. The organizers told me that they wanted me to perform one song, and the song they requested was "I Wish You Love."

This made me nervous because I thought, *this is a jazz song.* So I told one of the organizers of the event:

" 'I Wish You Love' isn't rhythm & blues. Why do I have to sing that song?"

They said, "Gloria, consider it rhythm & blues, because that's the song everybody wants to hear you sing. It's your signature song. You've got to sing it."

Of course, I obliged. The funny thing is, so many people request that song, and people really love it, but they assume it's my favorite, too. I think it's a beautiful song, but quiet as it's kept, my real favorite is "I'm Glad There's You." But I must admit, there is something magical about "I Wish You Love." Every time someone has recorded that song, it's been a hit. People really love it. And lyrically, it's just gorgeous.

The evening was incredible. The atmosphere in that hotel was electric. It's a wonder the place didn't levitate off the ground. There was so much fantastic energy flowing through there. All of my friends came to support me. My son, Richard, was by my side, and my precious "daughters," Earl May's girls, Carol and Robin.

There was music on top of music and everything had that rhythm-&-blues bass and guitar vamp. It was pumping all night. Then jazz singer Cassandra Wilson introduced me and I got up there to sing my "not R&B" number, "I Wish You Love." With a full orchestra, I sang the first few bars of the song, *Good-bye . . . no use leading with our chins*, and you could hear a pin drop. The vibe changed in the room. Suddenly, everyone was listening. The crowd loved it. Afterward, I was told by a lot of people that it was the highlight of the evening, which was very gratifying for me.

I saw so many old friends that night. It was like a high school reunion. So many of my old friends, musicians and singers that I had not seen in years. I think I knew almost everybody in there, or had worked with them or crossed paths with them on the road. So it was a really great feeling to be in such good company.

I had the chance to meet the Artist Formerly Known as Prince, who I've always loved. He reminds me of an old-fashioned soul that came back here. When I first heard his music, the first thing I said was, *This child has been here before*. Most of the people there that night I knew, but I really wanted to meet him. I love his approach to music. He's old in his thinking, even though he's a kid. He knows exactly what he is doing. And I always had the impression that he was nothing but sweet and kind. Now, I know firsthand, it is true. He told me how much he enjoyed my music and we talked for a few minutes. He lived up to my image of him, which made our meeting that much sweeter.

I find that the bigger they are the nicer they are. I remember meeting Lena Horne years ago. She is as nice as she can be. When you think of what she's accomplished, it is really astounding. She's a big, big name in the business. She is Lena Horne! But when you meet her, you never pick that up from her. You feel nothing but love. When she sees you, she's so warm and beautiful. If anything, she's bound to treat you like a bigger star than she is. She's always very gracious.

Somebody asked me that night, as I stood there, surrounded by phenomenal artists:

"Aren't you intimidated?"

"I am not intimidated by any singer," I said. "Never have been."

Since before I even knew exactly what I was doing, I knew I could sing. If you *know* that you're talented, regardless of whether you're getting the breaks, whether they blow up other people around you with explosions big enough to wipe out the whole sky, if you really know, no one can take that away from you.

I'm not intimidated by anyone.

The business is intimidating enough.

The whole evening was fantastic. It felt like a dream. Throughout the night, I had some very reflective moments, where I thought of my career and the life that I've lived because of the career. I looked around and saw all of my family and friends, and I felt closer to them than ever.

I have been blessed by some truly wonderful people in my life. My success has everything to do with the immense love that has been shared between my family of friends, the dedicated love of fans that have been with me since the beginning and of the new ones I've picked up along the way, my insatiable love of my music, and a true understanding of how to love myself. And it was clear to me that because of them, I made it through.

My manager, Duke, was with me that night. I thought of him.

Duke dedicated himself to black artists, particularly jazz artists. And despite the setbacks, he has made it his business to help artists who nobody else would. He even shared artists with other agents in the business. He never required that you be exclusive with him or sign an actual contract. If he could get you work, he would. Although Duke has a wonderful personality and a smile that welcomes you into his life, he is firm in his business dealings. He is a survivor. We have both learned to count our blessings and keep stepping, no matter how many rejections we face.

We still have the same vibrant spirit we had in the early years. I learned very early, in order to stay focused there is no room for comparisons. You will drive yourself crazy worrying about somebody else's career. While you've got your mind on their business, who's watching out for yours? It's a waste of time.

As much as I have been through in this wonderful thing called show business, Duke Wade taught me how to survive it all. He taught me to hold my head up high and trust in my Creator at all times. That's how he lives. Duke tells me all the time:

"Take the good with the bad and make the most of it."

When I pray, I always make a universal prayer. That way I don't miss anyone or anything, but I make a point to mention Duke and his family. They have always been there for me when I needed them, for more years than I can count. And hopefully, many more to come.

I thought of Danny Small.

Danny wrote a lot of the songs I recorded over the years, including one of my favorites, "Love, I Found You." When I heard that song, I begged him for it.

"Danny, I've got to sing that song. You've got to give it to me." He also wrote famous songs, like "I'll Take New York," "So This Is Love," and "Man of Mine."

He was a beautiful person. Danny taught me everything I know about vocal performance. When you hear me sing, you hear Danny. I owe my career to him. It was sad to see him go. He died before reaching the age of fifty.

I thought of my mother.

She would have been very proud to see me win the Pioneer Award. I thought of all the little contests she used to enter me in when I was a kid. And all of the songs she taught me in French. I thought of how she used to sing all the time and how beautiful her voice was. I missed her that night and I miss her now. But I knew she was somewhere smiling a quiet, reserved smile.

The entire evening was magic. It was the kind of night you wait your entire career for. Acknowledgment is always a golden feeling. And to be acknowledged by your peers is the absolute best. The Rhythm & Blues Foundation has made such great strides for artists. They represent honor and integrity and respect in an industry that is steeped in exploitation and corruption. I truly appreciate and admire their efforts. I thank God for them. Being acknowledged as one of the greats in the business and being considered a pioneer meant more to me than any other kind of award I could have received. I took great pride in accepting the Pioneer Award.

Back in '66, I recorded a little song called "Speaking of Happiness," which was written by Buddy Scott and Jimmy Radcliffe. It was released as a single and immediately shipped off to the European market, where it sold like hotcakes. Right before I received the Pioneer Award, I got a call from Jimmy's son, Chris Radcliffe.

Now, Buddy and Jimmy were something else. They would hustle and do whatever they had to to get their songs recorded. They wrote hundreds of songs down through the years. I'll never forget those days of them flying through the doors of the recording studio in the middle of the night with a song in their heads. And Buddy has a really nice voice, so he would stand there and sing the song to you and dare you not to love it. Actually, that's how I came to record "Speaking of Happiness." I was in the middle of a session and in walked Buddy and Jimmy, saying:

"Gloria, we got a song for you."

They taught me "Speaking of Happiness" right there on the spot and we recorded it in one take. It was really something. Buddy stood behind me at the microphone and the man sang the song into my ear, line for line. He would sing one line and I'd copy his phrasing and everything and sing it right into the mike just like him. I echoed him. We did the whole song that way, line for line. And as miraculous as it sounds, we didn't mess up once. And surprisingly enough, the mike never picked up Buddy's voice. We hit it in one take! It was beautiful. I've always loved that song. Those were fun, fun times.

When Jimmy Radcliffe died, Chris took over the family business. He started submitting their catalog of songs to film producers, soap operas, and television stations for a few years. He had a lot of success with it.

Chris called to tell me that Oliver Stone wanted to use "Speaking of Happiness" and "I Wish You Love" in his new film, *U Turn*. A couple years before that, in '95, the producers of *Se7en*, starring Morgan Freeman, used "Speaking of Happiness" on their soundtrack. Then, that same little song started popping up all over the place. Ford Motors was shooting a commercial for the international market and they wanted "Speaking of Happiness." I am very flattered by this new attention to such old material. As a vocalist, this kind of reaction to your voice and music is especially gratifying because you realize that you've contributed something timeless to the art form, that beautiful music never dies and your voice will continue to be heard as long as there is radio, TV, and film. None of these outlets were available to me when I first started out. Radio was it.

There was more good news. Early in 1998, a company called Collectables released four compact discs from albums I did in the sixties with Everest Records. When I first spoke to Jerry Green, president of Collectables, he told me that he was trying to get Everest to give him the masters of my recordings, but they refused to release them. So he asked me to send him the albums I had. I sent him seven albums and he paid me $7,000 dollars for them. He also gave me a contract for royalties.

Another pleasant surprise came when Verve, the jazz division of PolyGram Records, released a compilation album, entitled *Starry Eyes*, featuring a lot of my old hits, like "Joey, Joey, Joey," "Soul Serenade," "Some of

These Days," "I Cover the Waterfront," "Blue Afternoon," "For You," and "Blue Gardenia." The album features arrangements by Al Cohn, Hal Mooney, Bobby Scott, Bill Rubinstein, and Claus Ogerman. The release of this album created another opportunity for me to recoup some of the money that I should have received back in the sixties.

It's a very good feeling when you're treated like an artist, paid like an artist, and respected in your field. I am happy that I'm still here to bear witness that there are reputable record companies and those that really do honor the past.

I met some high school students recently, after a performance at Aaron Davis Hall at the City University of New York. I was coming out of the concert hall and they caught up with me. I always love talking to young people. I have all the faith in the world in them.

"Miss Lynne, we really enjoyed you," they'll say. "But we're not familiar with you or your music."

"Yes, but you will be. By the time you get to college, I'll be there. And even after that, I'll be there."

All of those years of recorded music will be right there waiting on them, when they're ready for it.

When I see the faces of young people beaming with excitement over my music, it makes the trip worthwhile: the struggles, the impossible odds, the successes, the good times, and all the laughs.

I've been fortunate to spend my life doing what I love.

When my first album came out, *Miss Gloria Lynne*, all the singers took me into their hearts. They were all I ever listened to and they could hear me and hear a little bit of themselves. I was part of all of them. They saw this young girl coming along, who had done her homework, and who knew and admired all of them. Their repertoires filled my head, and because of their music I made a life out of singing. Sarah, Ella, Dinah, Carmen. These were my people.

And I still fill houses!

God has been good to me. I've been blessed over and over and over again. I've gone places and done things I never imagined. Through it all, I kept reminding myself: *No matter how many times life knocks you down, keep your hand in God's hand and you will overcome it.* Everybody's going to have hardships. I've certainly had my share. But you can't let them take you, bend you, and break you.

Thinking back, I never dreamed that I'd reach the place in my career where people would be calling my name, "Glorious Gloria Lynne," among the legends and pioneers in jazz and pop. But it happened. With God's help, it has happened.

When I take a closer look at my life and consider all that I've been through, all that I've accomplished, and the choices I've made, I know that love got me through. I have always believed in and had deep respect for my talent. It has taught me invaluable lessons, guided me down roads I never thought I'd travel, and sustained me in ways that I never thought possible.

All of these years, I chased a dream and I finally caught it. I've been able to hold it in my hands and view it up close, and what I see, quite clearly, is a dream of love.

Selected Discography

RECORDINGS

Miss Gloria Lynne (Everest)
Lonely and Sentimental (Everest)
Try a Little Tenderness (Everest)
Impossible (Everest)
Pop Parade (Everest)
Gloria Lynne and Lena Horne (Coronet)
This Little Boy of Mine (Everest)
Day In Day Out (Everest)
Stormy Monday Blues (Everest)
Gloria Lynne at the Las Vegas Thunderbird (Everest)
He Needs Me (Everest)
After Hours (Everest)
I'm Glad There's You (Everest)
Live at Basin Street East (Everest)
I Wish You Love (Everest)
A Touch of Tenderness (Everest)
Go Go Go! (Everest)
Gloria Blue (Everest)
Gloria, Marty & Strings (Everest)
My Funny Valentine (Design)
Gloria Lynne and Her Friends Gloria De Haven, Tina Robin (Seeco)
Gloria Lynne Live! Take: 2 (Everett)
Intimate Moments (Fontana)
Soul Serenade (Fontana)
Love and a Woman (Fontana)
Here, There and Everywhere (Fontana)
The Gloria Lynne Calendar (Hi-Fi)

The Ballad, the Blues and the Beat (Blue Moon)
Where It's At (Fontana)
The Other Side of Gloria Lynne (Fontana)
Gloria (Fontana)
A Very Gentle Sound (Fontana)
The Best of Gloria Lynne (Fontana)
Happy and in Love (Canyon)
I Don't Know How to Love Him (ABC/Impulse)
Golden Classics (Collectables)
A Time for Love (Muse)
No Detour Ahead (Muse)
This One's on Me (Muse)
I Wish You Love/Go Go Go! (Collectables)
Try a Little Tenderness/I'm Glad There's You (Collectables)
Basin Street East/Live at the Las Vegas Thunderbird (Collectables)
Gloria, Marty & Strings/After Hours (Collectables)
Starry Eyes (Verve)
He Needs Me/This Little Boy of Mine (Collectables)

SOUNDTRACKS

Se7en	"Speaking of Happiness"
U Turn	"I Wish You Love" and "Speaking of Happiness"

ORIGINAL SONGS

"Watermelon Man" (lyrics, Gloria Lynne; arrangement, Herbie Hancock; music by Mongo Santamaria)
"All Day Long" (lyrics, Gloria Lynne; music by Kenny Burrell)
"That's a Joy"
"Oo Wee! What a Man!"

"Children of All Ages"

"America"

"Love Is Blind" (music, Gloria Lynne; lyrics by Ann Rubino)

"Lend Me Yesterday" (music, Gloria Lynne; lyrics by Ann Rubino)

"Come Get Your Share" (lyrics, Gloria Lynne)

"I'm All in Love with You"

"Ah! Yes"

"I Love You So"

"Winter, Summer, Spring and Fall"

"There Is a God in You"

"He's on Your Side"

"It's Autumn Again"

"Old Folks Can Rapp Too!"

"More Love"

"I Got Your Love"

"We Will Again"

"In My Lifetime"

"I Do a Little Music"

"Pappa"

"Say You Love Me"

"Record Company Blues"

"The Old Vinyl Record Stuck"

"These Are the Gifts"

"Stand Up for Your Rights"

"Kicking Life (Like an Old Tin Can)"

"Bad Won't Be 'Round Long (Good's Coming!)"

"Preachin" (lyrics, Gloria Lynne; music by Roy Meriwether)

"There's a Long Road"

"Come with Me"

"Love Your Fellow Man"

"Go One Step Beyond"

"Hey Baby! Make a Move on Me"

"Jewel" (lyrics, Gloria Lynne; music by John Woods)

"Mary Jane" (written for Mary Jane Kniser)
"Bus Buddies" (from original musical, *Bus Buddies*, by Gloria Lynne)
"I Like Everything That's Good"
"Jazz Is All Music" (from *Jazz Suite*)

Awards and Proclamations

Playboy Jazz Award, 1963
Bergen County Ad Hoc Committee Black Women's Organization
   Achievement Award, February 4, 1989
Zenith Award, May 1993
The Galaxy Award, February 4, 1995
The Key to the City of Camden, New Jersey, August 1994
Front Page Award from *New York Daily News*, February 24, 1994
International Women of Jazz, December 8, 1996
Rhythm & Blues Foundation Pioneer Award, 1997

PROCLAMATIONS, "MISS GLORIA LYNNE DAY"

Proclamation from Philadelphia, September 4, 1992
Proclamation from Delaware, October 22, 1992
Proclamation from New York City, July 25, 1995

Index

B
LYNNE
L

Lynne, Gloria.

I wish you love.